Capitalism's Endgame

The Catastrophe of Accumulation

Mark Hayes

Phillip Sutton

Lars Torvaldsson

Old Moles Collective

CONTENTS

Preface

This little book is in part an offspring of Covid19 and lockdown, when in 2020 a group of us started getting together online to talk internationalist politics. Like many in that strange and unnerving time we felt a strong need to break out of social isolation and discuss. Only some of us already knew each other at the outset and at first, our little gatherings were a bit like an online version of meeting down the pub for a chat with a few like-minded souls (beer included). There were no formal criteria for joining in; people were simply invited along on the basis of mutual trust and broadly sharing the same political space (we had all been involved, for many years but to varying degrees, in Left Communist politics). Usually this worked.

Little by little, our meetings became more or less regular and a bit more structured. In between we began thrashing out ideas in email threads. On the rare occasions when we felt a need to refer to ourselves as a group, we were 'Flotsam and Jetsam' – wreckage mostly from the 1970s washed up on the shores of the 21st Century. Let's be honest, most of us are old (well, oldish), and even the youngest is past the first bloom of youth.

As the ideas ebbed and flowed, three of us realised we shared a preoccupation with the notion of 'decadence', the point at which a given social form is no longer fit for purpose, no longer able to foster human progress. We were convinced, against its deniers and sceptics, that the decadence of capitalism was a reality today, but we were dissatisfied with the inability of existing groups to bring the concept up to date for the 21st century, and with what we felt was their narrow concentration on 'economics'. We began writing and discussing longer texts in an effort to grapple with new ideas, with the others dipping in from time to time as they felt inclined.

Eventually we felt we had something to say that would be worth laying before a wider audience. After a week together in a Welsh cottage in 2021 – a week of very long breakfasts thrashing out ideas, walks in the countryside, and visits to local sights, and pubs – we ended up with a rough plan and a deadline, which of course we missed.

Our discussions were not easy, and sometimes fraught. Should we really have been surprised? We hadn't realised how much we might disagree, or about what. Did it matter? In the end, we decided some disagreements were inevitable. After all, we are not a political group with a 'line' to defend, the questions we are dealing with are complex, and the best we can hope for is to spark off further interest and a broader debate. The 'Old Moles Collective' felt ready to hit the road.

In taking on the question of decadence we are very aware we are by no means the first, and cheerfully acknowledge that we owe many debts to both predecessors and contemporaries, including those whose political positions we do not share.

Our reflections are based on the theoretical groundwork undertaken in particular by the Gauche Communiste de France in the 1940s, then by the International Communist Current and the Communist Workers' Organisation in the 1970s.

In developing our own ideas, we have also benefited individually from discussions with the Controversies website on 'growth in decadence' and from work undertaken by the Internationalist Perspective group during the 1990s on economic development as a cause of ecological disaster. We have also drawn critically from the work of 'communisation' theorists and those in the 'autonomist' Marxist current. While we do not in the least share the political perspectives of the leftist *Monthly Review* magazine, the work of John Bellamy Foster, Paul Burkett and Kohei Saito on 'Marx's ecology' has also been seminal for us.

Finally, like Marx, we have made abundant use of official and academic statistics to support our arguments. Like Marx also, we are well aware that this is not without potential pitfalls. But whereas Marx had to spend hours in the reading room of the British Museum poring over the British government's Blue Books, the last five years have seen something of a revolution in the availability of online statistics and graphing tools. We have found the International Labour Organisation, the OECD, Groningen University's Maddison Project and Oxford University's 'Our World In Data' to be particularly useful sources. Wikipedia has, as always, been invaluable.

Last but far from least, we would like to acknowledge the comments, advice and support of our comrades, often critical but always invaluable.

MH, PS, LT

Introduction

If the doors of perception were cleansed every thing would appear to man as it is: Infinite.
For man has closed himself up, till he sees all things thro' narrow chinks of his cavern.[1]

In Dante's epic poem Inferno, the hero is guided through hell and has to brave the devil's arsehole before discovering the passage that leads him to the ascension of heaven. As he descends through the seven circles of hell, the poet witnesses the increasingly awful torments of the damned by fire and ice.

We began this project in 2021, after the hottest July ever recorded but with the promise that 2021 will be the coolest year this side of 2100. Heatwaves, droughts and wildfires spread across Siberia, southern Europe, and the West Coast of North America, while massive flooding caused devastation from Germany to Japan, presaging future torments by fire and water, of increasing severity.

We were also in the midst of a global pandemic, to which governments world wide responded with quarantines and lockdowns on a hitherto unimagined scale. These continue to disrupt the lives of millions, especially in China, and have given all states the excuse to impose a degree of social control which was once the stuff of wartime, or of Orwellian nightmare, all backed up by the latest technology.

At the same time, the world's leading industrial countries are engaged in a deadly game of escalating military tensions which once again threaten humanity with armed conflict, even nuclear conflict, on a global scale. The conflict which broke out in 2022 in Ukraine – in effect, a proxy war between Russia and the USA – is merely a foretaste of the devastating potential of modern warfare, and is threatening millions with famine by blocking Ukrainian exports of grain.

The four horsemen of the Apocalypse – Conquest, War, Famine and Death – are already abroad, brandishing nuclear weapons and riding on catastrophic climate change.

Inferno's inmates suffer not just physical torture, but also the psychological torments of despair, and in the present situation one could almost be forgiven for succumbing to it: humanity seems to be poised to achieve a distinction unique in the animal kingdom of being the only species to rush headlong, lem-

---

1   William Blake, 'Marriage of Heaven and Hell', in *Poetry and Prose of William Blake*, ed. Geoffrey Keynes, 2nd edition (London: Nonesuch Press, 1948), p.181

3

ming-like, to its own destruction, but with its eyes wide open, fully aware of the factors driving it to its downfall.

Who is to blame? There is no shortage of possible culprits: an utterly irresponsible capitalist class, of unparalleled greed and rapacity, whose only law is the maximum possible accumulation of wealth through the merciless exploitation of labour and pillaging the natural resources on which we all depend; a corrupt political and ruling elite, whose members are either too venal to care about anything but their own immediate self-interest, too cowardly to tell their electorates the truth about the dangers we confront, or too obsessed by ideology (notably religious ideology) to understand what is happening; finally, the great mass of humanity, blinded by consumerism, nationalism, religion, and too attached to their own petty comforts or ideological obsessions to look boldly at the future and take the steps that the situation demands.

One could look at things like this, but it would be a mistake. The catastrophe that humanity faces today is not the fault of individuals, be they greedy capitalists, venal politicians, or consumerist and fanaticised masses. It is not even the fault of capitalists as a class, since the capitalist class is itself the product of the social relations of production of which it is a part. Rather, it is due to the fact that this system of social relations, capitalism, has outlived its usefulness and is no longer fit for purpose. In a word, we are living in the epoch of capitalism's decadence – of its descent into barbarism.

Despair too would be a mistake because capitalism has engendered forces of creation as well as destruction.

It is in the nature of all living forms to progress through vibrant youth, to maturity, and finally to decline and death. Human societies are no exception, and there is no shortage in history of societies which have decayed and died, leaving nothing but ruins behind them. Others however, generate within themselves new social relations, new social forces, capable of resolving the fatal contradictions of the society within which they were born and of rising phoenix-like from the decay and ashes of the old. Capitalism is one such society.

Capitalism has remarkable achievements to its credit. It has unified human society across the planet, as never before in history; it has put into humanity's hands tools of enormous, almost godlike power. Yet it remains blind, driven by an inhuman dynamic: production for production's sake, unlimited expansion in a world which, being round, is by definition finite.

More than anything, capitalism has created a world wide class of associated labour. It is this class that sets in motion humanity's productive apparatus. By removing the fetters imposed by capitalism's social relations on humanity's social powers, and above all on the powers of associated labour, the future society has the potential to resolve the contradictions of the present and open the way to a new era of human existence.

The new society only exists in potential, however. It can become a reality only through the action of the class that embodies the future social relations: the class of world wide associated labour.

What does this mean? In most people's eyes 'Communism' has been discredited by the experience of the Soviet Union and of 'Capitalism with Chinese characteristics'; 'Socialism' is associated with the pale pink welfare statism of Social-Democracy, which has constantly betrayed its promises. Nowadays, the expression 'Post-capitalism' seems to be in vogue, but its contours are vague and in general no more than a capitalism-lite without the 'unpleasant' features, not realising that you cannot have one without the other, you cannot have your cake and eat it too.

If capitalism is decadent, then what comes next? What could come next?

'Men make their own history'. They are not merely automata driven blindly by economic forces, so that every revolution, every radical social transformation, is preceded by decades of intellectual ferment during which the ideas are forged that will allow humanity to break with the existing state of things. This does not mean creating utopian blueprints for the future, rather it is a matter of understanding the world in a new way: getting to the roots of the dynamic underlying what exists, and making conscious the 'real movement going on under our eyes'. Or, as Engels put it:

> The growing perception that existing social institutions are unreasonable and unjust, that reason has become unreason, and right wrong, is only proof that in the modes of production and exchange changes have silently taken place with which the social order, adapted to earlier economic conditions, is no longer in keeping. From this it also follows that the means of getting rid of the incongruities that have been brought to light must also be present, in a more or less developed condition, within the changed modes of production themselves. These means are not to be *invented*, spun out of the head, but *discovered* with the aid of the head in the existing material facts of production.[2]

Humanity is confronted with an unprecedented challenge, on an unprecedented scale: the veritable 'descent into hell' that menaces all human society in the decades to come can only be avoided by a profound social transformation. Nor is it just a matter of avoiding disaster: this transformation must also unlock humanity's titanic powers and liberate its potential. We cannot pretend to know how such a transformation will take place, but we are convinced that it can only

---

2   Friedrich Engels, *Anti-Dühring*, 3rd edition, London 1894 (Moscow: Progress Publishers, 1977), p.323 (Part III, 'Socialism', Chapter I, 'Historical').

be conscious, and so based on understanding. Only by throwing wide the 'doors of perception' will the class of associated labour be able to 'see the world as it is, Infinite' in its potentialities.

Our theoretical assumptions...
and difficulties

Our approach, and so our theoretical assumptions, are unabashedly Marxist, which is to say that they are inspired by the materialist conception of history first developed by Marx.

In its broad outlines, Marx's approach seemed to us clear enough: at some point in the future (Marx was writing in the mid-19th century, see p.240), it will be both possible and necessary to go beyond capitalism, to replace it with a more advanced social organisation which will both put an end to the old society's increasingly devastating contradictions, and allow humanity's productive forces to flourish. Or to put it another way, capitalism will enter its epoch of decadence and decline, and will be overthrown and replaced.

The decisive moment, when capitalism's continued existence could no longer be said to allow the development of the productive forces understood in the broadest sense, remains for us the outbreak of war in 1914. Fundamentally – and whatever interpretation one may prefer of Marx's analysis of capitalism's economic mechanisms – this represents the point where capitalism's inescapable need for constant expansion came up against the equally inescapable physical fact that the planet is round: henceforth, the drive to expansion must inevitably lead to catastrophic conflict between the major capitalist powers.

Clearly, this change of period did not happen overnight between the 3rd and the 4th of August 1914. At the end of the First World War, the ruling class in general still believed that it was possible to return to the pre-war *status quo*, and set about dismantling a large part of the state capitalist measures put in place to fight the war. The new period, characterised in particular by militarism and state capitalism, was only definitively established at the end of World War II.

In posing the question of capitalism's decadence in this way, we make no claim to originality. When the Communist International was founded in 1919, at the close of the most devastating war humanity had ever seen, and in the atmosphere of hope engendered by the October Revolution of 1917, it declared that a new epoch had begun: 'the epoch of wars and revolutions'. But the revolutionary experience was short lived, and it fell to the current known as the Communist Left, emerging as tiny minorities or isolated individuals from the wreckage of the Stalinist counter-revolution, to pursue the theoretical study of the new epoch.

However, this basic foundation inherited from Marx and the CI leaves much unsaid or undeveloped, and social evolution since then has raised many new questions. What exactly, for example, are 'the productive forces'? What are the 'fetters on production', and what would it mean, concretely, to remove them? What are the dynamics of 'the development of the productive forces'? How, perhaps most importantly, do we determine whether they have 'come into conflict with the existing relations of production' to the point where 'an era of social revolution' is a realistic proposition?

As we attempted to get to grips with these questions, none of which are either easy or straightforward, we felt the need to set out, in a separate article, our theoretical assumptions. Here, let us frankly confess, we bit off more than we could chew. The article in this collection by Phillip Sutton offers a brief overview of the materialist conception of history (neither Marx nor Engels actually used the term 'historical materialism'), re-examines some basic assumptions in the light of recent history and makes a valiant attempt to incorporate some of the reflections that emerged from our own long and sometimes difficult discussions on the subject. Nonetheless, it cannot and does not reflect our individual views on all aspects of this subject. Our discussions inevitably left many issues unresolved, and with hindsight this is hardly surprising: encapsulating the whole span of 200,000 years of human history in one article is a tall order, to put it mildly. An introduction is hardly the place to enumerate all these issues, and we will limit ourselves here to mentioning the two which seem to us most important.

The first, is the presentation of four successive modes of production (tribal society, slavery, feudalism and capitalism), which corresponds roughly to those used by Marx and Engels in the 19th century. Like all schemas, this one is inevitably incomplete and poses serious questions of historical interpretation – and indeed, of historical reality – which we have, unsurprisingly, been unable to resolve without launching ourselves into a whole programme of historical research. The schema is eurocentric inasmuch as the historical progression that it presents is completed by the emergence of capitalism in Europe. Nonetheless, our discussions raised issues as to the level of determinism in Marx's view of history and how to explain both apparent exceptions to the progression (especially that of China, which remained substantially in advance of Europe at the technical level – sometimes by centuries – and yet failed to develop into a fully-fledged industrial capitalist economy along European, and in the first instance British, lines), as well as the need for a more detailed analysis of how the development of the productive forces specifically led to new modes of production.

Another issue we confronted was the extent to which the ideology of any society is determined by the material processes of production, and how far does it in turn determine a society's future evolution: to what extent do consciousness and the ruling ideology influence events? Although we are all agreed that the evolution of society is not wholly deterministic,[3] but the fruit of the more or less conscious activity of human beings within given historical conditions, we have been unable to resolve this question to our mutual satisfaction.

This question is of far more than historical interest: indeed, one could almost say that from the standpoint of humanity's future survival, it is the burning issue of the day.

In his *Anti-Dühring*, Engels says the following: 'Modern socialism is nothing but the reflex, in thought, of this conflict [between the productive forces and the mode of production] in fact; its ideal reflection in the minds, first, of the class directly suffering under it, the working class'.[4] Bukharin, in his work on 'Historical materialism' says much the same thing and even elevates the progress of the workers' movement to the status of a historical law.

However convincing this may have seemed at the end of the 19th century (or in the early part of the 20th century), the complete disappearance today of anything that Engels would have recognised as 'socialism' poses a real problem. Either we must accept that material conditions have changed to the point where they are no longer able to generate a serious movement capable of going beyond capitalism, or else we must recognise that the relationship between the material conditions and the consciousness that arises out of them is much more complex, difficult, and painful than we once, rather naïvely, thought. We are understandably reluctant to accept the first conclusion, since it implies that there is no alternative to capitalism's headlong flight towards its own and humanity's self-immolation. The second conclusion demands our commitment to a battle which is yet to be fought out on both the practical and the theoretical levels.

These then are questions which remain open, and to which we may return in a future publication.

---

3   Here it is necessary to distinguish between 'hard' (or 'Laplacean') and 'soft' determinism. For Laplacean determinism (named after the 18th century French mathematician Pierre-Simon de Laplace), the future is entirely determined by the position and movement of its elementary particles; it is a popular hypothesis among theoretical physicists. For 'soft' determinism, while the present (including our consciousness) is determined by the past, human beings nonetheless have a certain freedom of action. This, in our view, is closer to Marx's statement in his *18th Brumaire* that 'Men make their own history, but they do not make it as they please'.

4   Friedrich Engels, *Anti-Dühring*, p.325

Rethinking capitalism's decadence

One thing on which we were all agreed, however, was that capitalism's evolution in its period of decline posed a real problem for the theoretical explanations proposed up to now by the Communist Left, whether they were based on Luxemburg's theory of markets or on the perhaps more conventional theories based on the 'falling rate of profit' developed initially by Grossman and Mattick.[5]

After all, if we look at the figures for world GDP since the beginning of the 20th century, we see a continuous upward progression in which crises like the 2007 banking crash appear as occasional blips, if at all. One might of course question the usefulness of such a measure inasmuch as catastrophic events such as world wars barely appear either; that said, the same holds true if we consider a more physical measurement such as primary energy consumption whose increase since the Second World War has been nothing short of vertiginous. Moreover, whatever the inadequacy of GDP as a measure there are physical facts on the ground: tens of thousands of kilometres of new highways and high-speed railways in China for example, not to mention the capital accumulation and concentration represented by the growing ranks of the world's billionaires.

At the same time, a society that threatens in the short term the survival of the species – either through cataclysmic war, or more inevitably through climate change and general ecological disaster – can hardly be considered to be in rude health. Human society is not some abstract construct that exists in books: its function is to allow the existence and development of humanity as a species. A society that can no longer do that is ripe for the 'dustbin of history': in short, it is decadent. The word itself is perhaps not the best – 'decline', 'obsolescence', 'descent', or more bluntly 'endgame' and even 'death agony' suggest themselves as alternatives – but as Shakespeare put it: 'A rose by any other name would smell as sweet', or in this case, as putrid.

This then was the problem we felt needed to be confronted: on the one hand, a capitalist economy which despite occasional crises continues to accumulate; on the other, the increasing devastation that this accumulation inflicts on the natural environment on which all life including our own depends. From the outset we have tried, if not to avoid any preconceptions (since pure empirical devotion to 'the facts' is an illusion), at least to keep an open mind and to follow wherever our research might lead.

---

5   Mark Hayes's article on 'The Accumulation of Catastrophe' refers to both theories at slightly greater length, with references to Grossman and Mattick's major works.

The blinkered, economistic view which treats anything outside economic statistics as somehow unreal left us profoundly unsatisfied. Instead, we have preferred to go deeper (though doubtless inadequately) into a properly materialist historical view which integrates questions of the economy, social change, ecology, climate change, and population growth, into a broader overall framework. This in turn has led us to try to think more deeply about the meaning of expressions like 'the productive forces', what their 'development' would mean, and what might constitute a 'fetter' on that development.

Let us reassure the reader from the outset that we do not propose a mere exegesis of Marxist texts, a sort of revolutionary version of Talmudic studies. If we cite Marx extensively it is simply because on almost any subject of social evolution, Marx has thought about it already, and in impressive depth, if only still in outline. Still, Marx was no biblical prophet and if, as he asserts, it is 'social existence' that 'determines men's consciousness', then it was not possible at the time he was writing to go further than to pose the question of capitalism's demise and to sketch in outline some of its contours. In consequence, while the immense fertility of this most powerful of social thinkers gives us our starting point, we will have no qualms in trying to push his premises further or even in contradicting them should this seem necessary.

In particular, there are three aspects of Marx's premises, at least as they have been interpreted since Marx, which seem to us incomplete or even missing altogether.

The first of these is the question of the 'material forces of production'. Generally speaking, Marxists have examined capitalism from the standpoint of political economy, on the assumption that capitalism's decline would be determined by its own internal contradictions, and that these could be measured using the statistical tools of the economist's trade: profitability, productivity of labour, GDP, inputs and outputs, and so on. We are by no means convinced that this is the case, and it seems to us necessary to re-examine, perhaps even redefine, the criteria we use to understand the implications of how decadent capitalism functions.

The second, is humanity's relationship to the rest of the natural world. There is a strong tendency to talk about 'nature' or 'the environment' as if it were something separate from us. We should be concerned about it, it is a source of enjoyment for us, but it is not 'us'. A moment's thought is enough to see that this dualist view of humanity on one side, nature on the other, makes no sense. We are part of nature, right down to the chemistry of our bodies which we share with all life on this planet. Marx understood this when he described the relationship between humanity and the rest of nature as 'metabolic', a process of constant exchange in which we modify the natural world and it modifies us. Because we are social animals, this metabolism is itself socially determined and today is reaching crisis point. Sadly, Marx's own rich insights into the ecological question and humanity's relationship with nature, have been largely ignored or underestimated in theories of decadence.

Finally, there is the question of consciousness which we touched on above. This is one of the most intractable questions posed by science today, so it is hardly surprising to find an unresolved tension in Marx's thinking on the subject. On the one hand, he tells us, 'social existence determines consciousness'; elsewhere he makes the point that the ruling ideas in any society are invariably those of the ruling class which has the material means of producing them. But Marx is no determinist. As he says (in *18th Brumaire*), 'Men make their own history, but they do not make it as they please; they do not make it under self-selected circumstances, but under circumstances existing already, given and transmitted from the past'. Human beings are conscious, or at least capable of being so, of themselves, of their activity; they can make choices about the future. Never has this been more true than in the epoch of capitalism's decay, so that in a sense the present is determined by the future, or as Marx put it 'The social revolution of the [21st] century cannot take its poetry from the past but only from the future'.

The structure of this book

The book is divided into three parts.

The first article attempts to set out the basic theoretical assumptions that guide our thinking.

The second section, which comprises several articles of historical analysis, might be titled a 'briefing for a descent into hell'.[6] It aims to provide a way of understanding the world in which we have been living since the opening years of the 20th century, which we characterise as the world of capitalism's endgame.

The final article summarises our main conclusions, and endeavours to show that the situation is not hopeless, that the society we live in, for all its danger and destructiveness, contains within it the premises for a very different, more optimistic future. This last article is in some ways the most important, since if the only future that can be imagined is disaster, then disastrous that future will be. However, the whole question is so vast that we felt it could only be dealt with separately; we will limit ourselves to a brief overview of some of the points we hope to cover later.

---

6   From the title of Doris Lessing's 1971 novel.

To our readers, now and in the future

Although those of us engaged on this project are in overall agreement on its general thrust, our individual sensibilities are different and we do not necessarily agree on the details: indeed, given the scope of what we are attempting it would be foolhardy to pretend otherwise. This is why, although all the articles have been the subject of considerable debate, they are all signed individually: we are a discussion group, not a political group with a defined platform, and each of us individually is in the end responsible for the ideas expressed there. Moreover, as we have indicated above, our discussions over two years have brought to light some fairly major disagreements, or at least difficulties, at the theoretical level. We are thus presenting ideas for further reflection rather than finalised theories. Our aim is above all to understand, recognising at the same time that whatever understanding we reach can only be provisional and subject to debate – that lifeblood of the workers' movement without which it cannot survive. Our hope is that the presently small and dispersed revolutionary movement will find them useful, that they will provoke debate and that they will contribute to a greater understanding of the problems we confront.

Such an understanding will be above all a matter for the future. There is indeed a potential for social transformation, but it will depend on the self-awareness of the world wide class of associated labour. Of that self-awareness, there is at present little sign, nor can we predict when it will reappear. But when it does, it will almost certainly be among new generations, those who today are only children or perhaps yet unborn. We address ourselves also to them, in the hope that they will be able to make use of our reflection and avoid our mistakes.

We are well aware of our own shortcomings and we make no claim to completeness. We will be eager to be argued against, contradicted. Only debate can knock down inadequate theories or strengthen good ones by obliging them to confront counter-arguments.

Historical Materialism and Capitalism in Decline

(Phillip Sutton)

Introduction

A key feature of capitalism that Marx identified in respect of its evolution is that capitalism could not facilitate the emergence of a new ruling class. It has effectively completed a cycle of expansion by exploiting societies and brought us to the point where, because no new exploiting class has been created and because the working class is the only exploited class, it is a revolutionary class which has no interest in creating a new system of exploitation, hence a new society based on common ownership of all property is possible.

Primitive communism was a society of common ownership but also of scarcity and the evolution through a cycle of societies based on exploitation and scarcity, has brought us to the point where science and manufacturing can actually go beyond scarcity and provide sufficient for all humanity, in other words a society of abundance. It is the marxist view that all societies experience periods of ascent and of descent and that capitalism in decline can only lead to socialism or barbarism.

But how do we start to assess this period of decline of capitalism?

The first section of this article aims to provide a grounding on the decline of capitalism by discussing Marx's theory of Historical Materialism and reevaluating, in the light of the recent evolution of capitalism, some conclusions by earlier marxists. We need to briefly review how previous societies with different modes of production experienced periods of decline. In particular, in our situation in a capitalism that is increasingly displaying an inability to organise itself rationally, we have also to reassess what the theoretical underpinnings for its decline actually are.

This reassessment questions views which say that the decline of a mode of production must be the decline of economic growth. We present the analysis that the decline of modes of production are all different and that capitalism's specific characteristics as a dynamic system mean we have not seen a reduction or slowdown in the economy. Instead we must recognise that capitalism continues to grow economically during its period of decline. This leads to an investigation of the role of relations of production as fetters on growth and the role of the productive forces themselves.

This article therefore also provides a grounding for other articles in this project which focus on population, capitalism's evolution over the past century and not least the economic impact of environmental threats.

Section 1 – Historical Materialism

To understand why capitalism is in decline and indeed why any mode of production declines, we have to explain the basics of Marx's theory of historical materialism and how it explains the development of human society.

Marx identified how humanity supports and reproduces itself and defined this as the mode of production. This is a simplified model of how a specific society is organised to produce the means of subsistence for life in that society. The means of production or the productive forces are the machinery or equipment used, the tools and raw materials, the class of workers and the technology that exists. This is the basis of any given society and sets the foundations for how people behave and think. In other words, how a population feeds itself and provides for its material needs is the basis of how to define that society.

This has often been taken, wrongly, to mean that 'economics', in the most limited sense, defines society.

Marx identified different societies in human history, societies that were based on different methods of organising and conducting the production of the population's needs and importantly was able to see that the consecutive societies in our history actually demonstrated a gradual social development.

Furthermore all societies have generated new material conditions and on this foundation new sets of beliefs and ideas develop. Please note that by the term 'material conditions', we mean the combination of the physical world and the social existence of humanity, ie human knowledge, behaviours and beliefs, at that time. In other words, even looking within today's world, if you are born in the UK people grow up with certain beliefs such as the idea that wage labour is normal, that it is normal for there to be rich and poor, or that there are standards of morality and ethics related to looking after yourself, your children, honesty, non-violence so on. Whereas if you are born in say Somalia after decades of war and famine and social collapse then your social attitudes are based more on absolute scarcity of resources and services, of droughts and famines, leading to an expectation of scraping a living and protecting yourself against others and often at the expense of others. These reactions are nobody's fault; they are completely dependent on the society we are born into and hence on real material conditions we face growing up and learning as normal. The same can also be said for people born into Roman society, where slave ownership was seen as normal, where the emperor's word must not be questioned, where work remained primarily manual and where wealth existed to provide a pampered lifestyle for the ruling class in society. Interestingly Roman society was a slave based society but it was not racially divided in the way we experience today. Both the slave workers and the ruling class were multicultural. In other words the dominant beliefs and ethics that develop in any given society tend to justify its mode of production and support the needs of its ruling class.

This view of history does not at all suggest everything is predetermined. All that is being said is that the material conditions at any given time in any given society have an impact on what can happen and on what people do and say. These conditions provide a framework for the possibilities for human activity but not precise determinations. It enables us therefore to see and understand the relationship between the physical world and the ideas of any given society as they progress and hence also the relationship between ideas and social change.[1]

There are three key elements of historical materialism to recognise: the mode or method of production in existence, the class structure that corresponds to it and the dynamic of progress in the development of the productive forces.

> The materialist conception of history starts from the proposition that the production of the means to support human life and, next to production, the exchange of things produced, is the basis of all social structure; that in every society that has appeared in history, the manner in which wealth is distributed and society divided into classes or orders is dependent upon what is produced, how it is produced, and how the products are exchanged. From this point of view, the final causes of all social changes and political revolutions are to be sought, not in men's brains, not in men's better insights into eternal truth and justice, but in changes in the modes of production and exchange. They are to be sought, not in the philosophy, but in the economics of each particular epoch.[2]

---

1   'The ideas of the ruling class are in every epoch the ruling ideas, i.e. the class which is the ruling material force of society, is at the same time its ruling intellectual force. The class which has the means of material production at its disposal, has control at the same time over the means of mental production, so that thereby, generally speaking, the ideas of those who lack the means of mental production are subject to it. The ruling ideas are nothing more than the ideal expression of the dominant material relationships, the dominant material relationships grasped as ideas.' (Marx, *The German Ideology* (1845), <https://www.marxists.org/archive/marx/works/1845/german-ideology/> [accessed 29 December 2022]

2   Engels, *Socialism Utopian and Scientific* (1880), <https://www.marxists.org/archive/

Here, Engels says that classes in society are identified by their position relative to how production is organised and wealth created, ie the relations of production.[3] What Marx and Engels were able to demonstrate was that history since the age of tribal hunter-gatherers has been the history of class societies. In each class society groups of advantaged individuals took control of the material resources that existed at the time (whether that was just land or, in later times, the ownership of slaves, buildings, weaponry or the means of production) and others who had no wealth but who had to work to be able to subsist. These two groups can be categorised as the ruling class and the working class although each society used different terms for these groups. It is in this sense of class relationships that Engels means that social change and political revolutions are to be found in the economics of an epoch.[4]

The 'Materialist Conception of History' is a theory that sets out to explain not only the roles that these classes perform within each individual society but also how distinct societies develop and transform. In other words, Marx's historical materialism is an analysis of societal development which helps us understand how different human societies form and ultimately how any given society reaches the limit of its development and either falls apart or gives way to a more dynamic society.

> In the social production of their existence, men inevitably enter into definite relations, which are independent of their will, namely relations of production appropriate to a given stage in the development of their material forces of production. The totality of these relations of production constitutes the economic structure of society, the real foundation, on which arises a legal and political superstructure and to which correspond definite forms of social consciousness. The mode of production of material life conditions the general process of social, political and intellectual life. It is not the consciousness of men that determines their existence, but their social existence that determines their consciousness.[5]

---

marx/works/1880/soc-utop/index.htm> [accessed 29 December 2022]

3   The relations of production are the totality of relationships within the mode of production between actors in society involved in the production and distribution of goods. Of further relevance here is the idea of the means of production, which are the physical factors, i.e. capital assets, raw materials and components, the available technology and the working class itself that are required to undertake production. The relations of production are how those means of production are acted upon by groups of people in society.

4   Note also the contradiction between this statement of the importance of economics with his later comment that people took his and Marx's view of the importance of economics too literally.

5   Marx, *Preface to a Contribution to the Critique of Political Economy* (1859), <https://www.-marxists.org/archive/marx/works/1859/critique-pol-economy/preface.htm> [accessed

Each mode of production forms a distinct society then, one which develops a combination of productive forces, new technologies and improved social systems to make use of those technologies. However historical materialism also recognises a progression of modes of production.

> History is nothing but the succession of the separate generations, each of which exploits the materials, the capital funds, the productive forces handed down to it by all preceding generations, and thus, on the one hand, continues the traditional activity in completely changed circumstances and, on the other, modifies the old circumstances with a completely changed activity.[6]

Marx is here placing the emphasis on the productive forces as the basis of social relationships in that society, 'civil society' as he termed it. However, historically as technology develops within any given society, it is possible for a new mode of production to develop within the old society which leads to a conflict between an old and a new exploiting class. What gradually emerges from that problematic situation is a new dominant mode of production, which has the capacity to develop technology and the means of production further. This new set of relations of production is introduced and developed by a new class; not necessarily consciously, for this new ruling class is following its own interests and developing its own position as a ruling class.

What this last paragraph has described is a period of ascent of the new relations of production followed by a period of conflict between the old and the new; the latter is actually a period of descent of the old and ascent of the new mode of production

What are the features of the descent of modes of production?

Marx's clearest statement regarding the limits to growth of a specific mode of production is as follows:

> At a certain stage of development, the material productive forces of society come into conflict with the existing relations of production or – this merely expresses the same thing in legal terms – with the property relations within the framework of which they have operated hitherto. From forms of development of the productive forces these relations turn into their fetters. Then begins an era of social revolution. The changes in the

---

1 January 2021]

6   Marx, *The German Ideology* (1845).

economic foundation lead sooner or later to the transformation of the whole immense superstructure.[7]

This is an important statement which is, or should be, the basis of any analysis of the changes in society during the course of history and of each society's decline. Note that the relations of production are the social relationships that people engage in to produce for the satisfaction of human needs, while the forces of production include not only manufacturing equipment but also the available raw materials, the available technology, the land and the working class itself.

We will return to this issue in Section 2 but first we should look with hindsight at the progression of the main societies in history that led up to capitalism i.e. primitive communism, slave society and feudal society. Whilst we do not wish to provide a fully detailed history of these forms of society, it will be constructive however to briefly review the factors that brought about the decay of each, to understand the implications for capitalism and its decay. Furthermore, in looking at the main progression of modes of production as presented by Marx, we do not intend to discuss those societies that certainly contributed to history but failed to lead directly to a new or progressive mode of production or failed to develop into capitalism. In this sense we are being eurocentric but that is only because Europe was the birthplace of capitalism; since its birth, capitalism has spread and now dominates the world.

Primitive Communism

The tribes that composed this form of society were essentially family-based and relied on communal property and communal preparation of the means of subsistence and reproduction. This form of lifestyle lasted for a long time so it was stable but clearly not dynamic in terms of expanding what the family could produce. It did however spread geographically throughout most of the world adapting to local conditions as it went. It was a society which remained primarily dependent on materials and foodstuffs that were readily available for them to be used in nature. Essentially they were small groups that may have had either sedentary or migratory lifestyles, in which the members of the tribe shared the tasks of hunting, gathering or growing food, cooking, childcare etc and property was seen as having a collective ownership.

This form of social organisation still demonstrated low productivity and, it is suggested, a short lifespan, being heavily dependent on available natural resources and with little defence against natural, environmental dangers. Its decline came with the emergence of permanent agriculture, which meant crops

---

7   Marx, *Preface to a Contribution to the Critique of Political Economy* (1859).

could be grown and stored for later usage. This step also meant the emergence of slavery as tribes came into conflict with one another and the losers became the property of the victorious tribe. It also led to the development of private property and the wealth of land and animals became important. Agricultural production began humanity's attempt to dominate nature and proved itself not only more productive than hunting and gathering but also created more powerful social organisations which the earlier family tribes were unable to compete with.

Bairoch suggests that hunter gatherer society had grown to its maximum capacity:

> These figures [for population growth] are certainly very low, but in the context of a hunter-gatherer society, they had reached a level where **continued population growth would be impossible without a radical modification of the economy.**[8]

In fact, given that hunter-gatherer tribes were classless, it seems that their society could not have clear or significant ascendant and decadent phases. However, there were relations of production in the sense of a division of labour among the tribespeople. But it was a stable society whereby small family-based tribes moved from place to place to obtain their means of subsistence and the society spread geographically as it expanded in population and searched for new food supplies. The most fundamental reason given for the change to agricultural farming communities is climate change. The change of period from Pleistocene to Holocene accompanies the emergence of agricultural communities in the period about 10,000 BCE.

> Agriculture came about because of the convergence of a number of seemingly unrelated phenomena that drove the evolution of a complex and expansionary economic system. These include the unprecedented climate stability of the Holocene, the evolution of human sociality, and our ability to cooperate with unrelated others. Once agriculture began to take hold, natural selection operating on diverse populations, driven by the economic requirements of surplus food production, favoured those groups that could best take advantage of economies of scale in production, larger group size, and a complex division of labour.[9]

The change of climate meant the environment facilitated the growth of the productive forces and of a new mode of production because it increased the

---

8   Bairoch, *Histoire économique De Jéricho à Mexico*, quoted in CMCI, 'In Defence of Historical Materialism' (2022), <https://afreeretriever.wordpress.com/portfolio/in-defense-of-historical-materialism-part-ii/3/> [accessed 10January 2023]

9   Gowdy, 'Our hunter-gatherer future: Climate change, agriculture and uncivilization' in *Futures* Volume 115, January 2020, <https://www.sciencedirect.com/science/article/pii/S0016328719303507> [accessed 29 December 2022]

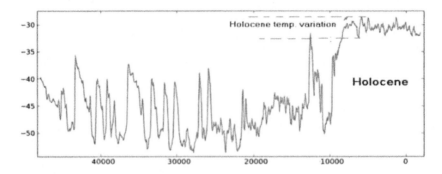

Figure 1: Temperature Variations Pleistocene and Holocene Periods
(NB Y axis based on ice core temperatures taken in Greenland)

From: Dalum Hjallese Debate Club, *History of Earth's Climate Chapter 7 Holocene* (2020)
<https://www.dandebat.dk/eng-klima7.htm> [accessed 29 December 2022]

average temperature and facilitated the capacity of the soil and climate to pro-duce foodstuffs that were of more use to humanity, in particular enabling wild corn and wheat to grow. Figure 1 indicates the change of temperature at this time. It is also the case that cows were first domesticated around 10,000 BCE at the start of this period, presumably based on pets kept in the previous period. Sedentary communities[10] existed alongside hunter-gatherers and pre-sumably this established not only the opportunity to increase the number of slaves, but also to spread and learn skills. Agricultural communities will have been more productive and hence more dynamic than the earlier tribes.

The argument here is that the temperature change from a wildly variable colder climate to the relative climate stability of the Holocene enabled the de-velopment of agriculture which was dependent on a more stable temperature: 'Only the Holocene could offer a stable climate for a long time, during which agriculture and civilization could develop'.[11]

No doubt there are more complexities to add to this picture but what is evident is that the change in climate, i.e. an external factor, facilitated the capa-city of human society to develop new methods of production.

---

10   For example, the Chinchurro society were sedentary fishermen who lived from about 9000 to 3000 BCE, and Göbekli Tepe and Çatal Höyük are dated to about 11,000 BCE

11   Dalum Hjallese Debate Club.

Slave Society

The next major form of mode of production was based on slavery. This type of society began with the early sedentary, agricultural communities as mentioned above but developed into the more structured kingdoms which began emerging around 5000 years ago, including the Mayan empire of middle America, the Chinese empires of the Far East to the various Middle Eastern empires, e.g. Egyptian, Babylonian and Persian. Most of these empires rose and fell without providing the basis for a slave-based mode of production, although some would have an impact on later empires in terms of new technologies. They used slaves but it was not specifically for production. Hence we should perhaps see the Greek, Athenian, and Roman empires as the peak of slave societies as they were fully developed modes of slave production.

The Roman empire was a particularly dynamic society that eventually created a large empire out of the regions surrounding the Mediterranean Sea. The empire based in Rome lasted some 1000 years until nearly 500 CE and the eastern half of the Roman empire, what is called today the Byzantine empire based in Constantinople, lasted for a further 1000 years after that. It was the dynamism of this empire that brought it into conflict with neighbouring tribes from northern Europe which were also starting to expand by the 4th century; a factor that was significant in its final downfall.

This was a centralised society based on Rome as the centre of the empire and controlled entirely by the ruling class in the city. Wealth drawn from the empire was not used to help these regions develop significantly; it was mostly used to support the luxurious lifestyles of Rome rather than to develop the regions significantly, even though agricultural development was an important element of the empire.

Slave society expanded by taking on more slaves and land, thereby gaining the labour to produce more buildings, foods and crafts etc. These slave societies therefore developed technologies based on labour-intensive crafts and warfare, hence ships, roads and buildings advanced tremendously over and above the basic skills of the earlier tribes and there were also significant advances in weaponry, clothing and handicrafts. Also, the dependence on slaves gave the ruling classes much more free time to develop intellectual skills that the tribal societies lacked. This is how both Greek and Roman societies left behind significant social, cultural and even technical advances for later societies. Although some of this technology and learning was lost following their collapse, the term 'dark ages' to describe the period is however now seen as inappropriate.

In terms of slave society, it is perhaps most useful for us to look at the decline of the last empire, Rome. The Roman empire had developed significant technological skills, eg buildings, agriculture, roads and transport, water supply, and social structures. Also it was a relatively 'open' society which developed the economic and political systems in regions it took over and extended some of the political and philosophical ideas developed in Greek society.

From 200 CE onwards however the Roman empire had become too large and too costly and problematic to control. It was overstretched and became more and more despotic in its control of new regions it took over. The borders of the western empire in particular were porous and its control was unpopular with the populations in these regions. As a result, it became riven with internal strife as the ruling class struggled to find policies to manage the bloated empire. The empire eventually split into a western empire and the Byzantine empire in the east (the wealthiest section and hence of more interest to the ruling class). Both sections became more centralised and more despotic and indeed the adoption of christianity by the eastern empire intensified this process (i.e. one god, one emperor, one set of morals). The treatment of the lower classes became more brutal with more taxes being raised to support the armed legions in their almost continual conflicts with barbarians on all sides. The lower classes were kept occupied by the bloody spectacles of the arena that were put on as social entertainment to distract them from the failing political systems of the empire.

Agricultural estates became more important with the breakup of the empire and there was an increased use of wages to pay agricultural labourers (*coloni*).

Regarding the decline of the Roman empire, it is clear, in terms of internal fetters, that the economic weakness of an expanded empire exacerbated the political and military demands of a slave society. Certainly the western empire generated too little wealth and became uneconomic and too costly militarily to manage, and this generated more and more political conflict in Rome. Slavery became a fetter on the expansion of the empire as it became too costly to expand the empire and add more slaves. For the western empire it was not the case that slave production was squeezed out by the encroachment of feudal-type production although there was an increased use of paid labourers (coloni) as more and more people left the towns. It was the external threats posed by the barbarian tribes around the borders of the empires, in combination with the great military cost of managing the western empire, that finally brought it down. The lands overtaken by the so-called 'barbarians' formed the basis of agricultural estates in which slavery was gradually eliminated by the need of agricultural communities for legal protections for the workforce.

Economically, the material growth of the empire became itself a fetter on further growth as the cost of maintaining it became too great. However the final collapse of Rome was political and military. In its decline there was a growth of the state and this complemented political incoherence and a growth of social disparity and social intolerance, all of which were compounded by the adoption of Christianity. The split into two empires also cut off the western empire from the wealth of the Middle East, which weakened it further.

According to the historian Edward Gibbon:

> The story of its ruin is simple and obvious; and, instead of inquiring why the Roman empire was destroyed, we should rather be surprised that it had subsisted so long. The victorious legions, who, in distant wars, acquired the vices of strangers and mercenaries, first oppressed the freedom of the republic, and afterwards violated the majesty of the purple. The emperors, anxious for their personal safety and the public peace, were reduced to the base expedient of corrupting the discipline which rendered them alike formidable to their sovereign and to the enemy; **the vigour of the military government was relaxed, and finally dissolved, by the partial institutions of Constantine; and the Roman world was overwhelmed by a deluge of Barbarians.**[12]

The eastern, Byzantine Empire remained in place until the 15th century but it was transformed by its adoption of christianity, even though it maintained its attachment to the concept of a Roman empire. The warfare against the Huns as it tried to retake Rome and against Arab invaders exhausted it financially and a Black Death-related plague killed it off as a major force during the 14th and 15th centuries. In this empire, slavery became quite rare by the first half of the 7th century and by the 11th century semi-feudal relations had largely replaced slavery. Christianity had helped transform the eastern empire with the adoption of some feudal-type features.

Feudalism

As discussed, the clash with external tribes across Europe and the collapse of Roman centralised systems led over time to a more decentralised, agriculturally-based society. Although initially the large Roman estates broke up into peasant holdings, these became concentrated as property of larger landowners who owned the smaller strips worked by peasants tied to their bits of land. The formation of estates attracted many workers from the collapsed armies and towns. Feudal society followed on gradually then after the collapse of the Ro-

---

12   Edward Gibbon, 'General Observations on the Fall of the Roman Empire in the West' in *The Decline and Fall of the Roman Empire*, Volume 3 (London: Strahan & Cadell, 1781), reprinted in 3 vols. ed. David Womersley (London: Penguin Classics, 1995), vol 2, p.509. The quote can be found at Online Liberty Library <https://oll.libertyfund.org/quote/edward-gibbon-wonders-if-europe-will-avoid-the-same-fate-as-the-roman-empire-collapse-brought-on-as-a-result-of-prosperity-corruption-and-military-conquest-1776> [accessed 29 December 2022]

man Empire in the 5th century. These estates became the basis of manorial estates and kingdoms of the feudal era, a process which was driven forward in particular by the transformation of the Byzantine Empire and by the empire of Charlemagne in northern Europe during the 8th century. Slave labour was seen as inhumane and serf labour was seen as a protection of the rights and responsibilities of the workforce. This transformation reflected the idea that if workers had a vested interest in their own work, productivity would be improved, and what emerged over time was a new type of labour as a new productive force in society. Land in the form of worked estates was also a very important productive force and whilst all property ultimately belonged to royalty, it was managed by the local nobility and lords of the manor, who also had rights and responsibilities in the form of provision of armed service and taxes. This form of production was fully established by the 11th century. Royalty and the local nobility formed the ruling class and the serfs were workers who were required to provide tithes to the ruling class for the privilege. In some regions, instead of actual tithes, the payment to the upper classes took the form of the requirement of unpaid labour (the *corvée* system). The various layers of feudal society were established in law and those that tried to escape this control became outlaws.

In terms of the descent of feudal society, we can see some similarity to Rome in that there was increased conflict between the layers of the ruling class and more and more power came into the hands of royalty and the catholic church. It was the development of merchant trade and craft skills in particular that led to the growth of towns and the financial mechanisms that came to challenge feudal practices. In fact during its apparent period of decadence from the 1200s to the 1600s, GDP is estimated to have doubled.[13] This change came from the economic and political expansion of bourgeois society.

In the general population there was also a reaction against the feudal system and there were many peasant revolts in Europe during the 14th century. The reaction against the power of the Catholic church and feudal structures grew both in the ruling class and the population at large. There was eventually outright conflict between the Catholic church and the new protestant religions, which effectively supported the emergence of capitalist structures and represented a more open society with individual rights and greater freedom of thought.

From the time of the Crusades (approx 1100-1200 CE) there had been an increase in international trade but it also led to one of the issues that weakened feudalism. The death of so many in the Crusades meant that back home there

13   'World GDP over the last 2 millennia', 2022, in *Our World in Data* <https://our-worldindata.org/grapher/world-gdp-over-the-last-two-millennia?time=1000.1700> [accessed 29 December 2022]

were insufficient knights (sometimes described as rent-a-cops) to keep the serf population in check.

Feudalism was weakened by other crises during the 14th century. The Great Famine (1315-1317) led to a decline in agricultural production, meaning the lords had to come up with new strategies to obtain sustainability. The Black Death (1348-1350) severely decreased Europe's population, thereby making labour a more costly commodity. As time went by, greater numbers of serfs escaped from servitude and worked in outlaw regions or in towns for money; greater use of money in society in general facilitated this together with peasant revolts, and all of these factors conspired to weaken the traditional setup of unfree labourers being tied to the land and working for the rich. By the end of the 14th century more agricultural labour was done by paid workers than unpaid serfs.

From 1600 onwards international trade and colonialism grew enormously. The increased influence of towns as merchants and crafts grew in strength all reflected the ideology and needs of capitalism.

Feudalism had entered its decadence because of internal contradictions including the immobility of labour and the disparity of wealth, but its end came about because of the growth within it of the more productive capitalist system which eventually came to dominate society.

During the period from the 16th century the population started to rise again reflecting the emergence of capitalist methods. It is clear that capitalism did not start or cause this decline of feudalism but it did bring it to an end.

There were many local conflicts between the bourgeoisie (literally the town dwellers) and feudal structures as towns grew in strength and importance. From the end of the 15th century, as capitalist methods came to dominate, agriculture saw the serfs being thrown off the land by capitalist landlords, and farmers and the serfs could do nothing but move into towns to find work and obtain any sort of subsistence available to them.

So in its descent we can see feudal society suffering similar problems of internal political conflicts which were compounded by the conflicts and machinations between leaders of the various feudal kingdoms and by the churches trying to hold onto power, but also specific external factors which feudalism had no means of managing.

In conclusion, the mechanisms that feudalism put in place weren't strong enough to fend off the enormous growth of productive forces by capitalism, which also came to be seen to represent economic and political freedom. The Renaissance in Europe also took its toll on feudalism, as people embraced art, technologies and change that marked an end of the religious controls and royal prerogatives of medieval times and a transition into the modern world.

It would seem that the real weakness of the feudal system lay in the comparison with capitalist systems and ideas as they grew within feudal society so for example various sectors of the emerging bourgeoisie were introducing, even experimenting with new forms of commerce and manufacturing techniques such as cottage industries, rented land and so forth. So feudal relations need to be seen as the fetters on the development of productive forces. The new and more effective systems set up by the bourgeois class in contradiction to the feudal systems offered all layers of feudal society the opportunities of individual enhancement and freedom. In particular it was the capacity of capitalist systems to demonstrate the lack of productivity of feudalism through the development of larger scale industry and trade. This is not to say that feudalism was not in decline, there was an internal decline but that did not lead to its collapse. It was capitalism that put the nails in the coffin.

So what can we learn from these periods of decline?

The fetters raised by the relations of production do certainly apply when we compare consecutive modes of production and appear to lead to a decline in economic growth, but they do not necessarily lead to the economic collapse of the old method of production. External factors and the new modes of production developing within the old society played important roles. This is a significant consideration that we need to apply to capitalism to determine if it applies here too.

It is evident that we must take account of external factors that could contribute to the end of capitalism. Today, an acceleration of environmental problems, e.g. climate change, pollution, famines and droughts, fires and floods, the destruction of natural diversity, overfishing, deforestation and so on, are all what we are calling external influences on the mode of production which threaten the continued existence of capital and of humanity itself.

It is the very scale of capitalist production today that brings it into conflict, not just with its internal economic contradictions but also with these external factors.

The Ascent of Capitalism

From the 13th century, features of what we can now identify as capitalism began to appear within feudal society. Capitalism began with the accumulation of wealth in the hands of merchants who made huge profits from the international trade in spices, crockery, silk etc, and who, through the use of joint stock and charter companies, established and exploited the resources of colonies. Eventually their wealth was used to manufacture rather than simply purchase goods to sell and so expand a manufacturing system that depended on free labour and large scale production.

This system of manufacturing gave rise to a ruling class who owned both the means of production and the end-products of the manufacturing process. They employed a workforce to do the work for them but wage payments only provided for their subsistence. As a result, the capitalists became wealthier and wealthier whilst the working class remained on subsistence. It is a dynamic system that fosters and depends on competition and produces continual growth in capital and therefore enables continuing rapid improvements in technology and productivity. Although money and indeed wage labour had existed beforehand, capitalism is the first system to base itself on paid labour and money capital and production for exchange. This enables capitalists to invest in and expand the means of production and to generate, through this accumulation of capital, an expanded working class.[14] It is this use of waged labour that makes capitalism so dynamic because it gives capital the capacity to continually expand and improve the means of production. This is unlike the slave and feudal societies, which, although they exploited a working class, tied workers to their 'rulers' without paying wages, leading to conservative, stable systems of production.

The development of capitalism up to the end of the 19th century saw the creation of two major 'institutions': firstly the nation state, with national boundaries which provided the legal and social framework to facilitate the growth of a manufacturing economy; and secondly, as capitalist national economies came to dominate home markets, a world market, in which capitalism fundamentally dominated and which meant that all nations were under capitalist control.

The Descent of Capitalism

It is clear from the review of previous modes of production that each one demonstrates differing characteristics in their decadence, so in that sense there is no definitive guidance from history. However it has become evident that Marx's phrase 'the relations of production are a fetter on the productive forces'

---

14   Previous modes of production were based on natural economies because production, whether for the benefit of individuals or for tribal chiefs or emperors, was primarily of use values rather than exchange values. In these societies, any exchange that took place was of surplus goods and secondary to the main process of production.

does not have to refer purely – or even primarily – to economic decay within the decadent period.

Indeed it can be argued that Marx's expression here relates simply to the comparison of an old mode of production in relation to a new mode of production. In this comparison, it is absolutely clear that the new society represents a relative improvement in economic productivity over and above what the previous society was able to achieve.

Within tribal society and feudalism it is not clear that the old mode of production was in economic decline or collapse, rather it seems that external factors had a great impact on their decline (for hunter-gatherers it was the establishment of agriculture and private property in the hands of larger tribes and for feudalism it was capitalism itself). What has become evident is that there are external factors with each respective mode of production which have had a significant impact on its decline or end.

Marx does also state that no new society can arise unless the old society has fully developed its productive forces, but this seems to suggest either that the old society is producing to its maximum or that it effectively stops production and stops being able to support its population. There is little evidence of either however as all previous societies have come to an end after a long period of decline and from confrontations between old society and new exploiting classes, so it is much better to base ourselves on his statement that the new society never replaces the old until all the conditions for the new are in place.

So in terms of capitalism, we can see that the creation of a worldwide working class engaged primarily in associated labour has been achieved and there is no new (or more efficient) mode of exploitation growing within it that can supplant it.

But what needs explanation is the fact that, in contrast to previous modes of production, capitalism has continued to grow economically during its period of decadence. In fact the economy is growing faster in the 21st century than it did in the 19th.

What Figure 2 indicates is that the capitalist economy continues to grow even during what we are calling the period of the system's decline. This is not an accident; it happens because capitalist production always produces more commodities than already exist. It is a system based on the accumulation of capital and this, just as Marx said, is a process that must absolutely continue. Hence we should not expect capitalism's decadence to be a simple economic decay. In fact, perhaps we should be asking why capitalism did not grow faster economically in its period of ascendance than it did? It appears that the formation of national economies and national institutions, and the growth of a world market, were the main historical achievements of its ascendance i.e. its political

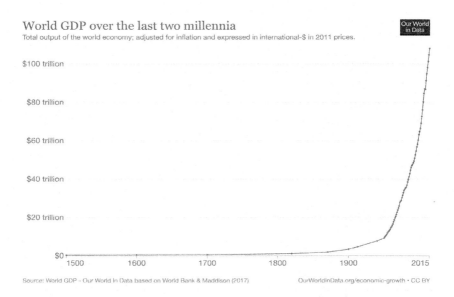

Figure 2: Growth of World GDP from 1500 to 2015

'World GDP over the last two millennia', 2022, in *Our World in Data* <https://ourworldindata.org/grapher/world-gdp-over-the-last-two-millennia> [accessed 29.12.22]

objectives, and the establishment of these structures also signified the elimination of the dominance of feudal institutions.

That capitalism has continued to grow both in ascendancy and decadence should not surprise us as it means simply that the accumulation of capital has continued on an accelerated basis as the graph of GDP[15] implies. Even if, as Marx again identified, the rate of profit that capital achieves has been falling precisely because the total mass of capital grows, this increased mass of capital means there will generally be an ever greater mass of profit produced. This should not be interpreted to mean economic crises do not occur, clearly they do, and it does not mean that disparities of income and the relative poverty of the working class do not worsen – these are permanent features of capitalism. It also does not mean that the relations of production do not act as a fetter on the productive forces in this period; it does mean however that these fetters can limit and divert growth into wasteful areas but they can never stop overall growth in the economy.

---

15   While GDP does not measure the actual accumulation of capital, it can be taken as an indicator of trends in the economy

By the end of the 19th century capitalism's domination of the world was completed with the colonisation of the vast majority of regions across the globe. The well-established nations had by and large completed their control over their home market and had pursued policies of expansion around the globe in search of additional resources, new commodities, cheap labour and new markets. This rise of capitalism was by no means peaceful or humane, capitalism never has been, but it was clearly an expanding system that was developing scientific, technical and manufacturing skills and social organisation in a way that no previous society had been able to.

Around 1914 something changed, wars of expansion turned into world wars of confrontation between colonial powers, and, instead of private capital, the state began to be the dominant force in each nation controlling the national economy as well as its international relations. The first half of the 20th century saw two world wars, an attempted working class revolution, economic crisis and increased ideological domination of the population. After World War II, there was a period of reconstruction followed by periods of economic crises and restructuring. By the early 21st century we have experienced a period of restructuring with the implementation of digital technologies and the globalisation of production. However political systems appear to have become infected with populist ideologies and the social systems are increasingly disorganised. What is clear is that we are not living in a rational system; there is too much going wrong and the ruling class does not appear able to cope.

So whilst we recognise that capitalism has continued to expand the productive forces and has enabled significant developments in scientific and technical knowledge, it is possible to identify over the past century of its decline various negative features, i.e.:

— the increased dominance of the state (state capitalism),
— the ideological control of society, and in particular, the ever-powerful weapon of nationalism,
— an increased dependancy on debt especially household debt,
— increased exploitation and the ongoing expansion of production, and in recent decades a massive increase in population (and the working class),
— and last but not least wars of attrition.

These are a mixture of political and economic factors which act as fetters on the transition of society to communism but not so much on the growth of capital as yet.

As in previous societies, we are now starting to see increasing political confrontations between sections of the ruling class, some of which are engaging in increasingly irrational policies (populism), as the insolubility of social problems, as well as social and economic disparities, intensify.

Lastly, the expression 'infinite growth in a finite planet' demonstrates perhaps the greatest threat to humanity from capitalism. We need to recognise that capitalism's ongoing capacity for growth and where this has now brought production and population levels are actually a major threat to a finite world. Capitalism has created a genuinely global system of production that could potentially benefit humanity but doesn't because of competition and the profit motive, but now this scale of production is leading to a major clash between this mode of production and the environment - whether that is the material world, pollution, the climate or the flora and fauna of the world.

The decadence of capitalism appears therefore to be very different to previous modes of production. Economic growth continues at a greater pace and scale than at any point in history, but that growth itself is one of the contradictions of capitalism that are provoking political, social and environmental crises, if not outright catastrophes.

To investigate this further we must first look afresh at the relations of production and the productive forces and their impact within capitalism

Section 2 – Fetters and Productive Forces in the Descent of Capitalism

Section 1 discussed the general theory of Historical Materialism and how it applies to capitalism in decline. Section 2 is intended to focus in more detail on key features in capitalism's decline and how they should be interpreted, in particular the question of the growth of productive forces as well as the fetters that impact upon them.

The Relevance of the Tendency for the Rate of Profit to Fall

If we are to understand in more detail this period as a period of decline, we then have to have an explanation for the growth of the capitalist economy, which we can clearly see from the constant rise in GDP, population and primary energy use over capitalism's life.[16] Actually this explanation is not hard

---

16   For some useful statistics on the growth of capitalism, the reader can refer to CMcl, 'Has Capitalism entered its Decadence since 1914?' <https://afreeretriever.wordpress.com/portfolio/has-capitalism-entered-its-decadence-since-1914/>.

to find in Marx's writings because whilst there is nothing in the model of capitalism that prevents continuing growth in decadence, there is, in fact, a law that says it must do so – the law of the tendency of the rate of profit to fall (TROPF).[17]

So what are the key points that Marx makes about the impact of the falling rate of profit?

> We have shown how the same causes that bring about a tendency for the general rate of profit to fall necessitate **an accelerated accumulation of capital** and, consequently, an increase in the absolute magnitude, or total mass, of the surplus-labour (surplus-value, profit) appropriated by it... It is evident that within the proportions indicated above **a capitalist disposing of a large capital will receive a larger mass of profit than a small capitalist making seemingly high profits.**[18] (our emphasis)

This is important because not only does it indicate that 'an accelerated accumulation of capital' is always present in capitalism, but it also generates an increased population. As a contribution to understanding the evolution of capitalism we can see that a small mass of capital can make a high profit rate, as was the case during capitalism's ascendant period, whereas a large mass of capital makes a low rate of profit but a larger mass of profit, as has been the case since the start of the 20th century and particularly since the 1950s.

To emphasise this point, the impact of the falling rate of profit (FROP) is that it leads not only to increased accumulation, and accelerated accumulation at that, but also to a continual increase in the mass of profit. Hence the overall economy may expand but individual firms experience increased pressure of competition and the situation of the working class deteriorates.

> The law that a fall in the rate of profit due to the development of productiveness is accompanied by an increase in the mass of profit, also expresses itself in the fact that a fall in the price of commodities produced by a capital is accompanied by a relative increase of the masses of profit contained in them and realised by their sale.[19]

We have here a key indicator that growth in capitalism in its period of decline is to be expected. It is a permanent consequence of the TROPF and must be present in both ascendancy and decadence. Is this not a very good descrip-

---

17   There is a debate as to what happens when insufficient profit is produced but proponents of the theory see the consequence as war leading to a reduction in the value of constant capital. In any case no one suggests that there is a set rate that would cause a crisis, let alone the decadence of capitalism

18   Marx, *Capital* Vol 3, Chapter 13 (1883) <https://www.marxists.org/archive/marx/works/1894-c3/ch13.htm> [accessed 29.12.22]

19   Ibid

tion of what has happened to capitalism over the past four centuries? Outside a fall in production, which has only happened since the 1950s during the Covid pandemic of 2020, the mass of profit must tend to grow. What does need to be taken into account here is also that at some point the TROPF will interact with other contradictions of capital and with the overproduction of capital to provoke crises and wars, which the CWO analyses as cycles of accumulation, in fact three of them, firstly prior to World War I, 1914-1945 and 1945 onwards.

It is obvious enough that in 1762 when Matthew Boulton built the first modern factory and the remainder of the economy consisted mostly of small craft workshops, it was relatively easy for capital to double in size because the increase was not that large. Today it is very much harder and takes longer to double in size, but the scale of capitalism today means that an average 3% growth in GDP per year leads to a much larger economy that doubles in size in little more than 20 years; this is a tremendous volume of growth.[20]

And the outcome, particularly over the past few decades, is that the rich get richer and the poor get poorer. This is not an empty slogan. Neo-liberalism since the 1990s, quantitative easing from 2008, the reactions to the Covid pandemic have all seen to it that the privileged benefit from all the government support and the rich soak up the cash that is pumped into the economy via banks and financial markets because all it does is make the assets they hold increase in value. By feeding the financial industries it further stimulates new profits for the rich because they can make greater profits in the financial markets than can be obtained through investing in industry. What is also clear though is that the growth in the economy and the increasing wealth of the ruling class do not mean that the working class is better off, in fact the opposite is true today.

Whatever phase of capitalism we are in, capitalism always continues to generate an increased rate of growth in the economy (aside from specific crises that is). This is what the bourgeoisie's own statistics on world GDP show,[21] and, even if we as marxists do not accept the figures as exactly showing capital growth, the trends are obvious. Marx summarises the problems caused by the 'unconditional development of the productive forces' thus:

> The real barrier of capitalist production is capital itself. It is that capital and its self-expansion appear as the starting and the closing point, the motive and the purpose of production; that production is only production for capital and not vice versa, the means of production are not mere

---

20   See the article by Mark Hayes, 'The Accumulation of Catastrophe'.

21   See Figure 2.

means for a constant expansion of the living process of the society of producers.[22]

The rate of profit is an indicator of accumulation in that because profit levels are falling, it drives individual capitals forward, but in a sense, it is also an indicator of the enormous level of economic growth of the economy as a whole. The growth of the mass of profit can only be a product of the exploitation of the working class and the increasing levels of surplus value created by capitalist production. It is what is called enhanced reproduction which is the norm for capitalism and possibly will be until the very end of its life.[23]

To summarise, it is evident that both economic growth and fetters on production exist within a declining capitalism. We can see these fetters in the way that capital produces for exchange and for profit and not for need, in the nation state and in the class struggle itself, but this does not prevent the increasing growth of capital. To argue that capitalism is capable of infinite growth is a perhaps dangerous prediction because capitalism itself continually generates fetters, contradictions and crises, but capitalism clearly generates new markets for itself as accumulation progresses. Hence we assert that growth in decadence exists and is not something that should be ignored and dismissed; it needs explanation and clarification by the communist left.

Understanding Fetters on Production

In the social production of their existence, men inevitably enter into definite relations, which are independent of their will, namely relations of production appropriate to a given stage in the development of their material forces of production. The totality of these relations of production

---

22   Marx, *Capital* Vol. 3, Chapter 13 (1883) <https://www.marxists.org/archive/marx/works/1894-c3/ch13.htm> [accessed 29.12.22]

23   Marx used the idea of simple reproduction to explain his model of capital and this is a scenario where only enough surplus value is created to replace the used raw materials and components (current assets) and repair the production machinery. In other words, the system has to make sure that the creation of surplus value precisely fits these needs and there can be no technical development, no population increase and no increase in capital assets. This is not how capitalism works. Let me propose another scenario where not enough surplus value is produced to undertake the tasks of simple reproduction, then there would be insufficient profit to keep production going, production would come to a rapid halt, the population would starve, and capital as a social system would collapse quickly if not almost instantaneously because no capitalist will manufacture if a profit cannot be produced. The last option here could only happen in a total collapse of the production system and the first option is impossible to anticipate, so the only viable reality is that capitalism keeps producing surplus value, increasing the population and accumulation so society and the economy keeps growing – at whatever rate the productive forces and the relations of production allow.

constitutes the economic structure of society, the real foundation, on which arises a legal and political superstructure and to which correspond definite forms of social consciousness. The mode of production of material life conditions the general process of social, political and intellectual life. It is not the consciousness of men that determines their existence, but their social existence that determines their consciousness. At a certain stage of development, **the material productive forces of society come into conflict with the existing relations of production** or – this merely expresses the same thing in legal terms – with the property relations within the framework of which they have operated hitherto. **From forms of development of the productive forces these relations turn into their fetters**. Then begins an era of social revolution.[24] (our emphases)

This is Marx's classic statement on the development and decline of modes of production and forms the basis of what has been the standard marxist position which emphasises that the relations of production are fetters that must cause a decline in economic growth. It was however written in 1859 when capitalism was still in its ascendant phase and Marx was still primarily writing about how capitalism was developing. At that time he had obviously no experience of what capital in decline would be like today and could only generalise from history, so it should not be surprising if his expectations for capital's decline are not totally correct.

This text does not question Marx's general analysis of historical materialism as he is completely correct to say that: 'The mode of production of material life conditions the general process of social, political and intellectual life'.[25]

Historical Materialism is an analysis of societal evolution and not the evolutionary study of humanity or ideas as such. When Marx raises the issue of stages of development and the fetters on productive forces it seems that in this regard there are different interpretations that can be placed on this analysis. This is what we wish to discuss here and relate to an understanding of capitalist decadence.

One interpretation by marxists of this statement is based on the last sentence of the quote above from Marx i.e. 'from forms of development of the productive forces these relations turn into their fetters'.[26] From this is drawn the conclusion that the decadence of a mode of production, and the primary influence on the evolution of that decline, is caused by the relations of production becoming fetters on production that brake or limit the growth of productive forces. This is an economistic view of the process of decline in the sense

---

24 Marx, *Preface to the Critique of Political Economy* (1859).

25 Ibid

26 Ibid

that ascendance and decadence are characterised by the state of growth of the economy.

This view is crystallised by Luxemburg for example:

> Capital accumulation progresses and expands at the expense of non-capitalist strata and countries, squeezing them out at an ever faster rate. The general tendency and final result of this process is the exclusive world rule of capitalist production. Once this is reached, Marx's model becomes valid: accumulation, i.e. further expansion of capital, becomes impossible.[27]

And by the ICC:

> According to the marxist view, the period of a society's decadence cannot be characterised by a total and permanent halt in the growth of the productive forces but by the definitive slackening of this growth.[28]

Bordiga presents a different view of the evolution of decadence in that he recognises that capitalism is still growing economically but will collapse at some point in the future. This view still depends on purely economic factors:

> The marxist vision can [...] be represented as a number of branches of curves, all ascending until they reach the top [...], after which there comes a sudden and violent fall and, at the bottom, a new social regime arises; we have another historic ascending branch.[29]

However, is this interpretation correct?

It clearly does apply when we compare one mode of production with its replacement. Each successive mode of production (ie tribal, slave, feudal and capitalist societies) demonstrates economic and social changes and improvements in the forces of production over and above the previous system, that much is certain. This can certainly be interpreted to mean that the old relations of production, embodied in the ruling class, act as a historic fetter on the progress of human society, but it seems unlikely that this is solely what Marx meant.

What we want to question therefore is just how accurate this economistic interpretation is when applied to the present period of capitalism's decline?

One problem is that the term 'fetter' is itself open to different interpretations when applied to the period of decline within any given mode of produc-

---

27   Luxemburg, *The Anti-Critique*, Chapter 6 (1915) <https://www.marxists.org/archive/luxemburg/1915/anti-critique/ch06.htm> [accessed 29.12.22]

28   ICC, *The Decadence of Capitalism*, Chapter 4, (2005 Edition), <https://en.internationalism.org/pamphlets/decadence> [accessed 29.12.22]

29   Bordiga, 'Meeting in Rome' (1951), quoted in GCI-ICG, *Theories of Decadence: Decadence of Theory*, 1985<https://libcom.org/library/theories-decadence-decadence-theory> [accessed 29.12.22]

tion. Is it a halt or a slow brake on the economy? Is it a reduction in the size of the economy? Is it a restriction on what is possible with the existing forces of production? Is it an internal or external limit to production? Certainly all of these are possible interpretations but the question is what happens in reality.

These questions pose the issue of just how the concept of a fetter on the productive forces should be used in understanding the process of decline of capitalism and how we should interpret Marx's statements. He said the relations of production act as fetters but is it about the conflict between waged labour and the ruling class? Is it the contradiction between exchange and use values? Is it profit vs surplus value? Is it imperialism and the destruction of war, or the nation state, competition, debt, inflation, non-capitalist markets or what?

At the start of the 21st century it is evident that despite periodic economic crises and issues caused by the contradictions of the capitalist mode of production, what has been taking place is an ongoing and indeed accelerating level of accumulation.[30] Unfortunately, those that adhere to the aforementioned interpretation of the role of fetters ignore the significance of the scale of economic growth in the 20th century in order to justify their own schemas and see only economic decay and decline in their view of decadence.

The CWO however presents their view of the decline as follows:

> Thus, if we start from the materialist view of history, it is clear that the motive force behind historical development is the material development of the productive forces. In all societies the forces of production develop and expand or become more complicated until, at a certain point, this development conflicts with the network of social relationships from which they had originally been engendered.[31]

This perspective clearly emphasises the level of development of the productive forces as the crucial factor in the evolution of society, in other words the development of productive forces disrupts the relations of production rather than the other way round.

A similar viewpoint was taken up by Internationalist Perspective (IP) in a series of articles discussing capitalist decadence during the 1990s:

> There is, however, in my opinion, an integral link between the permanent crisis of capitalism and the development of the productive forces. Rather than blocking or fettering their continued development, the relation

---

30   CMcl, 'Has Capitalism entered its Decadence since 1914?', 2021 <https://afreeretriev-er.wordpress.com/portfolio/has-capitalism-entered-its-decadence-since-1914/> [accessed 29.12.22]

31   CWO, 'Capitalism's Economic Foundations Part 1', 2022 <http://www.leftcom.org/en/articles/2022-08-31/capitalism-s-economic-foundations-part-i > [accessed 29.12.22]

between the two is such that the forces of production developed within the period of decadence become not only increasingly powerful and potent, but that they become increasingly dangerous, increasingly deadly, increasingly murderous, and this not just 'incidentally' or 'accidentally', but because capital in permanent crisis increasingly requires forces of destruction rather than forces of production in order to sustain itself.[32]

This perspective adds an important contribution, i.e. that the growth of capitalism is itself dangerous and a threat to humanity, which IP develops further:

The defining feature of capitalist decadence in this view, then, is neither a halting nor a deceleration in the development of the productive forces; it is, rather, the increasingly destructive tendency of the productive forces developed by capital, and not just because these become increasingly powerful [...] The underlying assumption here is that – at least at a certain stage in the historical development of technology – different courses of development of the productive forces are possible. This idea is entirely foreign to traditional or orthodox Marxism, with its productivist (and usually economic determinist) basis. For such Marxism, the productive forces developed by capitalism, decadent or otherwise, are neutral (between capitalist and communist deployment of them) because there is only one possible course or trajectory of their development, and thus any development of them at all, whether brought about by capitalism or not, is historically progressive.[33]

Pannekoek's analysis recognises that revolution and hence the decadence of capitalism is not simply an economic act or an act determined by economics, but a product of the acts of the working class and its experience of the society in general as based on that economic system:

For Marx the development of human society, and so also the economic development of capitalism, is determined by a firm necessity like a law of nature. But this development is at the same time the work of men who play their role in it and where each person determines his own acts with consciousness and purpose – though not with a consciousness of the social whole. To the bourgeois way of seeing things, there is a contradiction here; either what happens depends on human free choice or, if it is governed by fixed laws, then these act as an external, mechanical constraint on men. For Marx all social necessity is accomplished by men; this means that a man's thinking, wanting and acting – although appearing as a free choice in his consciousness – are completely determined by the action of the environment; it is only through the totality of these human acts, de-

---

32   ER, 'For a Non-productivist Understanding of Capitalist Decadence', *Internationalist Perspective* No 44 2005 <https://internationalistperspective.org/wp-content/uploads/2021/04/IP044.pdf> [accessed 29.12.22]

33   Ibid

termined mainly by social forces, that conformity to laws is achieved in social development. The social forces which determine development are thus not only purely economic acts, but also the general-political acts determined by them, which provide production with the necessary norms of right.[34]

This clearly reflects Engels' view as expressed in his letter to Bloch:

According to the materialist conception of history, the ultimately determining element in history is the production and reproduction of real life. Other than this neither Marx nor I have ever asserted. **Hence if somebody twists this into saying that the economic element is the only determining one, he transforms that proposition into a meaningless, abstract, senseless phrase**. The economic situation is the basis, but the various elements of the superstructure [...] also exercise their influence upon the course of the historical struggles and in many cases preponderate in determining their form. There is an interaction of all these elements in which, amid all the endless host of accidents [...] the economic movement finally asserts itself as necessary. Otherwise the application of the theory to any period of history would be easier than the solution of a simple equation of the first degree... [35] (our emphasis)

The argument by marxists that economic decline is the determinant of the decadence of any given mode of production is clearly contradicted here by Engels.

To conclude this section then, it is important to recognise that alongside the economic and social crises which we have seen in this period since the start of the 20th century, there has been an enormous increase in the overall productive capacity of capital, an increase which has been much greater than that achieved during the ascendant phase of capitalism. There has also been an enormous increase in population, something which Marx identified as a consequence of accumulation. What we have not seen is anything like the absolute halt or collapse in the forces of production that Luxemburg or Grossman, for example, suggest.

A view of decadence must therefore recognise and explain the contradiction between capitalism's continued tendency to grow and the fetters exerted on this growth.

What is noteworthy is that those who deny that capitalism is decadent in the 20th century tend to do so on the basis that economic growth is still continu-

---

34   Pannekoek, *The Theory of the Collapse of Capitalism* (1934), <https://www.marxists.org/archive/pannekoe/1934/collapse.htm> [accessed 29.12.22]

35   Engels, Letter to J Bloch (1890) <https://www.marxists.org/archive/marx/works/1890/letters/90_09_21.htm> [accessed 29.12.22]

ing. They recognise reality but their interpretation of capitalism's trajectory is equally economistic.

Historical Materialism and the Role of the Productive Forces

We must now consider the second aspect of Marx's statement from the previous chapter:

> At a certain stage of development, the material productive forces of society come into conflict with the existing relations of production.[36]

This is perhaps an aspect that has been too widely ignored, but Marx uses it more than once and indeed it can be seen to contradict the idea that it is the relations of production that act as a fetter and cause the slowdown or halt in the growth of productive forces, for example:

> The bourgeoisie cannot exist without constantly revolutionising the instruments of production, and thereby the relations of production, and with them the whole relations of society. Conservation of the old modes of production in unaltered form, was, on the contrary, the first condition of existence for all earlier industrial classes. Constant revolutionising of production, uninterrupted disturbance of all social conditions, everlasting uncertainty and agitation distinguish the bourgeois epoch from all earlier ones.[37]

In the following passage, Marx again places the emphasis on the growth and centralisation of capital (and labour) as the instigator of the end of the mode of production:

> There appears here the universalizing tendency of capital, which distinguishes it from all previous stages of production. Although limited by its very nature, **it strives towards the universal development of the forces of production, and thus becomes the presupposition of a new mode of production.**[38] (our emphasis)

Bukharin expresses the same thing in this way:

> Revolution therefore occurs when there is an outright conflict between the increased productive forces, which can no longer be housed within the envelope of the production relations, and which constitutes the fundamental web of these production relations i.e. property relations, owner-

36   Marx, *Preface to the Critique of Political Economy* (1859).

37   Marx, *The Communist Manifesto* (1848) <https://www.marxists.org/archive/marx/works/1848/communist-manifesto> [accessed 29.12.22]

38   Marx, *Grundrisse*, Notebook 5 (1857-61) <https://www.marxists.org/archive/marx/works/1857/grundrisse/ch10.htm> [accessed 29.12.22]

ship of the instruments of production. This envelope is then burst asunder.[39]

Gorter also placed the emphasis on technology and hence the development of the forces of production as the critical factor in the growth and the end of capitalism as a mode of production:

> But technology does not stand still. It is part of a faster or slower development and movement, the forces of production grow, the mode of production changes. And when the mode of production changes, the relations in which men face one another must necessarily change as well.[40]

And let us not forget that Gorter also provided a summary or definition of historical materialism:

> I have briefly summarised the content of our doctrine. It can be recapitulated in an outline form as follows:
>
> 1. Technology, the **productive forces**, forms the basis of society.
>
>   The productive forces determine the **relations of production**, the relations in which men confront one another in the production process.
>
>   The relations of production are at the same time **property relations**.
>
>   The relations of production and property are not only relations between persons, but between **classes**.
>
>   These relations of class, property and production (in other words, social existence) determine man's consciousness, that is, his conceptions of rights, politics, morality, religion, philosophy, art, etc.
>
> 2. Technology is undergoing continuous development.
>
>   Consequently, the productive forces, the mode of production, property and class relations, are also undergoing constant modification.
>
>   Therefore, man's consciousness, his conceptions and representations of rights, politics, morality, religion, philosophy, art, etc, are also modified along with the relations of production and the productive forces.
>
> 3. The new technology, at a certain stage of development, enters into conflict with the old relations of production and property. Finally, the new technology prevails.[41]

---

39   Bukharin, *Historical Materialism*, Chapter 7 (1921) <https://www.marxists.org/archive/bukharin/works/1921/histmat/7.htm> [accessed 29.12.22]

40   Gorter, *Historical Materialism for Workers* (1908), <https://www.marxists.org/archive/gorter/1920/historical-materialism.htm> [accessed 29.12.22]

41   Gorter, *Historical Materialism for Workers*, Chapter 3 (emphasis in the original).

We find the same view that the development of the productive forces is a key factor in social evolution expressed by Engels:

> Just as Darwin discovered the law of development of organic nature, so Marx discovered the law of development of human history: the simple fact, hitherto concealed by an overgrowth of ideology, that mankind must first of all eat, drink, have shelter and clothing, before it can pursue politics, science art, religion etc; that therefore **the production of the immediate means of subsistence and consequently the degree of economic development attained by a given people or during a given epoch forms the foundation** upon which the state institutions, the legal conceptions, the ideas on art and even on religion, of the people concerned have been evolved, and in the light of which they must therefore be explained, instead of vice versa, as had hither been the case.[42] (our emphasis)

It is correct that Marx and Engels themselves could not be clear about the conditions of capitalist decadence at the time they were writing, they were obviously influenced by what was happening in Britain during their lifetime. The following statement from the *Communist Manifesto* is however important:

> The productive forces at its disposal no longer play in favour of bourgeois property; they have, on the contrary, become too powerful for bourgeois institutions, which only hinder them.[43]

This quote is significant because it quite clearly starts from the perspective that even in the period of its ascendance the productive forces have become too large for capitalist society and disrupt the operation of the productive relations. Whilst it is quite true this section of the *Communist Manifesto* goes on to say that relations of production are a fetter on the productive forces, what we are arguing is that both the relations and the forces of production have an impact on the decline of a mode of production. We refer to the review of previous modes of production earlier in this article which suggests that other political, social and external factors also impact on the development of historic modes of production. As Engels suggests, other factors can and do come into play.

What we have to understand about historical materialism is that the productive forces are not a passive force in social development, they are in fact the driving force of social evolution. New modes of production and indeed changes within a mode of production do not occur because somebody thinks it would be a good idea to change the relations of production. The productive forces demand changes and generate classes that represent that change.

---

42   Engels, quoted in Franz Mehring, *Historical Materialism* (1893) (New Park Publications, 1975), p.8.

43   Marx, *The Communist Manifesto*.

To the extent that the labour process is solely a process between man and Nature, its simple elements remain common to all social forms of development. But each specific historical form of this process further develops its material foundations and social forms. Whenever a certain stage of maturity has been reached, the specific historical form is discarded and makes way for a higher one. The moment of arrival of such a crisis is disclosed by the depth and breadth attained by the contradictions and antagonisms between the distribution relations, and thus the specific historical form of their corresponding production relations, on the one hand, and the productive forces, the productive powers and the development of their agencies, on the other hand. A conflict then ensues between the material development of production and its social form.[44]

There is no question that economic decline as a product of internal contradictions is a feature demonstrated in previous periods of decadence but to argue that economic decline is the only factor in the decay of a mode of production is a narrow economistic approach.

While we have argued for the importance of the growth in the productive forces as the basis of social development, this is not the only factor to consider. The relations of production themselves can and do limit the productive forces in a period of decadence.

What we should recognise therefore is that it is not a question of 'either/or', it is a question of an ongoing interaction between the forces and the relations of production and the different roles played by each. Bukharin places the development of the productive forces at the core of society but recognises that the relations of production, as well as the superstructure, have a relationship which impacts the strengthening and weakening of an economy in different periods.

---

44   Marx, *Capital* Vol. 3, Chap 51 (1894) <https://www.marxists.org/archive/marx/works/1894-c3/> [accessed 29.12.22]

Types of Fetters acting on the Productive Forces

At this point therefore we need to consider how to understand the fetters and contradictions that exist within capitalism. We have looked at the factors in the 'core model' of capitalist production that Marx developed and we have identified that Marx and other marxists accepted the concept of factors 'external' to capitalism, but this is not a sufficient explanation. Those theories that focus solely on economic factors in the decline of a mode of production fail to examine the problem historically and focus only on a narrow interpretation of Marx and indeed rely simply on selected quotes rather than interpreting these quotes in the context of the remainder of his writings. Above all it is necessary to ensure that the concept of decadence is applied to the particularities of capitalism.

Although Bukharin suggests two categories of contradictions that can generate fetters on capitalism, we would now identify three:

1. the 'core elements' of capitalism, i.e. Marx's model and the contradictions that are generated from it,

2. the phenomena of capitalism that are generated by the operation of the core such as national economies, state capitalism, imperialist blocs etc, but which are not considered essential to Marx's model,[45]

3. 'external' factors, which are elements that capital does not create and which exist independently from it but impact upon it and are drawn into relationships with it.

1) Internal Fetters and Contradictions in the 'Core Model' of Capitalism

The ruling class, the capitalists, own all the means of production and they employ and pay the working class to produce products which then belong to the capitalists and are sold as commodities on markets to generate additional income for the capitalists. This additional value can be partly reinvested in new production and the cycle begins again.

These are the central relations of production in capitalism. It is the primary method of how goods are produced in the society. Furthermore, because money exists and is used to value commodities, it becomes possible for the ruling class to exploit workers and make a profit from the labour they provide, and because of this it has certainly been a more dynamic system for production than any in the past, which has significantly developed the productive forces.

---

45   This would have been less clear to marxists at the start of the 20th century in that the superstructure of global capitalism was changing significantly at that time

However, these elements of the capitalist model can also be negative factors in that they generate contradictions that can hold back social development. This may well vary periodically but, generally speaking, we see these contradictions impacting more severely on society in a period of decline, including the following:

- The working class and the ruling class are always drawn into conflict because the more the working class earns, the less profit the ruling class makes.
- Labour generates wealth for the owners of capital not for the workers.
- The falling rate of profit generates a continual need to increase the exploitation of the working class in competition with other capitalists.
- The objective of production is to make a profit and not to produce useful or socially necessary goods.
- Overproduction of capital is an inevitable consequence of the need for accumulation.
- Competition between capitalists is a key element of the market system.
- The centrality of money in production and distribution leads to the capacity to accumulate but also to wealth disparities and hence poverty.

These contradictions derive from the core relations of production: they are what creates capitalism's dynamism and drive it forward but they also pose fetters and restrictions on the capacity to produce and give rise to struggles between the classes.

A particularly important contradiction for capital is created by an important element of the way capitalism works, i.e. that the proletariat is a class of associated labour. This is specific to capitalism and the most important of the productive forces that capitalism has set in motion.[46] Associated labour is essential to capitalist organisation and profits.

However, because it unites the working class with a common interest in opposing the ruling class, it establishes the basis for the power of the working class to disrupt and potentially end this system of exploitation and so it also generates a working class that has a worldwide common interest in opposing the ruling class.

---

46 Associated labour: i.e. cooperative production by groups of workers organised in a division of labour. It is essential to passing beyond craft production in the early days of capitalism to the full flourishing of capitalist mass production. As above, the bigger the networks of associated labour, the more profitable it can become.

2) Phenomena of Capitalism as Fetters on Capitalism

Capitalism generates social and political structures to support its functioning and, as a consequence of being such a dynamic mode of production, these structures do not remain static. They find themselves continually changing with the development of new technological capacities, new production methods and new social needs. Capitalism has developed from a primarily mercantile phase to craft production to factory production and to mass production during the course of which it has gone from local to global production systems.

Each new phase of capitalism develops social structures which initially facilitate the expansion and development of the system but later come to be fetters on this development.

The National Economy

The creation of the nation by capitalism not only established unified legal and customs frameworks in which the economy and nation state could expand, it also unified populations hitherto divided culturally and linguistically. Technically, it created the new methods of transport, and 'that union, to attain which the burghers of the Middle Ages, with their miserable highways, required centuries, the modern proletarian, thanks to railways, achieved in a few years'.[47]

But by the early 20th century, the national economic structures had fully developed and the nation itself was becoming a barrier to the development of capitalism.

In recent decades, it has become clear that the largest industries e.g. aircraft and car manufacture, shipping, telecommunications, computing, no longer find it possible to operate in one country alone and, as a result, international joint ventures and global organisations selling on global markets have become the order of the day.

As we write in 2022, globalised production and market systems dominate the large industries but there is also a counter reaction to this shown in a tendency towards populism and nationalism in political life and a strengthening expectation for the support of local and national industries. Immigration is increasingly constrained, at the same time as economists are generally in agreement that the developed nations need to import young labour into an ageing workforce.

Hence the nation itself now stands as a barrier to the further development of capitalism. It is an economic, social, political and military framework which

---

47   Marx, *The Communist Manifesto*.

the bourgeoisie adopted for the revolutionary overthrow of feudalism and which the ruling class is basically incapable of doing without.

The Nation State and State Capitalism

The nation state initially acted to eliminate feudal controls and enable capitalist versions of freedom to become established but from the early 20th century the nation state took on the role of the manager of the nation and the national economy, and came to perform roles in controlling class and social conflict as well as economic management nationally and internationally. The state has also developed as a means of providing social support for the population which many see as positive contributions, e.g. health and social welfare services, pensions, fire services, roads and transport systems but which are actually established as supporting mechanisms for the war economy. A recent example of this enhanced social control would be the measures taken in the Covid pandemic which provided some (limited) support for the population as well as preventing the kind of economic downturn which would probably have occurred in the 19th century under similar circumstances. This growing role of the state in any nation also becomes a barrier to freedom by imposing laws and systems that serve to protect the *status quo* and the role of national ruling classes in society. The nation state as a reactionary institution becomes a fetter by maintaining the national focus, putting barriers in the way of genuine international development and by more and more clearly failing to provide solutions to the economic and social ills that capitalism produces.

Last but not least the power of each nation state expresses itself as the promoter of nationalism and ideological controls over the working class and society generally.

Globalisation

The ruling class is well aware of the barrier that the nation's existence places in the way of the maximum division of labour, competition, and rational exploitation of resources and technology. There has been no shortage of attempts to overcome it, from trade pacts like North Atlantic Free Trade Agreement (NAFTA) or the more recent Trans-Pacific Partnership, to international trade bodies like the General Agreement on Tariffs and Trade (GATT) or the World Trade Organisation (WTO), to customs unions of which the most important is the European Union.

Particularly during the second half of the 20th century we have seen a massive expansion of production systems globally. Companies no longer just manufacture their entire products in one factory but use raw materials and components produced in different parts of the world and sell the completed

47

products either regionally or internationally, facilitated by telecommunications networks and the reduction of transport costs by container shipping etc. This enables products to be manufactured more cheaply through mass production methods and economies of scale and the use of lower wage labour in less developed parts of the world, all of this in an attempt to maintain the rate of profit and increase the exploitation of the working class.

However these processes also generate weaknesses in that any minor interruption can cause massive disruptions in supply, e.g. the recent blocking of the Suez Canal by one container ship and also the shortages in the supply of processors due to Covid and Bitcoin requirements.

Trading blocs and international organisations reflect the incapacity of capitalism to avoid the process of internationalisation. Whilst they show the attempts of capitalism to go beyond the national stage, it is ultimately a system based on competition expressed at the national level and so there develops a contradiction between these two tendencies. Hence the United Nations is continuing to be hampered from encouraging an international response to the global climate change crisis, for example, and COP26 and 27 have failed to actually implement significant change despite all the good talk.

In fact international organisations are talking shops that give the impression that something is being done when nothing is being done. They bring the ruling class together in opposition to more radical change.

Towns and Cities

Towns were originally the focus for capitalist development, drawing in labour expelled from the land and enabling new production methods which formed the basis of capitalist development. They were also places that enabled workers to live near their workplaces.

However today, while capitalism depends on creating huge industrial centres, the resulting cities and megacities create slums, overcrowding, pollution and waste mountains across the world. Capitalism can offer nothing but larger and larger towns and cities which have become constraints on the future development and reorganisation of society. Instead of providing proximity to work they have created the necessity for continual and increasingly costly travel for their inhabitants. The countryside gets further away and holidays become a necessity.

3) External Factors

The Planetary Environment

> Now man, as an animal form, as well as human society, are products of nature, parts of this great, endless whole. Man can never escape from nature, and even when he 'controls' nature, he is merely making use of the laws of nature for his own ends. It is therefore clear how great must be the influence of nature on the whole development of human society.[48]

As we have discussed, while humanity is part of nature capitalism uses nature as if it owns it all, it uses nature for free in its productive process. The environment is not created by humanity, it exists as it is, or rather as common to all modes of production, so it is external in that it is not a construction and humanity can only use what is there. However external factors are not independent, they are drawn into a relationship with humanity and its modes of production and each mode realises its own consequences on nature.

In that sense the environment exists external to all modes of production but particularly it provides a limit for capitalism whose capacity for growth brings the earth closer to exhaustion of its resources and pollution of its ecology. It is an external limit, which can act as a stimulant for life and production (eg the Holocene) but today is becoming a fetter and a threat to what is possible for the development of humanity (the article 'Capitalism vs the Environment' develops this argument in greater depth).

New Modes of Production

It is true that in the past, new modes of production have begun development within the old, existing mode of production. This old society already in existence has a specific ruling class representing a particular method of production, but as the productive forces become too powerful for the old relations of production, there will come into existence a deadly conflict between the old ruling class and the class that is posing itself as the new ruling class and representing a new, more capable mode of production. There is then an antagonism, a class conflict, between the classes representing different economic and manufacturing relationships.

As such, the new mode of production whilst emerging within the old society is nevertheless antagonistic and in this respect can be considered external to the old society; it represents a movement that is not only completely opposed to the old system of production but also promotes its death knell. Hence feud-

---

48   Bukharin, *Historical Materialism*, Chapter 5a (1921), <https://www.marxists.org/archive/bukharin/works/1921/histmat/5.htm> [accessed 29.12.22]

alism was in decline from the 13th century onwards but those industrialists and politicians that represented capitalist relations were promoting a new form of society from the 16th century onwards and that new system came to dominate and effectively eradicate feudalism.

For capitalism this is not the case, there are only two historic classes in this society, the ruling class and the working class. There is no new ruling class representing a new property system that can challenge the bourgeoisie within capitalism. Hence the new society can only be built once the bourgeoisie has been relieved of its power and the working class sets about building a non-exploitative society. This demonstrates the reality hinted at in previous revolutions, that is that the new mode of production is definitively external and antagonistic to the old mode of production

Space

Some may find this subject a comical aside to a theory of historical materialism but it needs to be taken a bit more seriously than that. Space is an external factor to whatever happens on earth and just as we see the world market as a fetter on the growth of capitalism, it is also evident that space is a barrier which capitalism cannot easily overcome.

On the one hand, we are totally dependent on the sun for its light in the form of UV, X-ray and Gamma radiation as well as the infrared radiation that provides us with heat. These forces have obviously had a positive impact on the earth in the past as clearly light and warmth are essential to life. Indeed it is speculated that some of the basic foundations of life including organic matter and water were brought to earth in the past by meteorites.[49] Let it not be forgotten that the earth itself was created by activity within space; the afterglow of the Big Bang is now something that is visible to us through the latest James Webb Space Telescope. These factors are not fetters but stimulants or facilitators just as the nation and the nation state have been in the past.

Humanity however is not in control of these factors so they have to be seen as external to any given mode of production that develops on earth even if humanity, at certain points, interacts with these elements.

In *Historical Materialism*, Bukharin points out that the earth with all its natural properties is the environment for society. He argues that humanity's interaction with nature is expanded thanks to its technical development:

> Coal becomes a raw material only when technology has developed so far as to delve in the bowels of the earth and drag their contents into the light of day. [...] Before technology with its feelers had reached the iron-ore,

---

49   'Where did Earth's Water come from?' (2021) in *Carnegie Science* <https://epl.carnegiescience.edu/news/where-did-earths-water-come> [accessed 29.12.22]

this iron-ore was permitted to sleep its eternal slumber; its influence on man was zero.[50]

So too with space, by the 21st century, technical development has extended the interaction with the environment beyond our planet to near Earth orbit, which is now an important part of both the economy (telecommunications, meteorology, pest control and many other applications) and imperialist rivalry (military spy satellites etc). The European Space Agency is investigating the possibility of creating solar power stations in orbit and sending the power to Earth via microwave.[51]

Recognising positive contributions to life, it must also be accepted that such external factors have also had negative impacts on life and the planet itself, for example the extinction of the dinosaurs and various climate changes in history.[52] Meteorites strike earth on a routine basis[53] and they can vary in size between the dust particles that arrive every day to asteroids of 100 metres or so that hit every 2000 years. Scientists have therefore been researching methods of asteroid deflection and recently a test was conducted to assess the impact of such a planetary defence strategy by hitting an asteroid with a rocket.[54] It is suggested that a planet-killing meteorite half a mile wide or more could lift sufficient dust to cause a nuclear winter, although these are very rare thankfully. Space is an external factor in our environment and a significant barrier to capitalist expansion.

The Productive Forces
in the Descent of Capitalism

Having looked at the theory in general, let us look at what Marx had to say regarding the role of the productive forces in capitalism because as we have said, we need to identify the specific features of capitalism to understand both its process of ascendancy and decline. Let us look again at this quote from Marx:

---

50   Bukharin, *Historical Materialism*, Chapter 5a.

51   'Plan to research solar power from space' (2022) in *European Space Agency* <https://www.esa.int/Enabling_Support/Space_Engineering_Technology/SOLARIS/Plan_to_research_solar_power_from_space> [accessed 6.1.23]

52   See the Chapter on 'Capitalism vs the Environment'

53   Nasa, 'Asteroids Fast Facts', 2022 <https://www.nasa.gov/mission_pages/asteroids/overview/fastfacts.html> [accessed 29.12.22]

54   NASA, 'NASA's DART Mission Hits Asteroid in First-Ever Planetary Defense Test', 2022 <https://www.nasa.gov/press-release/nasa-s-dart-mission-hits-asteroid-in-first-ever-planetary-defense-test> [accessed 6.1.23]

There appears here the universalizing tendency of capital, which distinguishes it from all previous stages of production. Although limited by its very nature, it strives towards the universal development of the forces of production, and thus becomes the presupposition of a new mode of production, which is founded not on the development of the forces of production for the purpose of reproducing or at most expanding a given condition, but where the free, unobstructed, progressive and universal development of the forces of production is itself the presupposition of society and hence of its reproduction; where advance beyond the point of departure is the only presupposition.[55]

Marx is here saying that capitalism has a specific characteristic, 'the universal development of productive forces' and that this enables society to grow sufficiently to lay the basis for a communistic society. One of capitalism's most important features is its dynamism, its capacity to expand and grow. This is based on the system of waged labour which enables capitalists to profit enormously and to use that wealth to focus on technological, productive and scientific advances – not forgetting that this includes the expansion of and changes in the structure of the working class itself. No previous society had the capacity to develop either technical or social progress in such a dynamic way.

In this crucial respect capitalism must be understood as very different to previous modes of production which developed slowly over millennia.

Technology developed gradually step by step through hunter-gatherer systems to sedentary agricultural farming. Slave societies gradually developed building and weapon technologies (in fact, Greek and Roman societies developed the basic elements of technologies relating to steam, hydraulics and even mechanical computers but they just could not apply these to production, they remained as playthings for the ruling classes and were lost following their demise). Feudalism further improved agricultural technologies based on decentralised social structures. By centralising productive and administrative institutions, generating an accumulation of money and freeing up labour from the legal constraints of the past, capitalism became the most technologically dynamic society in history. Here again we should note that the productive forces play an active role in this history of capitalism, it is the level of technology and the capacities of a 'free' workforce of associated labour that enables future development.

Capitalism is therefore very different to previous modes of production which is why Luxemburg called it a commodity economy compared to previous natural economies.[56] We should not therefore expect capitalism to behave in

---

55   Marx, *Grundrisse*, Notebook V (1857-61)

56   Luxemburg, *The Accumulation of Capital*, Chapter 27 (1913) <https://

the same way as previous societies. When it comes to analysing its ascendancy and decline, it has specific characteristics which need investigation and identification.

> The means – unconditional development of the productive forces of society – comes continually into conflict with the limited purpose, the self-expansion of the existing capital. The capitalist mode of production is, for this reason, a historical means of developing the material forces of production and creating an appropriate world-market and is, at the same time, a continual conflict between this its historical task and its own corresponding relations of social production.[57]

Here Marx argues that the ongoing growth of the productive forces itself generates conflict with the way capitalist production can use that growth. What is more, these are not isolated statements that could be put down as mistakes or a lack of clarity, Marx holds firm to this explanation of social development and returns on many occasions to the theme, for example:

> We thus see that the social relations within which individuals produce, the social relations of production, are altered, transformed, with the change and development of the material means of production, of the forces of production.[58]

Again in *Theories of Surplus Value*:

> Over-production is specifically conditioned by the general law of the production of capital: to produce to the limit set by the productive forces, that is to say, to exploit the maximum amount of labour with the given amount of capital, without any consideration for the actual limits of the market or the needs backed by the ability to pay; and this is carried out through continuous expansion of reproduction and accumulation, and therefore constant reconversion of revenue into capital.[59]

And in *Capital* Volume 3, Marx has this to say:

> The contradiction of the capitalist mode of production, however, lies precisely in its tendency towards an absolute development of the productive forces, which continually come into conflict with the specific conditions of production in which capital moves, and alone can move.[60]

---

www.marxists.org/archive/luxemburg/1913/accumulation-capital/index.htm> [accessed 29.12.22]

57   Marx, *Capital* Vol. 3, Chapter 15 (1883) <https://www.marxists.org/archive/marx/works/1894-c3/ch15.htm> [accessed 29.12.22]

58   Marx, *Wage Labour and Capital* (1847) <https://www.marxists.org/archive/marx/works/1847/wage-labour/> [accessed 29.12.22]

59   Marx, *Theories of Surplus Value*, Chapter 17-14 (1861) <https://www.marxists.org/archive/marx/works/1863/theories-surplus-value/ch17.htm> [accessed 29.12.22]

60   Marx, *Capital* Vol. 3, Chapter 15 (1883) <https://www.marxists.org/archive/marx/

As we can see from these quotes, Marx posits the development of society on the conditions generated by the growth of the productive forces. His historical materialism is based not on the relations of production determining the forces of production but on the forces of production impacting upon the relationships that are generated.

It is surely obvious that when capitalism was comprised of small scale craft industries there was no need, for example, for mass distribution systems, personnel and wages departments, management theories etc. But this changed as capital developed the capacity to produce in factories on a mass scale using powered machinery and with large numbers of workers organised in a division of labour. Thereupon came about a need for far more complex organisational structures within businesses and in society as whole. Large factories arise because of the growth of technological capacities, not because there are masses of workers waiting at the gates. The role of technological change is relatively easy to see in the enormous impact that digital computerisation has had since the 1980s on the modern factory as well as the structure and divisions of labour within the workforce.

> The modern division of labour is determined by the modern instruments of labour, by the character, description and combination of machines and tools, i.e. by the technical apparatus of capitalist society.[61]

At the end of the 19th century, technological and social developments led to what Lenin and Bukharin termed monopoly and finance capital, when the concentration and centralisation of capital created new institutions and new business structures. The nation state took ever greater control over the management of the national economy and became the foundation for what we call today state capitalism. These developments therefore led to drastic changes taking place in capitalism's relations of production.

Lenin was clear that the new period of imperialism which he saw as a product of monopoly and finance capital, represented the decay of the capitalist system but that this would not prevent the growth of the productive forces.

> It would be a mistake to believe that this tendency [of capitalism] to decay precludes the rapid growth of capitalism. It does not. In the epoch of imperialism, certain branches of industry, certain strata of the bourgeoisie and certain countries betray, to a greater or lesser degree, now one and now another of these tendencies. **On the whole, capitalism is growing far more rapidly than before**; but this growth is not only becoming more and more uneven in general, its unevenness also manifests itself, in

works/1894-c3/> [accessed 29.12.22]

61   Bukharin, *Historical Materialism* (1921), Chapter 6 <https://www.marxists.org/archive/bukharin/works/1921/histmat/6.htm> [accessed 29.12.22]

> particular, in the decay of the countries which are richest in capital (Britain).[62] (our emphasis)

So from this we have the concept that capital must keep growing in both its ascendant and decadent periods. The accumulation of capital is an essential feature of capitalism – if it stops then capitalism doesn't exist! Our analysis of capitalist decadence must recognise and take account of this factor and not try to deny growth in order to cling to inadequate theories like those of Luxemburg and Bordiga.

Conclusion

Within the context of Marx's theory of historical materialism then, did he recognise such a thing as an external influence on a mode of production? Is the possibility of ecological apocalypse merely a factor of secondary importance within capitalism?

In reviewing Marx's writings on ecology and nature, it is very clear that he saw human beings as part of nature: he hence saw nature as an important external factor and he states that the mode of production depends upon it – this makes it far more than a secondary influence. In fact, Marx and others have argued that production absolutely depends on the natural world for all resources so it must have a significant relationship with each mode of production.

> To say that man is a corporeal, living, real, sensuous objective being with natural powers means that he has real, sensuous objects as the objects of his being of vital expression, or that he can only express his life, in real, sensuous objects […] Hunger is a natural need; it therefore requires a nature and an object outside itself in order to satisfy and still itself […] **A being which does not have its nature outside itself is not a natural being and plays no part in the system of nature**.[63] (our emphasis)

He understood that production in human society absolutely depends on the natural world for all its resources so there is a significant relationship between humanity and nature which forms an essential part of each mode of production.

> Actual labour is the appropriation of nature for the satisfaction of human needs, the activity through which the metabolism [*Stoffwechsel*] between man and nature is mediated.[64]

---

62   Lenin, *Imperialism, The Highest Stage of Capitalism*, Chapter 10, (1916) <https://www.-marxists.org/archive/lenin/works/1916/imp-hsc/ch10.htm> [accessed 29.12.22]

63   Marx, 'Critique of Hegelian Dialectic' in *Economic and Philosophic Manuscripts of 1844* <https://www.marxists.org/archive/marx/works/1844/manuscripts/hegel.htm>

64   Marx, *Theories of Surplus Value* (1861-1863) <https://marxists.architexturez.net/

Marx was therefore fully aware that humanity has a relationship with its environment and so that external factors impacted upon the development of societies as well as the capacity for modes of production to have a negative impact on the environment. In particular in the 19th century the issue was the impact of capitalism's advance into agriculture and its robbery of the Earth's resources.

> In the process of production, human beings work not only upon nature, but also upon one another. They produce only by working together in a specified manner and reciprocally exchanging their activities. In order to produce, they enter into definite connections and relations to one another, and only within these social connections and relations does their influence upon nature operate – i.e. does production take place. [65]

The key issue is how each mode of production uses and thus relates to nature. Production depends on nature as well as labour. So nature, the planet, space are all external factors that exist and in appropriate times must come into relationships with the mode of production in existence and, of course, be changed by it.

Bukharin in his work, *Historical Materialism*, also tackled this topic directly:

> The metabolism between man and nature consists, we have seen, in the transfer of material energy from external nature to society; the expenditure of human energy (production) is an extraction of energy from nature, energy which is to be added to society (distribution of products between the members of society) and appropriated by society (consumption); this appropriation is the basis for further expenditure etc, the wheel of reproduction being thus constantly in motion.[66]

In summary, it is just not correct to state that the productive forces grow more slowly in the period of capitalism's decadence simply because they are shackled by the relations of production. As the quotes from Bukharin and Marx earlier suggest, the productive forces within capitalism must keep growing and this growth must also impact upon the relations of production. In other words, historical materialism does not say that relations of production are the active factor and the forces of production are purely passive in this process, quite the reverse.

The world is limited in size and whilst its resources can be more efficiently used and requirements change with the development of technology, the different modes of production represent different stages in the growth of the productive forces. Not only are the internal contradictions different for each of

---

archive/marx/works/1861/economic/ch13.htm> [accessed 6.1.23]

65   Marx, *Wage Labour and Capital* (1847) <https://www.marxists.org/archive/marx/works/1847/wage-labour/> [accessed 29.12.22]

66   Bukharin, *Historical Materialism*, Chapter 5b (1921).

these modes of production but so are the external contradictions and influences. Capitalism, as a very dynamic system of production must keep accumulating and hence society must keep expanding, and as a result is now at the stage where it is confronting the limitations presented by the way it uses the earth itself. It is at the stage where it is irreversibly damaging the resources that are needed for humanity's survival.

What we have to be fearful of therefore, is not so much an economic collapse but the **continued growth of capital**. At the end of 2021 after the peak of the impact of the Covid pandemic has apparently passed (in Europe at least), the bourgeoisie is proudly boasting that after all periods of economic downturn there is always growth again. But this is simply a product of a system of 'accelerating accumulation' and says nothing positive about the abilities of the bourgeoisie to resolve the core economic contradictions of the system.

Bukharin clearly identifies the relationship of society to the external environment, the natural world, as the determinant in its development.

> It is quite clear that the internal structure of the system (its internal equilibrium) must change together with the relation existing between the system and its environment. The latter relation is the decisive factor; for the entire situation of the system, the fundamental forms of its motion (decline, prosperity, or stagnation) are determined by this relation only.[67]

Today, it is the very scale of capitalism that is changing its relationship with the environment and bringing it to the point where now it threatens humanity and the natural world that we live in. It is the fact that capital produces for profit not for human need that leads its growth to become a destructive tendency. This is why, despite all the international environmental conferences and the plans they generate, despite all the warnings from environmentalists, society is failing to come to terms with the problems humanity is faced with. Capitalism as a system that determines human behaviour does not allow for the type of changes necessary to solve these problems.

In terms of the material conditions within a declining capitalism, we should realise that fetters on the productive forces lead to a falling rate of profit, overproduction and a distortion of the forces of production due to capital's aim of production for profit. In the past few decades a confrontation between the continuing growth and scale of capitalism has become more and more apparent. What we are suggesting here is that there is a fetter external to capitalism: the finite natural world in which we exist. Concerning decadence therefore, it is the continuing growth of capitalism that poses the threat of the destruction of humanity and of the natural world because the natural world poses a limit to

---

67   Bukharin, *Historical Materialism* Chapter 3e (1921) <https://www.marxists.org/archive/bukharin/works/1921/histmat/3.htm> [accessed 29.12.22]

capitalism's ability to expand. **The problem is not that capitalist production has been slowed or unable to develop enough but its continued destructiveness**.

To conclude, at the start of the 21st century in capitalism we need to understand that the alternative of socialism or barbarism is becoming a reality. We have reached a stage where the continued growth of economic and social activity is coming up against the problem that the planet can no longer cope with the disruption it causes. There is no longer sufficient space on the planet to support life as it has been in the past and the environmental damage being caused today is staring humanity in the face. Yet the very intensity of relationships across the world and the new conditions created by the Ukraine war are also generating a serious threat of further catastrophic wars for humanity and the earth itself. The conditions in Syria and the Ukraine furthermore indicate that it is not just nuclear wars that can decimate our planet.

Yes, we can see economic contradictions holding back social development, but what is more and more clear today is that the twin threats of wars of attrition and ecological crisis are what will most likely lead us into barbarism; they are a direct product of the ongoing growth and accumulation that capital is achieving. They are fetters holding back the future communist development of the production forces. In fact they are such important fetters that cleaning up the earth will also dominate the early tasks of a communist society – if they don't prevent us from getting there in the first place.

The task for communism consequently will not simply be the further development of the productive forces which are today bloated by the need for profit, but also the redirection and restructuring of the productive forces to satisfy the actual needs of humanity. This will mean the elimination of the waste production demanded by capitalism, the transfer of resources and skills to productive uses, the development of underdeveloped areas of the globe as well as a global approach to solving the ecological crisis the world is facing. This may well mean at least in the short term the reduction of the levels of production that capital has reached.

Humanity in Nature

(Lars Torvaldsson)

A bald statement: food production is today the biggest single factor in the destruction of the natural world on which we depend for our survival.[1] It would be hard to imagine a more devastating expression of humanity's estrangement from nature.[2]

A social system which has, so to speak, gone to war with its own material basis, has clearly reached a point where it is no longer viable, even if the reality of its situation is not yet fully apparent.

How did we get here? We need to answer this question because only by doing so can we imagine a way out of this disaster. History never goes backward, it is impossible to return to a previous, supposedly more 'eco-friendly' state. But neither can we go forward blindly: that is what got us into the mess in the first place. Only by understanding our past will we be able to determine our future.

Human interaction with the land, with nature, is not only 'the foundation of all wealth' (to use Marx's expression), it is the foundation of human existence. There could be no clearer proof of the decadence of the present mode of human organisation – capitalism – than its relationship to the rest of the natural world: in a very real sense, capitalism, and notably capitalist agriculture, has gone to war against life in the reproduction of life itself. For at least the last forty years, this reality has been a growing crescendo in public discourse: as we write, in the aftermath of the 2021 COP26 Conference on Climate Change, it has become almost deafening. But its roots lie in the social relationships of cap-

---

1   Susan Jebb, Professor of Diet and Population Health at Oxford University. See <https://youtu.be/1fLHDI23ezQ> [accessed 05.01.2023]

2   A stimulating examination of Marx's concept of alienation (estrangement) can be found in the chapter in *Communism: not just a nice idea but a material necessity* published by the International Communist Current. What follows should be seen as a continuation of the reflection contained in that article, coming at the subject from a different angle. Indeed, our point of departure is already contained in that article, written thirty years ago: capitalism 'did not in itself produce the alienation between man and nature, which has a far older history, but it takes it to its ultimate point. By "perfecting" the hostility between man and nature, by reducing the whole natural world to the status of a commodity, the development of capitalist production is now threatening to destroy the very fabric of planetary life' ('The alienation of labour is the premise for its emancipation' in *International Review* no. 70, 3rd Quarter 1992, <https://en.internationalism.org/internationalreview/199207/1797/alienation-labour-premise-its-emancipation> [accessed 5 January 2023]).

italism – and humanity's relationship to nature is always a social one – more specifically in the profound modification of capitalism's functioning that took place during the first half of the 20th century: the militarisation of society, and of society's relation to nature.

The workers' movement has always been aware of the foundational import- ance of humanity's relation to the land: this can be seen in the writings of Marx and Engels, and of their successors: Kautsky, Bebel, and Bukharin for example. The struggle of the working class, however, has been directed more than any- thing against its economic exploitation or, as in 1917, against war; it has con- cerned itself with human society, not with nature.

This is no longer tenable. The question of humanity's relation to nature is already primordial and immediate, and confronts us with global problems. If humanity is to survive at all, then at some point the junction must be made between the class struggle against exploitation and war, the working class's own self-awareness, and a broader and deeper understanding of our place in the bio- sphere and of the vast social transformation that must be undertaken if human- ity is both to live and to flower. Timid premises exist, for example in China where workers have on occasions entered into struggle against pollution, but these remain local and limited in their perspectives.

The present crisis covers every aspect of human material existence: produc- tion, distribution, consumption. Only the class of associated labour, which sets in motion the mechanisms of production and distribution, and – of necessity – consumption, can find a solution, in part because that solution itself must be a radical reorganisation of production, distribution, and consumption. Because humanity only interacts with the rest of nature socially, through labour, its es- trangement from nature can only be resolved by ending its estrangement from its own nature, in other words by putting an end to the alienation of labour un- der capitalism.

Only the working class in action can resolve the crisis concretely. Yet prior reflection – theory – is a precondition for conscious action towards a goal. This essay does not claim to have solved all the questions it raises, far from it; there are, moreover, doubtless many questions that have been left out – sometimes deliberately – and many that we have only touched on. We are all too painfully aware of our own inadequacies. We hope only to help lay the groundwork for a historical and materialist understanding of humanity's place in nature, as a basis for that action.

Before we begin though, we need briefly to consider the two words 'hu- manity', and 'nature'.

It is common enough these days, and even fashionable, to talk about the need for a 'new relationship with nature', or to 'care for the environment'.

'Greenery' is everywhere: bankers, traders and economists lick their lips as often as not, at the mention of the coming 'green economy'. Yet behind such expressions lies a fundamental misconception, even, one suspects, a wilful blindness to the reality of humanity's place in nature, rather in the same way that using the word 'man' as a substitute for 'humanity' unconsciously pushes the female half of the species into the background and engenders an ideologically distorted way of thinking about the social world. We talk about 'the environment' or the 'natural world' as if we were not a part of it, as if there were humankind on one side and 'nature' on the other.

A moment's thought reveals the one-sidedness of this world view which we slip into so easily: we do not 'depend on nature', we are part of nature. Every human being who has ever lived only does so by eating, drinking, and defecating in a constant process of exchange with the world around us. In this, we are like every other living being, indeed at the deepest level we share the same body chemistry with all life on the planet. Our genetic material, which determines whether each individual is a human, a chimpanzee, a lizard or a tree, is written in the same DNA alphabet as that of all living organisms.

Marx's 1844 'Economic and Philosophical Manuscripts' contain an entire chapter on 'Estranged Labour' – that is to say, alienated labour – a theoretical principle which we can briefly summarise as follows: purposeful labour on the material world, to transform it according to human need (above all social need) is part of humanity's essence, its species-being to use Marx's expression. In capitalist wage-labour however, what the worker creates is surplus-value, a form of capital, which not only does not belong to him but increases the power of capital which stands against him as a hostile, alien power.

> Labour produces not only commodities: it produces itself and the worker as a *commodity* – and this in the same general proportion in which it produces commodities.
>
> This fact expresses merely that the object which labour produces – labour's product – confronts it as *something alien*, as a *power independent* of the producer. The product of labour is labour which has been embodied in an object, which has become material: it is the *objectification* of labour. Labour's realisation is its objectification. In the sphere of political economy this realisation of labour appears as loss of realisation for the workers; objectification as loss of the object and bondage to it; appropriation as estrangement, as alienation [...]
>
> The alienation of the worker in his product means not only that his labour becomes an object, an external existence, but that it exists outside him, independently, as something alien to him, and that it becomes a power on

its own confronting him. It means that the life he has conferred on the object confronts him as something hostile and alien.[3]

We can use Marx's concept of alienation as a means to examine the history of humanity's relationship to the rest of the natural world, which appears as a progressive estrangement from our species-being as a part of nature to the point where today we speak of nature as something external, other, alien.[4] Yet as Marx pointed out in the same chapter on 'Estranged Labour':

> Man **lives** on nature – means that nature is his **body**, with which he must remain in continuous interchange if he is not to die. That man's physical and spiritual life is linked to nature means simply that nature is linked to itself, for man is a part of nature.[5]

It must be understood then, that when we speak of humanity's alienation from nature, we do not think of nature as something external to humans. In a sense, it is humanity's alienation from itself and as such, it is a source of suffering.

Indeed for Marx, the alienation of labour and humanity's alienation from nature are closely related, though they are not identical. As he says:

> The relation of the worker to the product of labour as an alien object exercising power over him [...] is at the same time the relation to the sensuous external world, to the objects of nature, as an alien world inimically opposed to him.[6]

As he points out elsewhere, the world which we inhabit is **both** a natural and a social world. The 'nature' that surrounds us has been shaped from time immemorial by social human activity, so that our estrangement from nature is today first and foremost humanity's estrangement from itself, from its own activity in the natural world which the property relations of capitalism make appear as something foreign to us.

This alienation is a source of suffering, certainly, but not only that. History, as Marx pointed out, is not merely a succession of events, nor even a series of causes and effects. It is a dynamic movement, driven amongst other things by the internal contradictions inherent to all human society. History advances through these contradictions and their resolution in new social forms. As we

---

3   Marx, 'Estranged Labour', in *Economic and Philosophical MS of 1844* (New York: International Publishers, 1972), p.108.

4   There was a fashion, especially in the Stalinist tradition among philosophers like Louis Althusser, for trying to separate the 'young Marx' of the 1844 MS from the 'mature Marx'. In reality, we find the same ideas expressed in *Capital*, stripped of their post-Hegelian language (see the chapter 'Imagining the Future').

5   Marx, 'Estranged labour', p.112.

6   Ibid, p.111

will see, humanity's ever-greater separation from the rest of nature is thus also the condition for human self-awareness, for growing human knowledge of the natural world as a whole, and of our place in it, and for the increasing ability of labour consciously to shape the world. Just as the alienation of labour under capitalism accompanies the development of a world wide class of associated labour capable of overthrowing all alienation, so the paroxysm of alienation from the natural world that we experience today is the condition for humanity to take its place within nature as its conscious element, living with and guiding it.

In this article, we intend to focus on humanity's direct relationship to the living natural world, although we realise of course that the question of the environment extends much further than this.

Like everything else, humanity's alienation has a history. To understand it, we must therefore start at the beginning.

The first alienation:
the emergence of *homo sapiens*

From the Arctic wastes to the Amazon forest, archaic peoples[7] share an origin myth which may differ in its details but remains strikingly stable in its essentials. In the beginning, go the stories, nature was undifferentiated: there were animals, humans, and spirits, all of which could change their form such that humans could shift shape to become animals, spirits could take human form, and so on. At some point, a differentiation occurred and humans, spirits, and animals all took on their definitive forms. Only the shaman in trance could make the passage from one world to the other, could communicate with spirits, or take on animal form.[8] These myths express humanity's first awareness of its existence as a separate species, of itself as a distinct part of nature. This new consciousness was to have profound implications.

---

7 I have preferred the expression 'archaic peoples'. They were once generally described as 'primitive', but this seems inappropriate for two reasons: first, because there are no fundamental anatomical (and therefore mental) differences between any members of the species *homo sapiens*; second, because whatever the differences in material (or indeed spiritual) culture, the archaic peoples' technology has proved a successful adaptation to their ecological niche for millennia, while their knowledge of their environment is complex and sophisticated.

8 Australian Aboriginal myths are unusual, perhaps unique, in this respect, since the mythical beings of the time of creation are no longer considered to be present in the world of here and now. They belong to the 'dream time', which can be accessed still in dream but which does not affect the present.

The reader might reasonably object that 100,000 years is a very long time. Can we draw meaningful conclusions about humanity's origins on the basis of observations made at best 2000 years ago by Roman historians, or more usually by European travellers and ethnographers during the last two centuries? Let us try our readers' patience for a moment, to explain why this seems to us justified, and indeed unavoidable.

— Firstly, the geographical distribution among populations on different continents suggests either that their myths share a common origin which predates these populations' separation tens of millennia ago, or that a common hunter-gatherer lifestyle, albeit in profoundly different climatic and ecological conditions, determines a common origin-myth.

— Secondly, there are strong reasons to think that mythology is conservative and durable. In the ethnological record, Australian coastal peoples possess myths to explain events attributable to rising sea levels at the end of the last glaciation, 7-10,000 years ago.[9] In the archaeological record, we can observe the surprising stylistic homogeneity of cave paintings in Chauvet (France) and Altamira (Spain) which are separated by more than 15,000 years (or indeed, the fact that the paintings in Chauvet themselves span a period of 5000 years).

— Finally, we really have no other choice. Incontrovertible knowledge of the first origin myths will forever elude us. The best that we can do is to ensure that we remain within the bounds of probability and that we do not contradict the archaeological evidence.[10]

Having posed these inevitable caveats, what do these myths tell us?

This 'fall of man' (though it has no moral overtones) appears as a differentiation of once shifting natural forms: human beings can no longer change into animals and only the shaman has the ability to move from the human, to the animal, and to the spirit world. Humans are conscious of themselves as a separate species. They are conscious of their own activity as something specific from that of other animals. Human activity is no longer solely instinctive, it has become conscious activity. Other animals are not seen merely, and instinctively, as predator or prey, they become objects of learning through observation. Our species is no longer confined to an ecological niche defined by the slow rhythm of evolution by natural selection, it can occupy new niches that it creates through a conscious process of cultural adaptation. As Marx puts it:

---

9   See Chris Knight, *Blood Relations* (Yale University Press, 1995), pp.452-3.

10   On the methodology and use of ethnographic material, see Alain Testart, *Avant l'Histoire* (Gallimard, 2012), pp.58-62.

> The animal is immediately one with its life activity. It is not distinct from that activity; it is that activity. Man makes his life activity itself an object of his will and consciousness. He has conscious life activity.[11]

Like other characteristics once thought of as specifically human (tool use, emotions…), consciousness undoubtedly emerges in sufficiently complex brains, somewhere between the nematode worm *C. elegans* with its 302 neurones and *homo sapiens*. Other animals have been observed using tools (chimpanzees, crows), but no other animal chains together a series of actions separated in time and space to produce a tool for use in the future, as a human does in making a stone-tipped lance and a throwing stick, or a woven basket, or a gourd for carrying water. This ability depends on the interaction between the brain and the manual dexterity[12] provided by sensitive fingers and an opposable thumb, but it also depends on the ability of the human mind to form multiple mental images of an imagined future, and to choose between them: on conscious activity. As Marx puts it in a famous passage:

> Primarily, labour is a process going on between man and nature, a process in which man, through his own activity, initiates, regulates, and controls the material reactions between himself and nature. He confronts nature as one of her own forces, setting in motion arms and legs, head and hands, the natural forces of his body, in order to appropriate nature's productions in a form suitable to his own wants […] A spider carries on operations resembling those of the weaver; and many a human architect is put to shame by the skill with which a bee constructs her cell. But what from the very first distinguishes the most incompetent architect from the best of bees, is that the architect has built a cell in his head before he constructs it in wax. The labour process ends in the creation of something which, when the process began, already existed in the worker's imagination, already existed in an ideal form.[13]

That said, Marx's outlook suffers from a certain one-sidedness inasmuch as he concentrates on the human use and production of tools, and rather leaves to one side the archaic peoples' extraordinarily intimate and detailed knowledge of the natural world: of plants, their growth, their properties; and of animals and their behaviour. This knowledge, based on long observation and transmission

---

11   Marx, 'Estranged Labour', p.113.

12   See Engels, 'The Part Played by Labour in the Transition from Ape to Man' in *Dialectics of Nature* (Moscow: Progress Publishers, 1976).

13   Karl Marx, 'The labour process and the process of producing surplus value', in *Capital*, Volume 1 (4th edition, 1890), trans. Eden and Cedar Paul, ed. GDH Cole (London: Everyman, 1967), p.169-170. The point of quoting Marx so extensively here is not to seek 'proof from authority', but rather to illustrate the point that the findings of modern anthropology tend to confirm the theoretical premises of Marx and the early workers' movement.

from one generation to the next, is as much part of the human 'toolkit' as the lance or the basket. Moreover, human interaction with plants and other animals is and can only be social. Human beings only exist as social animals. Consequently, the emergence of self-awareness is not just an awareness of our 'separateness' from other animals, it is also an awareness of our individual separateness from other humans, and a conscious awareness of social rules which are not innate (as they largely are for all other social animals) but specific to every culture and transmitted between generations. With self-awareness comes also an awareness of death, of our own transience as individuals.

In this archaic period of humanity's social evolution, human productive powers remain largely natural productive powers; the social world and the natural world remain profoundly interwoven. Nature is envisaged according to a model based on human social relationships, and these relationships are themselves conceived according to a natural model. More concretely, archaic societies think of non-human animal species (and sometimes even plants) as being ruled by human institutions with human taboos, while human society is often divided into clans on the basis of totems derived from nature.[14]

How better to bring to life this intimate interaction between humans and nature, than these stories from among the Inuit, reported by Jean Malaurie.

> The one law to be respected here is never to counter the current of forces, the life force (*Sila*) in all its many aspects. Thus, Rasmussen[15] reports that the Earth – *Nuna* – is profoundly sensitive. It is living matter and death distresses it. Since the village is linked to the Earth, the rule is that the skins of dead animals should never be placed on the ground except in islands or areas separated from the village by a glacier, and according to Rasmussen, if this rule is not followed then the spirits of the dead beasts will afflict the Earth.
>
> Another rule is that of hospitality towards captured animals. The polar bear and the seal are not 'really' killed when they are harpooned. In the hunters' minds, the animals have let themselves be killed only in appearance, in order to visit their human brothers and to help them. Consequently, everything in the igloo must be done to respect them, and even to amuse them. Songs are sung to them in a low voice and words like 'knife' carefully avoided. The seal needs fresh water, which is brought to him in a bowl. The decapitated head of the bear must be turned towards

---

14   Cf Alain Testart, *Le communisme primitif* (Éditions de la Maison des Sciences de l'Homme, 1985), p.506. In *Avant l'Histoire*, Testart suggests that the absence of human representations in the Chauvet cave paintings are the marks of a society based on totemism; each different animal represents a social grouping of humans.

15   Malaurie's book is dedicated to the great Danish explorer and anthropologist Knud Rasmussen (1879-1933)

the interior, so that the animal has no difficulty in returning home, so Rasmussen tells us; he adds that sometimes the bear is given a hunter's equipment, since the bear may, should he need to, take a human form.

In Alaska (on Saint Lawrence Island), they go even further: knowing that the bear likes to smoke, the pipe is lit and placed in its mouth. An old hunter from Savoonga informed me that his father always used to do this. They would prepare various instruments which could never be used thereafter: a bow drill and a knife for a male, a scraper and a needle for a female. Only after four days for a male, five days for a female did they consider that the spirit of the animal had returned to its own people and that the taboos could be lifted.

All these rules of 'correct behaviour' are intended to avoid contradicting the will of *Sila* and its various expressions.[16]

This sense of the animal world's proximity survived in legend and religion long after the hunter-gatherer societies from which it sprang had disappeared: we need only think of therianthropes like the Minotaur or the Egyptian god Anubis, or shape-shifters like Dracula and the were-wolf. It survives today, instinctively, in young children who have no difficulty in relating to animals as persons in their own right: this may in part explain the enduring popularity of the Narnia stories or Beatrix Potter's delightful animal humans. Clearly though, it is no longer grounded in a profound observational knowledge of the natural world, nor is it present to us on a daily basis as it was for our hunter-gatherer ancestors, dependent for their survival on constant and intimate interchange with the plants and animals whose environment they shared.

Because other species were all imagined on the human model, relations with them had to be constantly negotiated as they were with other human groups, through elaborate ritual and even self-deception. Death was always dramatic, killing, whether of animals or humans, always incurred blood-guilt. We have seen the Inuit example above, when it comes to hunted animals. Ethnographic testimony on intra-human conflict and murder confirms it:

> Because he was a spiritual danger to himself and anyone he touched, a Huli killer of New Guinea could not use his shooting hand for several days; he had to stay awake the first night after the killing, chanting spells; drink 'bespelled' water; and exchange his bow for another. South American Carib warriors had to cover their heads for a month after dispatching an enemy. An African Meru warrior, after killing, had to pay a curse remover to conduct the rituals that would purge his impurity and restore him to society. A Marquesan was tabooed for ten days after a war killing.

---

16   Jean Malaurie, *Les derniers rois de Thulé* (Plon, 1989), pp.405-406 (my translation). Malaurie is a French cartographer and ethnohistorian whose remarkable book describes several years living among the Inuit of northern Greenland in the early 1950s.

A Chilcotin of British Columbia who had killed an enemy had to live apart from the group for a time, and all returning raiders had to cleanse themselves by drinking water and vomiting. These and similar rituals emphasise the extent to which homicide was regarded as abnormal, even when committed against the most bellicose enemies.[17]

Does a lioness suffer pangs of conscience when she brings down an antelope? Does a male chimpanzee feel the need to purify himself when he kills the offspring of a vanquished rival? Do wildebeest negotiate with the savannah grass they trample on? The uniquely human relationship to the rest of nature springs from an awareness of difference, an estrangement.

All species interact with each other in the world wide ecology of life. As species change, they occupy new niches, out-compete rival species which disappear, or enter into symbiotic arrangements with others to the benefit of both. Invasive species entering a new environment may out-compete those already in place. Humans are no exception, but they have altered the world consciously. Compared to the frenetic pace of present day capitalist society, the tens of millennia of human cultural evolution that preceded recorded history seem static, unchanging, timeless. Seen from another perspective, the opposite is true. Some 60 millennia, a mere blink of evolutionary time, have seen humanity spread across and out of Africa, becoming the planet's most invasive species and its ultimate super-predator. Men hunted and killed, both animals and each other. Indeed, many researchers consider hunting by humans responsible for the disappearance of megafauna around the world: since humans first arrived there Australia's giant wombats, kangaroos or crocodiles have all gone extinct, like the mammoth and the giant cave-bear.[18]

Alienation is a source of suffering. Other animals know fear, but they do not fear death as an end to existence, nothingness. Alienation is the knowledge, not only of the human species' difference within nature but also of the individual's difference within its species, and therefore of loneliness, the separation from other humans, the absence of love and affection. But the first alienation, the awareness of separation, is also integral to the human condition. Only because 'his own life is an object for him [...] is [man's] activity free activity'.[19]

---

17   Lawrence Keeley, 'Attitudes towards War and Peace', in *War before Civilization* (Oxford University Press, 1996, Kindle edition).

18   See for example Andermann, T., Faurby, S., Turvey, S. T., Antonelli, A., & Silvestro, D. (2020), 'The past and future human impact on mammalian diversity' in *Science advances*, Volume 6, no. 36, <https://doi.org/10.1126/sciadv.abb2313> [accessed 05.01.2023]. The major exception is Africa, where, so the extinction hypothesis suggests, the megafauna co-evolved with humanity and acquired an instinctive awareness of the danger that this apparently insignificant and inoffensive biped represented.

19   Marx, 'Estranged Labour', p.113.

The first alienation is inescapable, it is what we are, our species-being. Yet our hunter-gatherer ancestors' very conditions of life forced them to overcome the separation from nature that self-awareness imposed, by integrating themselves into the rest of the natural world through myth, myths which were determined by and yet also determined the permanent negotiated metabolic relationship between humans and all other life.

There is another aspect to this first alienation which was to become critical for human social development. A cultural understanding of the world could not be 'merely' technical, it had to be founded on an explanation of the world and human society: not just what it is, but why it is as it is. It is characteristic of human consciousness that it constantly creates mental images of future options: 'what will happen if I do this, or that?'. In other words, we make choices based on our images of a world that does not yet exist. These images are conditioned by the social world in which we live – our imaginations are constrained by reality – but they are not absolutely determined by it.

Human cultural evolution[20] both conditions and is dependent on mental images of the future: on changing ways of understanding the world.

There is a particular aspect of this understanding of the world which has echoed down the ages, transmuted by social evolution, and which we want to highlight here.

Nobody who has seen the cave paintings in Chauvet (which date back to about 37,000 BCE) or elsewhere can fail to be impressed by the omnipresence of the feminine principle: stylised pubic triangles or vulvae are everywhere; animals stream out of clefts in the rock-face, directly from the belly of the Earth-mother; clefts suggestive of vulvae are deliberately highlighted with red ochre in evocation of menstrual or birth blood. The world, for our hunter-gatherer forebears, is not created by an all-powerful male god, but issues forth, literally, from the body of the Earth, the Inuit *Nuna*, and is continually renewed. What can this imply if not that all humans, and animals, are quite literally brothers and sisters, blood relations? Killing, whether of animals or humans, incurs blood-guilt which amongst humans often led to vendetta. The emotional ideology of hunter-gatherers resorts to all sorts of intellectual subterfuges to shake off the guilt. To take just one example, 'some traditional Diné Indians – practitioners of the Navajo Coyoteway ceremonial – would blame the lethal accuracy of their arrows on "bird people"' who "contributed" the guiding tail feathers that had been attached at the rear of the arrow shafts'.[21]

---

20   Cultural evolution in the broadest sense, including different social structures and different tool kits.

21   Karl Luckert, *Stone Age Religion at Göbekli Tepe* (Triplehood, 2013), p.48.

Yet at the same time, these societies are based on hunting in ways which go far beyond the simple necessities of food. The importance of meat in their diets varied widely of course, depending on the environment, from relatively trivial, perhaps 20% in areas of abundant vegetation, to almost exclusive in the Arctic. The prestige attached to meat, on the other hand, is uniform. Even societies where the majority of the food intake is provided by gathering, essentially by women, accord greater prestige to meat, and not just to any meat: it is common enough for women to hunt small game. This prestige we might call an 'ideology of meat', and it is still with us. Ever since the beginning of agriculture a diet rich in meat has always been the privilege of the ruling classes, even to the point of ruining their health. Today, bourgeois society has democratised what were once aristocratic privileges (at least in its ideology), and meat consumption has been separated from the killing of animals. Who then, is to share the blood-guilt for 80 billion living beings slaughtered annually, out of sight and out of mind?

The second alienation: agriculture

In the multitude of people is the king's honour,
but in the want of people is the destruction of the prince. (Proverbs 14.28)[22]

It was the Marxist prehistorian Vere Gordon Childe (described at his death in 1957 as 'the greatest prehistorian in Britain and probably the world') who first coined the expression 'Neolithic Revolution' to encompass the invention of agriculture and the emergence of urban societies based on farming. Justifiably so, in our view, for the emergence and spread of agriculture profoundly modified every aspect of human existence, from its diet to its beliefs and its social-political organisation. From the broadest standpoint, we are still living in the society created by the Neolithic: a society dependent on agriculture for its sustenance, and divided into ruling and exploited classes. The decadence of capitalism, which has brought us to a point where agriculture itself is undermining the natural foundations on which farming is based, also closes the historical cycle opened by the Neolithic.

What prompted the Neolithic Revolution, a revolution at the rhythm of prehistory, spread over millennia? Childe himself attributed it to demographic

---

22   The quotation is taken from James C Scott, *Against the Grain* (Yale University Press, 2017), p.150. It emphasises the point that the increase in population made possible by agriculture also made possible the emergence of a class society where power was dependent essentially on the ability to control large masses of people (see below).

70

pressure on existing food sources, but it is almost certainly a mistake to look for a single factor in any fundamental social evolution, still more so when the archaeological record is so fragmentary and the change itself is spread over so wide an area and so great a span of time. The question is far too complex for us to treat here, although as the map shows (see Figure 3 overleaf), agriculture's near-simultaneous appearance in different centres suggests that some global factor was at work; since it corresponds roughly to the rise in temperatures at the end of the Younger Dryas about 12,000 years ago, then climate change would be a good candidate.

While no single factor can explain the Neolithic Revolution, we can suggest three that had to come together to make it possible. The first is climate warming, which in turn made possible the second:

> ...the agricultural revolution, so-called, of around 11,700 years ago [...] was made possible by certain changes in the amount of carbon dioxide in the atmosphere, a certain stability of the climate, and a degree of warming of the planet that followed the end of the Ice Age [...] The temperature of the planet stabilised within a zone that allowed certain kinds of grass to flourish. Barley and wheat are among the oldest of such grasses.[23]

The third was human familiarity with the newly plentiful grasses which were to form the bases of the agricultural states; in the Fertile Crescent, the Neolithic toolkit was already present millennia before the switch to agriculture.

The point we want to insist on here, however, is that agriculture both prompted and depended on new ways of thinking about the world. These constitute our 'second alienation', in that they increased the estrangement between humans and the rest of nature.

Agriculture does not just depend on technique, or even on new natural conditions. It also constitutes a radical overthrow of the hunter-gatherer view of the world and especially of humanity's place within it as one animal amongst many (or perhaps we should rather say, as one type of human among many).

---

23 Dipesh Chakrabarty, *The climate of history in a planetary age* (University of Chicago Press, 2021), p.40.

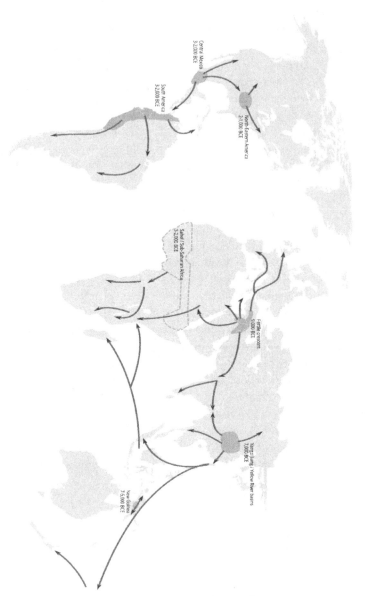

Figure 3 - Expansion of agriculture
CC-SA Wikimedia, adapted from Diamond, J. (2003). 'Farmers and Their Languages: The First Expansions'. *Science* 300: 597–603

The 'second alienation' is thus simultaneously a change in the way human beings think of the world, and a fundamental change in the way human beings reproduce their own existence. There is a reciprocal relationship between ideas (imagination) and society's material base. Humans had to think about nature differently in order to develop agriculture and the development of agriculture engendered this new way of thinking. The same holds good today. The working class will never be able to transform the world without first developing the perspective of something different. That perspective is born (engendered, made possible) from the potential existing within society today, but at the same time will be modified and made concrete as humans try to put it into effect.

Animals are no longer 'another kind of human' (so to speak), each with its own characteristics but living, marrying, and dying as humans do, with which humans must interact by contractual relations and negotiation. They are subjected to humans, they live in enclosures built by humans for human convenience, and their reproduction is controlled by humans to the point where humans create new species: they no longer hunt the aurochs and the mouflon, they herd their own cows and sheep, which they themselves have created through selective breeding. The same is true for crop plants, which in some cases were personified in the same way as animals.

This new view of humanity's relation to nature finds expression in the Book of Genesis (1.28):

> Then God blessed [Adam and Eve], and God said unto them, Be fruitful and multiply, and replenish the Earth and subdue it: and have dominion over the fish of the sea, and over the fowl of the air, and over every living thing that moveth upon the Earth.

Domination, however, does not extend to the whole of nature: not all species are domesticable, indeed the number of species susceptible to domestication is in fact fairly limited compared to the comestible range. The process of domestication leads to a distinction between the wild and the tamed. The tamed are human property over which man (I use the word advisedly) has 'dominion'. Everything else is not only wild, it is an enemy. Wild animals hunt livestock or destroy crops; wild plants compete for nourishment with grain crops and vegetables.

As people more and more live in a world of their own creation, so 'Nature' becomes something separate from and opposed to man. Wild nature is to be hunted, excluded, extirpated. Tame nature becomes property, first of humans in general, then of individuals, lineages, or institutions.

In one sense, however, the old identification of human and animal worlds survived. For, if it were now permitted for humans to corral, breed, and slaughter other animals, why should they not do the same with other humans?

Humans too, could be corralled into cities or temple farms, they could be slaughtered en masse in war; and human breeding could also be controlled, on condition that human females became the property of the male. Man's 'dominion' over nature was an extension and a reflection of a new social relationship between human beings: man's dominion over woman and the dominion of the ruling over the exploited classes.[24]

Agriculture – and by this we mean, specifically, the breeding of new grain crops and the taming of herd animals – was much less of a progress for the people involved than was once thought; so it must surely have seemed at the time. Grain production made it possible to feed more people, but on a more limited and less nutritious diet: not all the plants, or animals, that had made up the Palaeolithic diet were suitable for domestication, and the domesticated plants and animals took over space that once carried a broader ecosystem.[25] In consequence, people were smaller and suffered more from deficiency diseases.

Not only was their diet poorer, the first farmers were exposed to a storm of new zoonotic diseases. It was when humans first began living with animals rather than hunting and eating them, that the first major zoonoses appeared in the human population.

It is evident that density dependent diseases such as measles which requires a population of 300,000 to persist arose around the time that the first cities were established. And measles which probably originated in sheep and goats is just one of a host of ills that leaped from herds to humans as population densities and proximity to livestock increased. We share 26 diseases with poultry, 32 with rats and mice, 35 with horses, 42 with pigs, 46 with sheep and goats, 50 with cattle, and 65 with our oldest companion, the dog.[26]

The transition from hunter-gatherer to the first agricultural city-states was undoubtedly more protracted and less continuous than was once thought. Social hierarchy preceded agriculture, in societies which began to master the storage of gathered food,[27] and the imposition of state power on the farming population was often resisted and avoided, with cities collapsing as the population escaped back to a previous way of life. It has been suggested that 'state forma-

---

24   See Luckert, *Göbekli Tepe*, p.113 and following.

25   'In east Africa, the Hadza, one of the last remaining hunter-gatherer tribes, "eat from a potential wild menu that consists of more than 800 plant and animal species"'. From Dan Saladino, Eating to extinction, in *The Economist*, 23 October 2021, <https://www.economist.com/books-and-arts/2021/10/23/human-diets-are-becoming-less-diverse-a-new-book-warns> [accessed 05.01.2023]

26   Tim Flannery, 'The first mean streets' in *New York Review of Books*, 12 March 2020.

27   For a discussion of this point, see Alain Testart, *Les chasseurs-cueilleurs ou les origines des inégalités* (1982, Société d'Ethnographie).

tion becomes possible only when there are few alternatives available to a diet dominated by domesticated grains'.[28]

The switch to agriculture is often seen as an escape from the scarcity of the hunter-gatherer economy, but in fact the nomadic pre-agricultural peoples led a much less precarious existence than might be supposed. They had – and indeed still have, though in vanishingly small numbers – a profound and detailed knowledge of their surroundings which even today's professional naturalists envy; they were adaptable, because they had fallback solutions should a particular food supply fail, and they were mobile. Their world was governed by broad rhythms – the seasons, animal migrations – with which they were deeply familiar, but was otherwise unpredictable and constantly shifting.

> It was not that [Australian Aboriginal] man was dominating nature; but neither was it that human society stood helpless in the face of nature's powers. Rather, human society was flexible enough and sensitive enough to attune itself finely to the rhythms of surrounding life, avoiding helplessness by replicating internally nature's own 'dance'. Nature was thereby humanised, while humanity yielded to this nature – this was not mere projection of a belief system onto the external world. This was how things felt – because, given synchrony and therefore a shared life-pulse, this was at a deep level how they were.[29]

In adopting agriculture as a way of life,

> *Homo sapiens* traded a wide spectrum of wild flora for a handful of cereals and a wide spectrum of wild fauna for a handful of livestock […] [Agriculture] represented a contraction of our species' attention to and practical knowledge of the natural world, a contraction of diet, a contraction of space, and perhaps a contraction, as well, in the breadth of ritual life.[30]

The mobile, shifting existence of the archaic peoples is reflected in their conception of God and Creation, which is flexible and hard to grasp, or simply indeterminate. Insofar as 'God' can be said to exist at all, he (or she) is ambivalent, morally ambiguous, often sexually ambiguous also, and generally hard to pin down.[31]

How different was the life-experience of the farmers in the first city-states of Sumer! Dependent on a limited number of crops, unable to move should the bad weather conditions cause those crops to fail, and corralled in a state dominated by a ruling priestly or royal caste, they were constantly in fear of uncer-

---

28   Scott, *Against the Grain*, p.21.

29   Chris Knight, *Blood Relations*, p.465.

30   Scott, *Against the Grain*, p.89.

31   See Mathias Guenther, *Tricksters and Trancers* (Indiana University Press, 1999), especially chapters 3 & 4 on Khoisan cosmology and the Trickster god.

tainty. The world they lived in was largely man-made: tilled fields, permanent dwellings, the city behind its walls and the palaces and ziggurats at its centre. In this world, the gods take on a more stable form, indeed they are identifiably human with human passions and emotions, rivalries; the gods of Greek mythology resemble nothing so much as the royalty of the ancient cities, with all their human defects writ large. The indeterminacy of the hunter-gatherer creation myths and the omni-presence of the feminine principle give way, as in the Book of Genesis, to the conscious act of a single (male) God imposing order on the world.[32]

There is one specific aspect of the new relationship between human society and an external 'nature' that we want to highlight here: the disappearance of a sense of measure, or proportion, as expressed in sacrificial offerings.

An important mechanism of archaic societies is the gift; indeed, it would hardly be an exaggeration to call them 'gift economies'. Gifts, however, are not 'free': a gift necessarily creates a reciprocal obligation, a debt. This is not a debt in the sense that we understand it: a precise, contractual agreement to repay a specific sum on or by a set date. In archaic societies, a gift is not an exchange, it is not offered 'in exchange' for something. However, every gift inevitably implies a counter-gift of indeterminate value, at some unspecified time in the future: in short, a debt. The whole society, in fact, is knit together by a constantly shifting web of mutual reciprocity.[33] These gifts are not a commercial exchange in our sense, and certainly not the imaginary system of barter dear to classical economists. Through gifts, people exchange things that everyone has, or can make, or can cultivate. The purpose of the exchange is not the gift, but the giving. Giving, to begin with, implies visiting and socialising; the aim is to create feelings of friendship, and through these constantly renewed sentiments, to weave society together.[34]

Gifts may be given between individuals, or between social groups (clans). Since, in these societies, there is no absolute distinction between people and other animals, inevitably, gifts also pass from human clans to clans of animals, spirits, and so on, to ensure the continued 'friendship' and reciprocity between human beings and other species.

---

32   At least in Middle Eastern and Meso-American mythology. Chinese creation myths, in which the 'myriad beings' (i.e. the natural world of plants and animals) emerge from the nothingness of *wuji* through the operation of the yin-yang principle are a very different kettle of fish – but that is a vast subject, far too complex for us here.

33   The whole question of gifts, especially ritual gifts like those involved in the Melanesian kula, has provoked a vast debate ever since Marcel Mauss's groundbreaking *Essai sur le don* published in 1922, and we can't even begin to go over it here.

34   See Marcel Mauss, *Essai sur le Don* (Quadrige/PUF, 2007 [reprint from *L'Année Sociologique*, seconde série, 1924-1925), p.102.

There is, however, a problem which has to be negotiated over and over again: the reciprocity must be one of equality, more or less. If the gift is greater than the gift in return, or more importantly if the gift is such that the receiver can never give a gift of equal value, then to receive means to accept a relation of inferiority, even dependence. Generosity is a virtue, but it is double-edged: as the English expression says, 'it is easier to give than to receive'.

What happens when hunter-gatherer societies develop the means to stock their surpluses? To be able to store a surplus makes it possible to accumulate wealth, in the form of food to start with. Inevitably, the old egalitarianism breaks down as differences in skill or fortune allow some to stock more than others. The social ideal of disinterested generosity breaks down to be replaced by competitive giving in the potlatch. The generosity of the wealthy, affecting to despise wealth to the point of sheer destruction, enforces the dependency of the common people and the poor.

The same competitiveness, the same immoderation enters the relations between humans and gods, and so between humans and nature. The ziggurat, the pyramids, the enormous temples and the monstrous sacrifices, so many extravagant gifts to the gods from which equally extravagant presents can be expected in return. The sacrifice becomes the hecatomb that we encounter in Homer: literally, a 'hundred-bull sacrifice'. Perhaps nowhere did this deregulation reach such heights as among the Aztecs, who slaughtered tens of thousands of human beings annually, in mass sacrifices intended to maintain the balance of nature, to ensure that the sun continued to rise and set.[35]

Agriculture laid the foundation for the division of the human community into the ruling classes and the exploited. It reduced people's biochemical interaction with the environment to a limited number of food crops and animals. It underlies the first radical separation of humans from the land through the division of labour and the creation of towns separate from the countryside. Yet, just as the first alienation was the condition for humanity to become human, so agriculture and the division of labour laid the foundation for an immense step forward.

Dominion could go wrong, leading to over-exploitation and exhaustion of the land, and even to civilisational collapse, of the Maya cities for example. However, it also introduced a new and more positive aspect to the relationship between humans and the rest of nature: agriculture necessarily implies the nurture of plants and animals; we do not just live within the natural world, we acquire a responsibility to love it, to participate in its growth and development. This is something that the first farmers surely had to discover, and accounts for the fertility rites centred on goddesses like the Greek Ceres.

---

35 GC Vaillant, *The Aztecs of Mexico*, (Harmondsworth: Penguin Books, 1950), p.200.

Over the millennia, agriculture based on observation and adjustment thus developed into balanced and sustainable systems, so much so that in 1889 an adviser to the government of the British Raj in India, Dr John Augustus Voelcker, could write:

> there is little or nothing that can be improved [...] Certain it is that I, at least, have never seen a more perfect picture of careful cultivation. I may be bold to say that it is much easier to propose improvements in English agriculture than to make valuable suggestions for that of India.[36]

And in 1940, Sir Albert Howard, who had also served as agricultural adviser in India, opined that:

> The agricultural practices of the Orient have passed the supreme test, they are almost as permanent as those of the primeval forest, of the prairie, or of the ocean.[37]

We admire to this day the extraordinary rice terraces of China; we can equally admire the old and sadly now abandoned terraces of chestnut plantations in the French Ardèche.

New knowledge appeared. Dependent more than ever on the natural cycle of the seasons, humans took to studying the skies and the rhythmic dance of the stars and planets. Astronomy was born, and with it the first observatories. The development of handicrafts made possible the development of trade: people gained knowledge of others, of a world much vaster than before, much stranger, filled with a multitude of cultures. Trade and astronomy created new needs, especially new needs for knowledge and understanding: writing and mathematics were born.

Agriculture may well have meant a 'deskilling', a loss of broad knowledge about the natural world as a whole; yet it also demanded a deepening knowledge of how the natural world worked, without which the selective breeding and nurture of animals and plants would not have been possible. The need to organise agricultural society led to the invention of writing, and the way was open to a collectivisation of knowledge no longer dependent on the oral memory of a single person or a single tribal group. There was more to be known than any one person could possibly know, and just as tools extended humanity's physical powers, so writing extended its mental powers. Thanks to writing, humans could communicate both over distance and over time, holding conversations with the dead and with those not yet born.

There is no going backwards in history. We cannot return to a hunter-gatherer existence... but nor would we want to.

---

36   Quoted in Vandana Shiva, *Who really feeds the world?* (North Atlantic Books, 2016), p.2.

37   Ibid, p.2. Dr Shiva sees Howard as the father of modern sustainable farming.

This dominion however was still not a radical separation. The vast majority of the population (perhaps around 90%) worked the land, intimately tied to the natural rhythm of the seasons on which they depended. Energy use was limited by the natural world: the inexhaustible power of wind and water mills, the muscle power of humans and animals, and combustible energy drawn essentially from wood. Health depended on a vast plant-based pharmacopoeia.

The immediate dependence on living nature is reflected in the symbolism of mediaeval art. Every animal and plant has a symbolic meaning which interlaces human and natural qualities: rosemary is a therapeutic herb but also symbolises remembrance; the strawberry symbolises the blessed souls in heaven; the goat represents lust (but because it stood on mountain-tops could also stand for the far-seeing Christ); and so on. For the inhabitant of the mediaeval landscape, symbolism, meaning was to be found everywhere.[38]

The third alienation:
agriculture as industry

Sheep [...] these placid creatures, which used to require so little food, have now apparently developed a raging appetite, and turned into man-eaters. Fields, houses, towns, everything goes down their throats.[39]

We have described capitalism as an 'economy of pillage' and this is no mere term of abuse. Capitalism has always functioned by applying 'v' to 'c', labour to machinery. But the 'classic' Marxist formula 'c+v+sv' leaves out the value of the commons, which capital acquires and abuses for free. By 'the commons' we mean both natural resources as inputs, but also the ability of Earth systems to absorb outputs. For example, a deep-sea fishing fleet like those that have ravaged the cod banks of the North Atlantic incorporates constant capital in the form of ships, nets, freezing equipment, etc, and is set in motion by variable capital in the form of wages paid to sailors. The fish itself, however, is free. More than that, the entire ecosystem of which the cod form a part is also free. When industry pours CO_2 into the atmosphere, it pays nothing: waste disposal is free. When companies sell bottled water, they pay for the plastic bottles, but

---

38   'For anyone capable of reflection, the perceptible world was barely more than a mask, behind which everything really important happened, but also a language intended to express through signs, a deeper reality'. Marc Bloch, *La Société féodale* (Paris: Editions Albin Michel, 1939), p.133 (my translation).

39   Thomas More, trans. Paul Turner, *Utopia* (1516) (Harmondsworth: Penguin Classics, 1965), p.46.

the damage done to the world's ecosystems by billions of tons of plastic waste is free.

This pillage, or free appropriation, of the commons dates back to the beginning of capitalism, to the process of primary accumulation so graphically described by Marx in *Capital*: indeed Marx first took note of economic questions in his article on the 'theft' of wood by Silesian peasants (in reality their resistance to the appropriation of the forest commons by the landowners) written for the *Rheinische Zeitung*.[40] It is one of the factors driving capitalism's rapid colonial, then imperialist, expansion across the planet during the 18th and 19th centuries.

Industrial capitalism is responsible for the third alienation, engendering the most radical alteration of humanity's relation to the natural world since the Neolithic.

Although capitalism's origins lie in the finance and manufacture in the mercantile towns and cities of medieval Italy, Germany, and Flanders, its development would have been impossible without the overthrow of medieval attitudes to the land. For feudal society, the importance of land had not changed much since the Biblical Proverbs:

> What the feudal noble wanted was not land alone, but land and people. The more densely his land was populated, the greater the number of persons to pay taxes and render services, the larger was the military following which he could maintain. The efforts of the medieval noble were not directed to expelling the peasant, but to attaching him to the soil and attracting as many new settlers as possible.[41]

The whole of feudal society was organised around ties of loyalty: to family, to retainers, to overlords, and these ties were expressed through land, and through the multiple agricultural services attached to the land.[42]

This is antithetical to the requirements of capitalism. Capitalism needs free labour, that is to say workers who are 'free' from any attachment to the land, 'free' from any ownership of the tools of production, and 'free' to starve when they cannot be employed to produce surplus value. Capitalism also demands that land should be 'free':

---

40 Other examples which have often been underestimated include the pillage of human labour by the Atlantic slave trade, and the role of loot from India in financing accumulation in the 18th century (see above).

41 Karl Kautsky, 'Land hunger – feudal and capitalist', in *Thomas More and his Utopia* (1888), <https://www.marxists.org/archive/kautsky/1888/more/ch02.htm> [accessed 05.01.2023]

42 These are the 'sacred ties' whose destruction by capitalism Marx remarks on in the *Manifesto*.

Commodity production imparted to the soil itself the character of a commodity and consequently a value which was not determined by the number of inhabitants it nourished, but by the surplus it yielded. The smaller the number of its cultivators in proportion to the yield, and the less pretentious their standard of life, the larger the surplus and the greater the land value.[43]

Hence the evolution of legal and mental attitudes to land, transforming it from the inalienable appurtenance of a family or a fiefdom to a property which could be bought and sold like any other.

In a money economy, the relation of the workforce to the land was the same as to a machine. The purpose of labour is no longer to cultivate agricultural products but to produce surplus value. The fewer the workers and the less they are paid, the greater the surplus value. Rather than farming his estate, it was thus far more profitable for a feudal lord to convert his estate into a great sheep farm run by one or two families of shepherds, supplying the wool industry of Flanders or the Cotswolds with its raw material, which prompted Thomas More's acid remark in his *Utopia* about 'man-eating sheep'.

The separation of workers from the land, as described in Marx's chapter on 'Primary accumulation' in *Capital*, was carried out with a brutality and a cynicism that would have made Genghis Khan blush.

Whereas the Neolithic saw humanity largely abandon its original state 'in nature' for a sedentary existence tied to the land, capitalism expelled the workers from the land and condemned them to an existence at the mercy of an abstract economy. Moreover, by separating the workers not just from the land but from the tools of their trade, capitalism alienated them both from nature and from their own nature as human beings engaged in actively shaping the world for the satisfaction of their own needs. Estranged from the land, the worker was also estranged from both the product and the process of labour. Exploitation deprived the mediaeval peasant or artisan of a greater or lesser share of the fruits of his labour, but he still had mastery over the labour process itself and had an intimate knowledge of its preconditions and its product. For the factory worker, the division of labour carried to a hitherto unimagined degree disintegrates the labour process into discrete parts but renders the whole obscure.

Industrial agriculture's threat to the land

Marx described the capitalist production process in the formula c+v+sv: the application of variable capital (wages that buy labour power) to operate constant capital (machinery, raw materials and so on), so producing surplus value,

---

43   Kautsky, *Thomas More.*

effectively unpaid labour time. But in extractive industries (mining, agriculture, fishing, for example), the constant capital is not the ore, the nutrients in the soil, or the wild fish: rather it is the cost of land purchase, the mining or farming tools, and so on. For capitalism, mineral resources are treated as a free gift of nature, as if they were inexhaustible. They are cost free, since the only costs involved are based on the labour needed to extract them and the rent paid to the owner of the land under which they live. No payment is made to the future generations to whom the extracted minerals will no longer be available. The land is not a living entity, a biotope, it is merely abstract capital; value is extracted from the land by applying labour to it, and when the land is exhausted it is abandoned just as a worn-out machine is consigned to the scrap-heap. As Engels put it:

> Classical political economy, the social science of the bourgeoisie, in the main examines only social effects of human actions in the fields of production and exchange that are actually intended. This fully corresponds to the social organisation of which it is the theoretical expression. As individual capitalists are engaged in production and exchange for the sake of the immediate profit, only the nearest, most immediate results must first be taken into account. As long as the individual manufacturer or merchant sells a manufactured or purchased commodity with the usual coveted profit, he is satisfied and does not concern himself with what afterwards becomes of the commodity and its purchasers. The same thing applies to the natural effects of the same actions. What cared the Spanish planters in Cuba, who burned down forests on the slopes of the mountains and obtained from the ashes sufficient fertiliser for one generation of very highly profitable coffee trees – what cared they that the heavy tropical rainfall afterwards washed away the unprotected upper stratum of the soil, leaving behind only bare rock! In relation to nature, as to society, the present mode of production is predominantly concerned only about the immediate, the most tangible result; and then surprise is expressed that the more remote effects of actions directed to this end turn out to be quite different, are mostly quite the opposite in character.[44]

In effect, agriculture ruins the land the more it expands productivity. As Marx pointed out:

> ...every advance in capitalist agriculture is an advance in the art, not only of robbing the worker, but of robbing the soil; every advance in the fertility of the soil for a given period of time, is simultaneously an advance towards the ruin of the permanent sources of this fertility. The greater the extent to which a country tends to start its development upon the foundation of large-scale industry (as does the USA for instance), the more rapid

---

44   Engels, 'The Part Played by Labour in the Transition from Ape to Man' in *Dialectics of Nature*, (Moscow: Progress Publishers, 1976), p.183.

is this process of destruction. Capitalist production, therefore, is only able to develop the technique and the combination of the social process of production by simultaneously undermining the foundations of all wealth: the land and the workers.[45]

Today we would update Marx to include, in the sources of wealth, the oceans and the atmosphere.

Capitalism's industrial processes, moreover, multiplied the power of human labour to set in motion energy derived from external sources. Indeed, an increase in productivity, which means that the same amount of human labour sets in motion a greater amount of constant capital, must always mean an increase in energy use. At first, this still meant energy from animal and plant sources: draft animals for motive power and burning wood for heat, the first dating back to the Neolithic, the second being part of humanity's very existence. But the essence of capitalism being production without limit, it soon outstripped nature's ability to grow more trees. In Scotland, for example, the Great Caledonian Pine Forest had once covered 1.5 million hectares of the Highlands. By 1900, exploitation for charcoal, fuel and timber had reduced this to about 16,000 hectares.[46] The only solution was to turn from organic to fossil fuels.

Industrialisation has historically been dependent on fossil fuels, first coal, then oil and gas. Without the increasingly massive use of energy derived from coal, capitalism's takeoff in the early 19th century would have been impossible. In effect, this transformed an economy of husbandry into an economy of pillage dependent on burning energy sources laid down over millions of years. The pillage of the natural world was in continuity with the social relationships of pre-industrial capitalism and the expansion of the proto-capitalist European nations across the world: vast quantities of gold and especially silver were poured into the world's commercial networks by the Spanish pillaging of the Aztec and Inca empires, and the ruthless exploitation of the South American silver mines; Britain's industrial takeoff was in part capitalised by the sack of the Mogul Empire's accumulated wealth; slave labour (the pillage of human beings) on sugar and cotton plantations was integral to capitalism's early development. The new industrial proletariat was fed by decimating the enormous banks of cod discovered off Newfoundland, and by mechanisation of the newly cultivated lands of the Americas.

The relationship to the land and the natural world changed: the mechanisation of agriculture and the use of imported fertiliser increased the productivity

---

45   'Machinery and Large scale industry, Section 10, Large-scale industry and agriculture', in Marx, *Capital*, p.547.

46   Seen on an information panel on Auchnafree Estate in Perthshire, Scotland

of farm labour. By the early 20th century, only about 5% of the total British population still worked the land.[47]

The tool was originally a means of extending the powers of the human body. Industrialisation under capitalism has created tools which could no longer be set in motion by the individual, and turned the human body and mind into a component of the industrial process. 'Estranged labour reverses this relationship so that it is just because man is a conscious being, that he makes his life activity, his **essential** being, a mere means for his **existence**'.[48] Labour becomes abstract, something alien to the worker.

This separation of the human body, human existence, from what is essential to it – that is to say, labour, conscious activity to change the world in conformity with human need – is concomitant with a mechanical vision of nature. Human labour processes are no longer a complete whole, from raw materials to finished products after the manner of the artisan. They are broken down into component parts, simplified, rendered abstract; the worker is a cog in a machine, not a living being engaged in natural processes. Time, and the precise measurement of time, acquires a new importance; time also becomes abstract, no longer measured by the natural rhythms of sunrise and sunset, of years and seasons, but by the abstract rhythm of the clock's minute hand. It is no accident that the paradigmatic technology of the epoch was the clock (as today it is the computer). The whole of nature, 'man's natural body' as Marx put it, is seen as a machine whose component parts can be manipulated without regard for the whole, and which can become the subject of private appropriation right down to the molecular level, as we can see today in the practice of patenting genomes.

Just as the worker is separated from the production process, and reduced to the status of a cog, so Cartesian philosophy separates the mind from the body. For Descartes, the body is merely a machine with no faculty for thought or even feeling. For Kant, '[So] far as animals are concerned, we have no direct duties. Animals are not self-conscious and are there merely as the means to an end. That end is man'.[49]

---

47 In 1901 there were 2.42m people employed in agriculture out of a total population of 41.43m. See Max Roser, 'Employment in Agriculture' (2013) in *Our World in Data*. <https://ourworldindata.org/employment-in-agriculture> ' and Max Roser, Hannah Ritchie, Esteban Ortiz-Ospina and Lucas Rodés-Guirao, 'World Population Growth' (2013) <https://ourworldindata.org/world-population-growth> [accessed 05.01.2023]

48 Marx, 'Estranged labour', p.113 (emphasis in the original).

49 'Duties to animals and spirits', quoted in Jason Hickel, *Less is more* (Cornerstone, 2020), p.318.

We cannot, however, view capitalism – or indeed any historical development – one-sidedly. Stripping the sacred from nature was necessary if human understanding was to be established for the first time on a truly materialist basis; dismantling nature into its component parts was the only way to pierce the clouds of tradition. Francis Bacon may have sought to 'bind nature to service', and to 'force her out of her natural state' for human ends,[50] nonetheless he also insisted that only by observing nature could knowledge of nature be gained.

Trade and taxation prompted the development of mathematics in the days of Sumer and Babylon. The increasingly abstract process of capitalist production, encouraged a further development of abstraction. By applying new methods of production, capitalism was wresting new powers from nature, encouraging a questioning and rethinking of the knowledge of the ancients, whose superiority had previously been considered axiomatic. It was an era of discovery and a vast effort of classification in the sciences, allied to a painstaking naturalism in the arts. In *De Humani Corporis Fabrica* (1543), Vesalius published the first accurate and superbly detailed drawings of human anatomy; Carl Linnaeus created the taxonomic system that remains in use to this day; Robert Hooke's *Micrographia* (1665) revealed for the first time the teeming world of microscopic organisms, and the incredible complexity of nature's component parts.[51]

Moreover, this is not all there was to science. The European 'age of discovery' broadened people's appreciation of the limitless variety of nature, if they had eyes to see. It is no accident that Darwin's theory of evolution, in which all life – including humanity – is interrelated in one great web of being, began to take shape during his circumnavigation of the globe in HMS Beagle (1831-36).

In the 21st century science has astonished us by revealing something of the full extent of life's inter-connection: the role of mycelia in plant life, and the importance of the bacterial biome for animal life, to name but two examples. However, the basic principle is not new, rather it has been obscured by the domination of a mechanistic viewpoint driven by ideology and the demands of capitalist industry. Already in 1800 the great German naturalist Alexander von Humboldt was writing that 'Everything is interaction and reciprocal',[52] and in 1866, inspired by Humboldt and Darwin, the brilliant scientist Ernst Haeckel

---

50   See Hickel, *Less is More*, p.68.

51   Hooke is emblematic of the heroic age of early science. The worlds of art, science, and technology had not yet separated: Hooke himself was an accomplished lens-maker, the author of Hooke's Law of elasticity and Newton's rival in the physical sciences, the draughtsman of the engravings drawn from life in *Micrographia*, and the architectural partner of Christopher Wren in the rebuilding of London after the Great Fire of 1666.

52   Andrea Wulf, *The invention of nature* (London: John Murray, 2016), p.59.

published his *Generelle Morphologie der Organismen* in which he coined the term 'oecologie': ecology. Organic and inorganic nature, he wrote, constituted a 'system of active forces'; ecology was 'the science of the relationships of an organism with its environment'. After visiting his hero Darwin, Haeckel declared himself more than ever convinced that the natural world was 'one unified whole – a completely interrelated "kingdom of life"'.[53] An intuition that could be sidelined in the 19th century has become a critical element of social consciousness in the 21st.

The militarisation of the metabolism

If we take human society as a whole, from the point of view of the biosphere, it is hardly an exaggeration to say that while prior to 1914 it could appear as an invasive species, sucking nutrients from the ecosystem at the expense of others, since 1945 it is more akin to a toxic spill actively poisoning the environment, and the human species itself.

As we have seen, and as Marx had already pointed out, capitalist agriculture was never viable in the long run, involving as it did the constant leaching of nutrients into crops consumed at great – even transcontinental – distances from the farms, without any corresponding return of waste matter to the land. By the end of the 19th century, agriculture in Europe and the United States was largely dependent on the application of guano from South America, to replace the nitrates extracted by intensive farming of corn and wheat.[54]

Capitalist agriculture had clearly reached breaking point. Nonetheless, up to this point agriculture still remained reliant on an essentially natural cycle, and on the natural motive power of horses and oxen. All this was about to change as capitalism entered into its phase of decadence and decline.

The period 1914-45 profoundly altered capitalism's structure and functioning. Having spread their tentacles across every corner of the planet bar Antarctica, the octopi of world imperialism could only expand outwards at the ex-

---

53   Ibid, p.307-8

54   Guano, the accumulated excrement of sea-birds and bats, would almost merit a section to itself. An excellent fertiliser due to its high concentrations of nitrate, phosphate, and potassium, guano was mined in staggering quantities from sea-bird breeding-grounds on coastal islands off-shore from Chile, Bolivia, and Peru. The value of the guano trade was such that in 1856 the USA passed the Guano Islands Act, arrogating the right for any US citizen to claim possession of a guano-bearing island; from 1857 onwards the USA annexed up to nearly 100 such islands in the Pacific and Caribbean. It also led to the War of the Pacific between Chile and Bolivia, ending in the 1884 Treaty of Ancon whereby Chile stripped Bolivia of its entire Pacific coastline.

pense of their rivals. This led, inexorably, to two planetary wars, the most destructive and widespread in human history.

Capitalism's history since 1945 has been shaped fundamentally by militarism, state control, and imperialist rivalry, and nowhere more so than in the alteration of humanity's place in nature, which is our subject here.

How, more precisely, did this new period shape the world of agriculture?

Militarism. World War I had shown conclusively that the days of short, sharp,
confrontations leading to decisive victory were over. The 'model' of the 1870
Franco-Prussian war, which the Germans tried to reproduce in August 1914
and which had encouraged the belief among all the belligerents that the war
would be 'over by Christmas', was clearly obsolete. The next war would be
planetary, a long, grinding affair, pitting the entire productive, social, and psychological capacity of nations against each other. In the meantime, opposing
camps would live in a permanent state of war readiness and armed competition.

'An army marches on its stomach'. The saying is variously attributed to Na-
poleon or Frederick II of Prussia, but never was it more true than during
World War II; never before had such vast armies been supplied across such
distances, and in so many parts of the world, and never before had the armies
been so dependent on the industrial production of the civilian population.[55]

In this competition, food production and supply, both to the armies in the
field and to the civilian population in the factories, would be as critical as
weapons: both guns and butter, so to speak.

The militarisation of agriculture (of which more below) came full circle. The
USA militarised the world's food supply, partly in order to dump its own surpluses and partly as a deliberate instrument of foreign policy. Starting in 1954
with the passage of Public Law 480, allowing the Federal Government to dis-
tribute food aid abroad (both for free and at preferential prices), the United
States has used food aid as an instrument of imperial power. This was quite explicit: at the time, the (Democrat) Senator Hubert Humphrey declared:

> I have heard... that people may become dependent on us for food... To
> me that was good news, because before people can do anything they have
> got to eat. And if you are looking for a way to get people to lean on you
> and to be dependent on you, in terms of their cooperation with you, it
> seems to me that food dependence would be terrific.[56]

---

55 Much of what follows is based on the history of food and nutrition in the combatant
    countries in Lizzie Cunningham, *The Taste of War*, (Allan Lane, 2011), especially the fi-
    nal chapter "The Aftermath", and on Vandana Shiva, *Who really feeds the world?*.

56 'The Food Weapon', in NACLA's *Latin America and Empire Report*, 9:7, 12-17, 1975.
    NACLA is the North American Congress on Latin America, founded in 1966 (see
    nacla.org). <https://doi.org/10.1080/10714839.1975.11724007>

During America's wars in Indochina and South-East Asia, food aid was used especially to prop up friendly dictatorships and to disguise direct military assistance. Withholding food aid from Chile, and refusing credits to the Chilean government for food purchases in the USA, was used to stir up popular discontent against the Allende regime; following the CIA-supported army coup in 1973, food aid was used to support the infamous Pinochet regime.[57]

Food aid, and the export by the USA and Europe of subsidised agricultural products, has had the effect of flooding the world's markets with grain at rock-bottom prices, which in turn has been driving small peasant producers out of business, or has been forcing them into production of cash crops for sale to the developed markets. We thus have the absurdity of French beans grown in Kenya being flown to supermarkets in Britain (at immense cost in air fuel), rather than feeding the local population. The effects on the poor of relying on imported grain are today being made abundantly clear with the food blockade imposed by Russia on Ukraine. Clearly, the Russian ruling class has learnt the American lesson![58]

With this past history, when we consider that American (and European) agribusiness are both massively subsidised, that this subsidised food is forcibly dumped on the 'Global South' economies under the auspices of a 1995 WTO Agreement on Agriculture drawn up by Dan Amstutz, previously Vice-President of Cargill – one of the world's largest grain traders – and that the major seed companies (Monsanto, Bayer, DuPont, Syngenta and Dow) are aggressively patenting seeds of every description, it is hard not to come to the conclusion that the world's food supply is being increasingly weaponised by the major powers and especially by the United States. Or perhaps we should say, once again, that there is no solid boundary between the apparently civilian and the openly military.

In August 1974, the CIA produced a confidential report (which happily was leaked) on 'Potential Implications of Trends in World Population, Food Production, and Climate'. Ironically, at the time the climatologists consulted by the CIA expected decades of cooling in the immediate future, but they still predicted crop failures and food shortages as a result. In consequence, said the CIA, 'there would almost certainly be an absolute shortage of food':

> … In a cooler and therefore hungrier world, the U.S. near-monopoly position as food exporter […] could give the U.S. a measure of power it never had before – possibly an economic and political dominance greater than that of the immediate post-World War II years […] Washington would ac-

---

57   Ibid.

58   Since this was written, Russia has been forced to abandon its embargo, at least for the time being, under pressure from Turkey.

quire virtual life and death power over the fate of multitudes of the needy.[59]

As it turns out, the world is getting hotter not cooler, and the effects on the world food supply will almost certainly be still more catastrophic than the CIA imagined. But what is significant here is the Agency's view of climate change: not a threat but an opportunity to reassert American dominance.

State control. In the thirty years following 1914, capitalist states had to face the challenges of all-out war, economic breakdown, and social breakdown or even workers' attempts at the whole system's revolutionary overthrow. The only way to do so was by immensely extending the state's ability to plan and control, not just the economy, but every facet of social life. Government being impossible without some degree of consent on the part of the governed, after 1945 state planners had to avoid the social breakdown that had followed the previous war. Once again, food production would be key: the victory of democracy was all very well, but democracy butters no parsnips. The war and its aftermath caused the worst and most widespread food shortage in human history. In Britain, people were hungry, in continental Europe, the USSR, China and Japan, they were starving, and in India the Bengal famine of 1943 killed an estimated 2-3 million people. Even in the USA, civilians experienced food shortages. All this was a result, not of inadequate agriculture, but of war, and it inflicted a psychological trauma whose effects are hard to gauge, but surely no less real for all that.

The other challenge to the planners was the demobilisation and conversion of the vast apparatus of military production, above all in the United States which had been the 'arsenal of democracy' and which had become, in large part thanks to the war itself, far and away the world's dominant industrial power.

Imperialist rivalry. As such, this was of course nothing new: capitalist nations had always been rivals and had always fought wars, ever since the Anglo-Dutch wars of the early 17th century, perhaps the first specifically inter-capitalist wars in history. What was new in 1914, was the geographical constraint which would henceforth be a determining factor in capitalism's evolution.

There would be no more Indias to ransack for accumulated wealth, no more African populations shipped in their millions to the slave plantations of the Americas, no more limitless North American prairies or Russian steppes for capitalism to absorb in its innate dynamic of limitless production for production's sake. This was all the more true after 1945, in that Western capitalism – and capitalism up to 1900 had been overwhelmingly dominated by Western Europe and the United States – was now excluded from the vast and largely under-developed (from a capitalist viewpoint) Eurasian regions now controlled

59   Ibid.

by the USSR, China, and to a lesser extent India. No longer able to expand in breadth (geographically), capitalism could only expand 'in depth', by absorbing more and more sectors of economic activity.

This meant – amongst other things – intensifying capital accumulation in economic sectors which remained under-capitalised. This was true in particular in agriculture, which remained dominated by small-scale farming: in 1920, even the USA could only count 225 tractors in the entire country,[60] and in 1945 nearly half the French population still lived on the land.

Clearly, the model we have outlined here is extremely schematic. The different factors – military, economic, social and geographic – are intertwined and condition each other in ways which it is not always possible, or even desirable, to disentangle. It indicates, nonetheless, a profound modification in humanity's metabolic relation to the rest of the living world. More than that, it has profoundly modified humanity's own, internal, bodily metabolism. Capitalism, in a sense, has gone to war with its own physical foundation, indeed with the necessary physical foundation of all human society, and even of all life. That war is leading to the planet's sixth mass extinction, and while it has broken into the mainstream public discourse only relatively recently, it can be dated back to the 1950s.[61]

The militarisation of agriculture

The industrialisation, and militarisation, of life processes is not the only facet of capitalism's war on nature, far from it. Industrial pollution, the pillage of natural resources, and the unbridled consumption of fossil fuels, all enter into the picture as we are well aware. Here we have deliberately chosen to limit the scope of our argument to the production and consumption of food, since this is so central to our existence and our relationship to the planet as a whole.

The consequences of this new period in capitalism's existence were a radical transformation and extension of industrial agriculture in three domains: fertilisers, pesticides, and food processing.

Fertilisers. Without nitrate fertilisers, industrial agriculture is severely hampered by the need to counter nitrogen depletion in the soil, either by leaving the land fallow or by planting legumes which fix nitrogen naturally. By the end of the 19th century, naturally occurring nitrates began to be in short supply, and chemists were searching for alternative, manufactured sources. The

---

60   Michael Pollan, *The Omnivore's Dilemma*, (Penguin, 2016), p.38.

61   The biologist Rachel Carson's groundbreaking *Silent Spring* was published in 1962. It was, it must be said, completely ignored by the Communist Left.

result was the construction of the first chemical plant producing artificial nitrates in Oppau, Germany (1913), using the Haber-Bosch process. They did not have much immediate effect on agriculture, but during World War I the Oppau plant turned to producing nitrates for explosives, and World War II led to a massive increase in nitrates production for this purpose. What was to be done, at the end of the war, with the enormous stocks of ammonium nitrate intended for explosives, and the now unnecessary production capacity?

> The great turning point [...] in the industrialisation of our food, can be dated with some precision to the day in 1947 when the huge munitions plant in Muscle Shoals, Alabama, switched over to making chemical fertiliser [...] The chemical fertiliser industry [...] is the product of the government's effort to convert its war machine to peacetime purposes.[62]

The US federal government now spends $5 billion a year subsidising corn farmers to produce below cost, but the real benefit goes to companies like Cargill and Coca-Cola.[63]

Pesticides. The same holds true for chemical pesticides. The first chemical herbicide was 2,4-dichlorophenoxyacetic acid, commonly known as 2,4-D, developed as a defoliant during World War II for the same purpose as Agent Orange during the Vietnam War: to deprive the enemy of foliage cover. The glyphosate used today under the Roundup label, was developed as a less toxic alternative to 2,4-D.

> Since 1974 in the U.S., over 1.6 billion kilograms of glyphosate active ingredient have been applied, or 19 % of estimated global use of glyphosate (8.6 billion kilograms).[64]

Over the last half century, industrialised agriculture has poured 8.6 billion kg of poison into the planet's soil.

There is, however, no escaping the laws of evolution. The massive application of glyphosate has inevitably led to the emergence of glyphosate-resistant strains of the pests it is supposed to combat. The solution is first, more glyphosate, second the introduction of more powerful (and therefore more toxic) pesticides (a new version of 2,4-D is under preparation for precisely this reason). It is obvious where this is heading: new herbicides will lead to more resistant plants which in turn will lead to more toxic herbicides, then newly res-

---

62 Pollan, *The Omnivore's Dilemma*, pp.41, 54. In the first section of the book, Pollan concentrates on the aberration of industrialised cultivation of corn in the USA, but this could act as a paradigm world wide.

63 Ibid, p.54.

64 Benbrook, C.M. 'Trends in glyphosate herbicide use in the United States and globally' in *Environmental Sciences Europe*, vol 28, article 3 (2016). <https://doi.org/10.1186/s12302-016-0070-0>

istant plants... this cannot go on forever. Like the 'war on drugs' and the 'war on terror', the 'war on weeds' fought in this way, is one that cannot be won.

Roundup is intended to be used on GM crops that are Roundup-resistant: it kills everything else, in particular it is toxic for the micro-organisms, mycelia, and plants that are essential to healthy soil.

The first chemical pesticides used against insects (notably DDT) emerged from research into nerve gases, again during the war. The European pesticide market alone is worth €8 billion annually, which explains why it has so far proved impossible to ban neonicotinoids responsible for the catastrophic decline in the populations of bees and other pollinators.

Food processing. Like the nitrates industry and nerve gas research, the food processing industry received an enormous boost from the war, especially in the USA and Australia. Of all the populations involved in the war, the Americans were among the least enthusiastic:

> Generous meals were one of General George Marshall's[65] strategies for dealing with an army of drafted men who preserved a strong civilian mentality [...] They expected to be well looked after in the armed forces, and soldiers and their families formed a powerful pressure group within the United States [...]
>
> In response Marshall adopted a placatory policy which made 'troop welfare [...] an essential part of modern warfare'.[66]

Troop welfare meant, most importantly, abundant food. Consequently, the armed forces spent a great deal of effort developing the rations fed to soldiers, from the B-rations of military camps to the K-rations issued to combat troops. In the process they revolutionised and vastly expanded the food processing and packaging industry, both in the USA and in Australia which supplied about half the food rations for the US forces in the Pacific War. Along with fertiliser and pesticides, food processing became another industry in desperate need of a market when the war came to an end. It is hardly an exaggeration to say that whenever you eat a McDonalds or a ready-prepared meal, you are eating a descendent of the K-ration. This had the effect of banalising regional diets since, by their nature, army rations had to be standardised and the effect was then carried over to the militarised version of the civilian diet.

Australia's position as food supplier to the Pacific Theatre did not come to an end in 1945. NATO planners preparing for the next war, sometime in the 1950s, expected Australia to supply 1 million US troops. Inevitably, the country ended up with an overactive farm sector and a food processing industry which

---

65 US Chief of Staff during the war, best known today for his role in running the eponymous post-war Marshall Plan

66 Cunningham, *The Taste of War*, p.415.

had to find an outlet for its surplus. Preparing for the next war also meant massively increasing food production, since all the combatant countries bar the USA were acutely aware of the problems they had faced with food supply during the war itself. An enormous increase in farm output was achieved through programmes of mass mechanisation and huge inputs of chemical fertilisers and pesticides.

The industrialisation of food processing

Standardisation is fundamental to capitalist industrialisation. The extreme division of labour means breaking down a complex operation into smaller standard operations which can be performed more rapidly with less training by human workers, thus reducing the cost of labour; the more standardised the operations, the easier they are to mechanise, and the more standardised the product the greater are the economies of scale that can be achieved. Applied to agriculture, capitalist industrialisation based on standardisation finds itself in a fundamental contradiction with life processes, which are characterised by flexibility, diversity, constant non-standard adaptations to change; indeed the whole point of sexual reproduction is to increase resilience through diversity. Hence, the frenzied expansion of militarised capitalism into agriculture, food processing, and consumption brought humanity abruptly into contradiction with the processes of life itself.[67]

Consider for a moment the food chain as it existed up to World War II in Britain, the most precociously industrialised country which imported substantial quantities of food. A typical Londoner would buy fresh food grown in one of the market-gardens that ringed the city, from a market stall or a small shop, cooking it at home or eating out in a local café. Staple foods like meat or wheat would probably be imported but would be mostly sold through small outlets: local bakers and butchers.

The point is that all these small businesses, while they exist in an entirely money economy based on commodity production, are not in themselves objects of capital accumulation.[68] A small grocer or butcher with a regular clientele, even if they employ a few salaried workers, may live very well but does not accumulate capital. Constant capital (the shop, the goods for sale) is maintained

---

67   This has led us to a point where 'most humans now get 75% of their calorie intake from just eight foods: rice, wheat, maize, potatoes, barley, palm oil, soya and sugar'. *The Economist*, review of Dan Saladino, *Eating to Extinction* (see note above).

68   'We know that the means of production and the means of subsistence are not capital so long as they remain the property of the individual producer. They only become capital under conditions in which they can at the same time serve as the means of exploitation and subjugation of the worker' (Marx, *Capital*, p.850).

but barely increased. If surplus-value is extracted at all, it is destined to increase the shopkeeper's income but is inadequate for reinvestment.[69] A one-man food truck in the City does not accumulate capital; Sodexo, which distributes a range of identical sandwiches to innumerable service stations and other outlets, as well as running company canteens, does accumulate capital.

The small farm or shop is antithetical to capitalism, which exists only to accumulate, and which must constantly expand its accumulation. To do so, it must constantly produce more with fewer workers setting in motion ever more constant capital.[70] This is the inexorable logic of capitalist society.

Now consider what this means for food production. A small farm engaged in mixed agriculture may very well be more efficient in terms of energy inputs and waste production than a large agribusiness. Crop rotation and animal manure avoid the use of chemical fertilisers, the judicious (and often sophisticated) combination of plants encourages beneficial insects and birds which serve as pest control, hence no pesticides. The sun provides energy for plant growth. Plant waste is composted and animal waste is returned as fertiliser. On a farm in the American corn belt, however,

> when you add together the natural gas in the fertiliser to the fossil fuels it takes to make the pesticides, drive the tractors, and harvest, dry, and transport the corn, you find that every bushel of industrial corn requires the equivalent of between a quarter and a third of a gallon of oil to grow it – or around 50 gallons of oil per acre of corn (some estimates are much higher). Put another way, it takes more than a calorie of fossil fuel energy to produce a calorie of food; before the advent of chemical fertiliser [the same farm] produced more than two calories of food energy for every calorie of energy invested.[71]

The same is true of industrialised meat. Animal feedlots in the US fatten tens of thousands of animals for slaughter; the manure they produce has such high levels of nitrogen and phosphorus, not to mention heavy metals and hormone residues, that it is toxic to crops.[72]

Such a system is clearly both unsustainable in the medium term, and bordering on the insane. It also puts into perspective the incredible increases in

69   There are exceptions of course: the giant British supermarket chain Sainsbury began with just such a small shop in Holborn, in 1869.

70   This is basic Marxism, which we won't expand on here. See the essay on Surplus Population.

71   Pollan, *Omnivore's Dilemma*, p.45. Pollan adds, tongue in cheek, 'From the standpoint of industrial efficiency, it's too bad we can't simply drink the petroleum directly'.

72   Ibid, p.77.

productivity[73] achieved by industrialised agriculture since 1945. This is productivity measured in purely capitalist terms: more output for fewer workers. It takes no account of energy efficiency nor of pollutants since capitalism does not pay the full cost of energy, nor of waste.

The continued search for productivity gains in agriculture will aim to reduce labour still further: one person will run multiple farms on-screen using robotic tractors; cows are already trained to plug themselves into automated milking machines. Patented GM crops and the inevitable pesticides will drive more small farmers to debt and suicide (an endemic problem in India). Food production will continue to drive climate change (it already accounts for over 25% of global emissions[74]).

Consequences of the industrialisation of food processing

Transforming food into a commodity like any other, subject to the same imperatives of industrial production has profound consequences. Its nutritive value is of secondary importance, the only real criterion for the product is that it should sell in as large quantities as possible, and that its production should be at the lowest possible cost. But there is another, crucial, aspect in the cost of food: food is a fundamental, and necessary component of 'v' (variable capital, ie wages), since workers must necessarily eat to live and to go on working. Reducing the price of food therefore also reduces the cost of labour. Hence the interest of the industrial capitalists in repealing the British Corn Laws in the 1830s, so removing import tariffs on wheat and reducing the price of bread, the staple of the workers' diet.

The crudest forms of cost reduction (described by Engels in his groundbreaking *Condition of the working class in England*), such as the adulteration of flour with inedible waste like sawdust, have largely given way, in modern industrial countries, to the use of cheap food additives such as sugar and cornflour. These are edible, but damaging to health or even downright toxic in the long run.

---

73   See Cunningham, *The Taste of War*, p.491: 'By 1959 American farm production had grown by 60% of the pre-war average. In 1963 one farmworker could feed thirty people, whereas in 1940 he had been able to feed only eleven [...] Wheat yields in Britain rose by 75%'.

74   Hannah Ritchie, 'Food production is responsible for one-quarter of the world's greenhouse gas emissions' (6 November 2019) in *Our World in Data* <https://ourworldindata.org/food-ghg-emissions> [accessed 5 January 2023]

This does not mean that the criminal adulteration of food has disappeared; quite the reverse, it has attained monstrous proportions.

China recently (2008) witnessed a serious scandal over the addition of melamine into powdered milk.[75] In Europe, we can cite the Spanish cooking oil scandal of 1981 (although it seems that in reality the epidemic was caused by overuse of pesticides, which was deliberately concealed by the government),[76] the Austrian wine contamination scandal in 1985 in which diethylene glycol was added to wine to improve its flavour,[77] the Italburro butter scandal, or the dumping by EU countries of food including powdered milk and meat contaminated with radioactive fallout from the Chernobyl disaster.[78] The fraudulent Italian food industry alone is said to be worth €60 billion per year.[79]

The Covid19 pandemic has also made this abundantly clear: the majority of fatalities among any but the very old during the pandemic have been attributed to pre-existing conditions, notably cardiac problems and diabetes. These in turn are closely linked to the ongoing epidemic of obesity. According to the WHO, the number of obese adults has increased from 200 million worldwide in 1995, to 300 million in 2000, and to 650 million in 2018.[80] One of the main underlying reasons for this worldwide epidemic (which only escapes the designation pandemic, presumably, because there is nothing new about it) is not the criminal adulteration of food but the perfectly legal use of foodstuffs, notably sugar, which in more than small quantities should be considered as toxic drugs,[81] by the world's biggest food and drinks producers (Coca-Cola, Pepsi, Danone, etc). Nor is the epidemic limited to rich nations, on the contrary. Obesity is a disease of poverty within rich nations, and of poor nations; it is the fifth risk factor by

---

75 '2008 Chinese milk scandal' in *Wikipedia*, <https://en.wikipedia.org/wiki/2008_Chinese_milk_scandal> [retrieved 22 December 2022]

76 Bob Wiffenden, 'Cover-up' in *The Guardian*, 25 August 2001, <https://www.theguardian.com/education/2001/aug/25/research.highereducation>

77 '1985 diethylene glycol wine scandal' in *Wikipedia* <https://en.wikipedia.org/wiki/1985_diethylene_glycol_wine_scandal> [retrieved 22/12/2022]

78 Dirk Banninck, 'Contaminated foodstuffs dumped on world market' in *Nuclear Monitor* no. 349-350, 5 April 1991, <https://www.wiseinternational.org/nuclear-monitor/349-350/contaminated-foodstuffs-dumped-world-market> [accessed 05 January 2023]

79 Tom Mueller, *Extra virginity: the sublime and scandalous world of olive oil*, (London: Atlantic Books, 2012), p.45.

80 See 'Controlling the global obesity epidemic', World Health Organization, <https://www.who.int/nutrition/topics/obesity/en/> [retrieved 22 December 2022] and 'Obesity and overweight', World Health Organization, 9 June 2021, <https://www.who.int/news-room/fact-sheets/detail/obesity-and-overweight> [retrieved 22 December 2022]

81 See this documentary by Arte (in French) <https://youtu.be/6f3NvV05k28>

number of deaths world wide, but the third in Mexico (behind high blood sugar and high blood pressure).[82]

Here we are confronted with one of the most absurd and sinister contradictions of industrialised capitalism: scientific knowledge of human nutritional needs has never been greater, our technical and scientific understanding of the biosphere allow us to feed the entire world population more adequately than ever before, and yet the food industry is deliberately, knowingly, poisoning the world's population with toxic quantities of foodstuffs unsuited to the healthy development of the human body; among other effects, the omnipresence of preserved food means that we ingest ever greater quantities of additives intended to alter its colour and flavour, and to increase its shelf life. To take one example among a multitude (as you can see if you look at the ingredients list of any processed food): E171, or in real life, titanium dioxide. Who in their right minds would knowingly eat something like that?

The possibility of going beyond

Capitalism engendered new ways of thinking about the world. It has also, for the first time, brought into being a class of world wide associated labour which can, potentially, go beyond capitalism, close the cycle of class societies opened by the Neolithic Revolution, and so resolve the deepening contradiction between humanity and its 'natural body' created by our three layers of alienation.

In striving for a theoretical understanding of capitalism as it had emerged, and as it functioned in the present, Marx and Engels were working towards the resolution of this contradiction, in theory and one day in practice. Engels was so convinced of the importance of integrating historical materialism (and so the comprehension of human history) into an overall theory of nature, that he set out to write a *Dialectics of Nature*. Sadly this work was never finished, although the chapter on 'the transition from ape to man' stands on its own as a seminal reflection on human evolution. In it, Engels writes that:

> …at every step we are reminded that we by no means rule over nature like a conqueror over a foreign people, like someone standing outside nature – but that we, with flesh, blood and brain, belong to nature, and exist in its midst, and that all our mastery of it consists in the fact that we have the advantage over all other creatures of being able to learn its laws and apply them correctly.

---

82   Hannah Ritchie and Max Roser, 'Obesity' (2017), in *Our World In Data* <https://our-worldindata.org/grapher/number-of-deaths-by-risk-factor?country=~MEX>. Retrieved from: <https://ourworldindata.org/obesity> [accessed 22 December 2022]

And, in fact, with every day that passes we are acquiring a better under-standing of these laws and getting to perceive both the more immediate and the more remote consequences of our interference with the tradi-tional course of nature. In particular, after the mighty advances made by the natural sciences in the present century, we are more than ever in a po-sition to realise, and hence to control, also the more remote natural con-sequences of at least our day-to-day production activities. But the more this progresses the more will men not only feel but also know their one-ness with nature, and the more impossible will become the senseless and unnatural idea of a contrast between mind and matter, man and nature, soul and body, such as arose after the decline of classical antiquity in Europe and obtained its highest elaboration in Christianity.[83]

Marx, considering humanity's place in the organic and inorganic whole of nature, wrote in his *Economic MS of 1861-63* that 'actual labour is the appropri-ation of nature for the satisfaction of human needs, the activity through which the metabolism [*Stoffwechsel*] between man and nature is mediated' and in *Capital* he wrote of the 'independent process of social metabolism, a metabolism pre-scribed by the natural laws of life itself'.[84] Labour is a social process, such that the metabolic relationship between human beings and nature is, by definition, essentially a social one.

Unsurprisingly, Marx's preoccupation with this social metabolism came to the fore in his critique of capitalist industrial agriculture, where humanity's rela-tionship to the land is at its most immediate. Capitalism, he said, 'completely severs the old bond of union between agriculture and manufacture, which were held together when both were in their infancy. At the same time it creates the material requisites for a new and higher synthesis, a union of agriculture and in-dustry, upon the basis of their antithetically elaborated forms'.[85]

From today's perspective, faced with an existential threat to human society as a result of climate change, the collapse of biodiversity, and pollution, Marx's foresight can seem remarkably prescient:

> [by] destroying the natural and spontaneously developed system for the circulation of matter from the soil to human beings, and from human be-ings back to the soil, [capitalist production] necessitates the systematic res-

---

83   Engels, *Dialectics of Nature*, p.180.

84   Quoted in John Bellamy Foster, 'Marx's theory of the metabolic rift', in *Marx's Ecology* (New York: Monthly Review Press, 2000, Kindle edition).

85   'Large-scale industry and agriculture', in Marx, *Capital* p.547. Anarchists too were pre-occupied with the question, as we can see in Peter Kropotkin's work *Fields, farms, and factories*.

toration of such a circulation as a regulative law of social production, and its restoration in a form adequate to the full development of mankind.[86]

The preoccupation with agriculture as interchange between humanity and nature remained important in the Second International, as we can see in Karl Kautsky's writings on the agrarian question and in August Bebel's *Woman in Socialism* which (rather strangely given its title) devotes much of its argument to agriculture. It continued to be a concern in post-revolutionary Russia, before the revolutionary impetus was crushed by Stalinism and science had to bow to the dictates of pseudo-marxist ideology (in the form, notably, of Lysenko's theories). In his 1921 *Historical Materialism*, Nikolai Bukharin wrote:

> No system, including that of human society, can exist in empty space; it is surrounded by an 'environment', on which all its conditions ultimately depend. If human society is not adapted to its environment, it is not meant for this world.[87]

Russian scientists of the day were at the forefront of modern ecological science: in 1926 the Russian scientist Vernadsky published *The Biosphere*, one of its founding works, while the geneticist NI Vavilov established the world's first seed bank, with more than 150,000 samples, in Leningrad.[88]

Another future?

Is standardisation in itself inimical to life? In a sense, the contrary is true. What is DNA after all, if not nature's standard for encoding the characteristics of living cells, without which neither plants nor animals could live or reproduce.

DNA, however, is a standard whose essence is to permit – more, to encourage – the development of infinite variety, through the process of evolution: the real variety of life processes and, for humans, individual life experience, rather

---

86   Ibid.

87   Nikolai Bukharin, 'Society', *Historical Materialism* (1925). One could, however, take issue with Bukharin's statement that 'Man's environment is society, in which he lives; the environment of human society is external nature'. This puts the individual human being at one remove from any but its social surroundings, which ignores the importance, and influence, of the direct physical connection between the individual body and other organisms. <https://www.marxists.org/archive/bukharin/works/1921/histmat/4.htm > [accessed 5 January 2023]

88   Both Bukharin and Vavilov are cited in Foster, *Marx's Ecology*. Bukharin was executed in 1938 during the Moscow Trials. Vavilov, tragically, died of starvation in the Gulag. His seed bank was saved by the extreme dedication of his team of conservationists, who stored it in a cellar during the siege of Leningrad and kept guard over it throughout the 900-day siege; by the end, nine of them had died of starvation, surrounded by seeds.

than the fictitious variety offered by capitalist advertising where multiple brands of an essentially identical product (like washing powder, or fashion) are presented as so many life choices. Capitalism by its nature tends to reduce our multiple manners of reacting to the world, to one: profitability determined by the ability of the associated working class to set in motion ever greater quantities of capital. Applied to the production of food, this has separated humans from the rest of life, and has set them at war with their own bodies.

Yet like all life, capitalism is contradictory. While its destructive tendencies have been inherent from the outset, and have caused incalculable suffering, it has also given birth to a science able, potentially, to embrace nature's unity more fully and in greater depth than could ever have been imagined, allowing people (in Engels' words) 'not only [to] feel but also [to] know their oneness with nature', and to abandon 'the senseless and unnatural idea of a contrast between mind and matter, man and nature'.

Capitalism has created, potentially, technologies which, guiding nature and working with it rather than struggling against it in a vain attempt to dominate it, could liberate humanity from toil.

This 'oneness with nature' which our forebears knew intuitively, can only be both conscious and sensual, concrete. It does not mean dissolving into some New Age mysticism, nor does it mean an illusory return to a society of pre-industrial farmers. It is, however, incompatible with the demands of capitalist profitability.

The techniques exist to repair the land: they are already being applied, more or less experimentally and on a small scale, through the methods of permaculture and regenerative farming. These techniques are not susceptible to capitalist accumulation that agribusiness demands, precisely because they require close attention to the infinite variety of the land at the local level.

Repairing the land will only be possible, on the global scale that humanity needs, by the application of much highly skilled human labour: concrete labour, men and women dirtying their hands in the soil, caring day by day for life. It can only be associated labour, unconstrained by the limited horizons of pre-industrial peasant existence; it will be dependent on the universities, the laboratories, the factories, the energy supply and the universal means of communication to which capitalism has given birth and which await their liberation from the straitjacket of profitability and the nation state.

This association both demands and makes possible an end to the contradiction between town and country which has always been central to the communist perspective.

What that might look like, we hope to examine in a future volume.

The accumulation of catastrophe

(Mark Hayes)

Understanding growth in capitalism's descent

Introduction

The aim of this text is to offer a coherent explanation of economic growth in what Engels described as the 'descending curve' of capitalism.

This may seem misguided at a time when the global economy is clearly facing serious problems due to the cumulative effects of the ongoing Covid-19 pandemic, the war in Ukraine and the worsening effects of the climate crisis. But in our view understanding the nature and the consequences of growth in capitalist decadence is absolutely essential: the fact is that capitalism is the most dynamic mode of production in history, and it is this dynamism – its continual need to revolutionise society – that is at the root not only of its descent but also of its destructiveness.

Engels's description of the 'descending curve' or 'descent' of a mode of production seems particularly helpful to us because it allows us to express capitalism's decline or decay in dynamic rather than static terms and to give a sense that it has a trajectory.[1] But we should note straight away that the whole idea of a descending curve was explicitly rejected by Amadeo Bordiga, who saw it as a gradualist, reformist vision; writing in 1951 he argued that:

> The Marxist view can be represented (for sake of clarity and simplicity) as a series of continuous curves ascending to peaks (singular points or cusps in geometry) followed by sudden, almost vertical, descents; after which, from below, a new social regime, another historically ascending branch, appears.[2]

---

1   'Only when the mode of production in question has already described a good part of its descending curve, when it has half outlived its day, when the conditions of its existence have to a large extent disappeared, and its successor is already knocking at the door – it is only at this stage that the constantly increasing inequality of distribution appears as unjust, it is only then that appeal is made from the facts which have had their day to so-called eternal justice.' (Engels, *Anti-Dühring*, 'Subject Matter and Method' (Progress, 1977), p.184.

2   Bordiga, 'Theory and action in Marxist doctrine', *Bollettino Interno*, no. 11, September

Without examining this view in any detail here, it does seem to us to ignore all the evidence of long periods of decline in previous modes of production, accompanied by a fall in population, in which the new relations of production gradually developed within the old society.

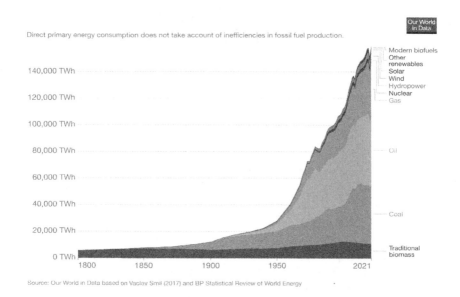

Fig. 4 Global energy consumption as an indicator of economic growth

H Ritchie, 'Global Primary Energy Production 2022', Our World in Data, <https://ourworldindata.org/grapher/global-primary-energy >

Bordiga denied that capitalism was in decline; instead he argued it would continue to grow 'until a sudden and immense explosion that ends the epoch of the capitalist form of production, and changes the profile of the curve.'[3] This would give us the task of coherently explaining the whole history of capitalism in the 20th century, with its world wars, profound economic crises, and all the abundant evidence of its descent into barbarism; so in summary we think we need to reject Bordiga's argument. But his vision of growth followed by sudden collapse does appear to capture one unique feature of the decline of capitalism

1951, <https://www.international-communist-party.org/English/Texts/51TheoAc/51TheoAc.htm>

3   A Bordiga, 'Dialogue With the Dead', 1956, *Bibliotheque Internationale de la Gauche Communiste*, <http://www.sinistra.net/lib/bas/progra/vale/valeecicif.html>, our translation.

which, unlike previous modes of production, is characterised, not by the stagnation or collapse of production but by continued economic growth and a rising population. This is clear, for example, if we look at primary energy consumption as an indicator of growth (see Figure 4).

So if we really do believe that capitalism is in its 'descending curve', how do we explain this apparent paradox?

In brief, each successive mode of production has its own history and laws of development. Unlike previous modes of production, capitalism strives towards the unlimited growth of the productive forces of humanity – but for its own limited purposes, without any regard for the satisfaction of human needs. Capital's only purpose is its own self-expansion: the reconversion of the greatest possible amount of surplus value extracted from wage labour into capital. Driven by competition and the tendency for the rate of profit to fall, every capitalist produces an ever-growing mass of commodities that must be sold and converted into money; only when this has been achieved can expansion (accumulation) take place. But capitalism's own relations of production limit the capacity of society to consume; the workers must by definition produce more than they can themselves consume, otherwise there would be no profit. Nor, if expansion is to take place, can the capitalists simply consume all the surplus value; the market, Marx argues, must therefore be continually extended. But this only leads to an expansion of production, recreating the same problem at a higher level; in this way the growth of productivity constantly threatens to outstrip the capacity of the available market.[4]

This fundamental contradiction of capitalism creates an inherent tendency towards overproduction. In theory of course, if capitalism had an infinite space to expand into, this would not be insurmountable. Unfortunately for capitalism however, the material conditions in which it arises include the fact that the Earth is round and not very large; while the first capitalist powers to arise could expand into the vast non-capitalist areas of the world, which provided an outlet for their ever-increasing supply of commodities, as well as vital sources of raw materials and labour, the resulting integration of these areas into capitalism, so that they ceased to absorb its surplus products and themselves became drawn into capitalist production, could only exacerbate the tendency within the system to overproduce.

So our main line of argument here is that the more that capitalism develops, the more it comes into conflict with the inherent limits on consumption due to its own social relations, which at a certain point become a definitive barrier to the further development of all the powers of production that have become available to humanity; the growing conflict between these now obsolete rela-

---

4   See Marx, *Capital* Volume 3, Chapter 15 (Penguin, 1981), pp.352-353

tions of production and the further development of humanity's productive powers expresses itself, in Marx's words, in 'bitter contradictions, crises, spasms' and 'The violent destruction of capital not by relations external to it, but rather as a condition of its self-preservation', which is 'the most striking form in which advice is given [capitalism] to be gone and to give room to a higher state of social production.'[5] The longer that capitalism is allowed to continue, the more violent these contradictions, crises and spasms must become, and the greater the scale of the destruction of capital – i.e. of the wealth accumulated by the labour of generations of workers and peasants. It is thus capitalism's dynamism that precipitates its descent and is therefore the starting point for understanding the nature and consequences of the phenomena of economic growth in capitalism's descending curve.

Lastly, there is another specificity of capitalism's development that for us underlines the validity and usefulness of Engels's description of the 'descending curve'. Unlike previous class societies, no new relations of production can develop within capitalist society; having created the material basis for production to potentially satisfy human needs, and brought into existence a class of associated, exploited labour, the revolutionary transformation of society is only possible through the violent overthrow of bourgeois class rule and the conscious eradication of capitalist relations of production: money, commodities, wage labour etc. In the absence of a successful proletarian revolution, the trajectory of capitalism's descending curve can only be towards barbarism.

Before we develop our main argument, we want to look at previous debates in the left communist movement, to test their approach to understanding the phenomena of growth in capitalism's descent.

1. Do world wars in capitalism's descent have an economic function?

Very briefly, since the 1970s, debates on the decadence of capitalism within the left communist movement have tended to polarise between supporters of the theories of Henryk Grossman and Paul Mattick on one side, and of Rosa Luxemburg's theory of capitalism's need for non-capitalist buyers on the other:

- for supporters of what we will call the Grossman-Mattick thesis, world wars in the period of capitalist decadence have the economic function of destroying capital to restore profitability;[6]

---

5   Marx, *Grundrisse*, 'The Section on Capital, Section Three' (Penguin, 1973), p.749

6   See for example the Communist Workers' Organisation, 'The economic role of war in capitalism's decadent phase' in *Revolutionary Perspectives* no. 37, 2005.

— for supporters of Luxemburg's theory of capitalist accumulation, world wars have the economic function of creating an outlet for capital in the absence of sufficient non-capitalist buyers.[7]

These theories were adopted and developed by surviving left fractions of the communist movement in the 1930s onwards as part of their attempt to understand the conditions of the new period of capitalism, which appeared to be dominated by a cycle of crisis-war-reconstruction, and focused on exactly which of the inherent contradictions of capital analysed by Marx best explains the economic roots of imperialism and the period precipitated by the First World War: either the tendency for the rate of profit to fall or capital's problem of realising surplus value, i.e. of finding markets.[8]

In Marx's analysis, of course, these explanations are not mutually exclusive, and the polarisation of debates has been at least partly due to the fact that those who emphasise capital's problem of realising surplus value tend to adhere to Rosa Luxemburg's theory of capitalist accumulation, which in this author's view is incorrect, encouraging those who emphasise the falling rate of profit to dismiss the whole problem of realisation as somehow 'outside' of capitalism, or even Marxism.[9]

Basing ourselves on Marx, we can agree that in capitalism's descent the destruction of capital in wars can play a role in restoring profitability – in specific conditions – and that wars certainly do provide outlets for capital; but based on a preliminary study of empirical evidence it seems to us that neither of these theories on its own is able to adequately explain the phenomena of economic growth in capitalist decadence:

1. In common with previous modes of production, capitalism's descending curve does not begin with a generalised economic crisis.

   The 'long depression' of 1873 to 1896 certainly signified a change in the nature of capital's economic crises, from its previous 10-year cycle of periodic crises to a more generalised crisis of overproduction, but

---

7   See for example the International Communist Current, 'The cycle of war-reconstruction' in *The Decadence of Capitalism*, second edition, 2006.

8   For Grossman, see *The Law of Accumulation and Breakdown of the Capitalist System* (1929); for Mattick, see in particular Chapter XIII in *Marx and Keynes: The Limits of the Mixed Economy* (1969); for Luxemburg, see *The Accumulation of Capital* (1913)

9   See for example the CWO, 'The Accumulation of Contradictions or the Economic Consequences of Rosa Luxemburg' in *Revolutionary Perspectives* no. 6, 1st Series, 1976. For a critique of Luxemburg's theory see Phillip Sutton, *A Critique of Luxemburg's Theory of Accumulation* (Amazon, 2020). See also M. Hayes, 'Debate on Luxemburg: "impossibility" of accumulation or overproduction?', <https://markhayes9.wixsite.com>

the decade leading up to World War I saw signs of a temporary economic recovery (Figure 5).

2. Despite the destruction of capital in World War I there was no renewal of economic growth.

World War I ended with the ruin and impoverishment of the European belligerent powers, victors and vanquished. Their industrial production fell by more than a third – a greater drop than in any economic crisis in the history of capitalism.[10] It has been estimated that the war destroyed over a third of the wealth of humanity.[11] But there was no concomitant renewal of economic growth.

The notable exception was the United States, which had suffered no physical destruction and few losses itself, and emerged from the war as the world's most powerful economy; the specific reasons for this, and the implications for subsequent phenomena of economic growth, will be explored in more depth below.

3. The destruction of capital in World War II does not appear in itself to be able to explain the ensuing economic boom.

Most western European economies returned to pre-war levels of production by 1952 but the destruction of capital alone does not appear to explain the fact that from 1950 capitalism was able to achieve growth rates unprecedented in its entire history while delivering real wage rises for two decades in line with productivity.

The above at the very least raises questions about the thesis that world wars in decadence have an economic function – either in destroying sufficient capital to restore profitability or by creating outlets in the absence of non-capitalist buyers – and the validity of the schema that phenomena of growth in this period can be described as part of a cycle of crisis-war-reconstruction.

If we look more closely at profitability, assuming the Grossman-Mattick thesis is correct we would expect to find supporting evidence for it in the trend since the late 19th century; that is, we would expect to see:

- a decline in profit rates leading up to World War I demonstrating that periodic crises and competition were no longer sufficient to avert the growing crisis of profitability;

- a recovery of profit rates after World War I as a result of the massive destruction of capital;

- a renewed drop in profit rates in the 1930s demanding an even greater destruction of capital;

---

10   Sternberg, *Capitalism and Socialism on Trial*, p.178.

11   W Woytinsky cited in Grossman, *The Law of Accumulation* (Pluto, 1992) p.15

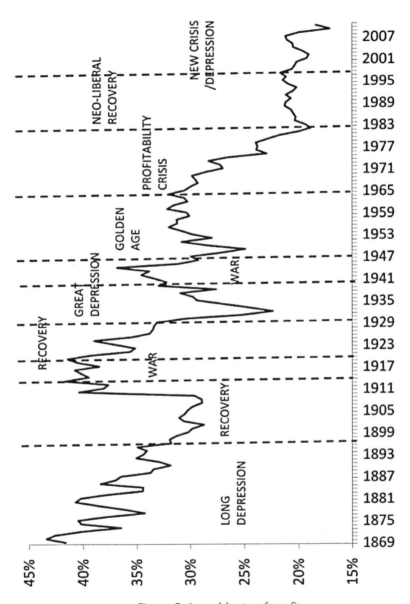

Figure 5: A world rate of profit

From 'A world rate of profit: a new approach', on M Roberts' blog,
<https://thenextrecession.wordpress.com>, July 2020

- a corresponding recovery of profit rates following the unprecedented destruction of World War II.

If we refer to the results of attempts to produce an overall Marxist view of the rate of profit's evolution, we must first of all note that over the long term the world rate of profit indeed shows a clear downward trend, just as Marx predicted (see Figure 5). But they also show:

- that profit rates in the core capitalist countries, which had declined steadily after the crisis of 1873, showed signs of stabilising in the years leading up to World War I;
- they fell sharply from the end of World War I, except for a spike in the mid-1920s, to a low point in the early 1930s;
- they then rose to a high point during World War II (although lower than in World War I), before falling again until around 1950, i.e. the start of the post-war economic boom.[12]

There is some supporting evidence here for the argument that profit rates stabilised or recovered in the run up to both world wars due to the build up of armaments production and a war economy, especially in the 1930s, which will be examined in more depth below. But there does not appear to be a strong correlation between the destruction of capital in the two world wars and a restoration of profitability in the ensuing post-war reconstruction, and from this brief examination we must conclude that we have not found strong evidence to support the thesis that wars have the economic function in decadent capitalism of destroying capital in order to restore profitability.

To repeat, this does not mean that the destruction of capital in wars does not play a role in restoring profitability in specific conditions, just as wars undoubtedly provide outlets for capital, but it does raise questions about the ability of the Grossman-Mattick thesis to explain phenomena of economic growth in capitalist decadence. At the very least we need to make a clear distinction between the physical destruction of capital due to the direct effects of war (bombing of railways, factories, infrastructure, etc), and the massive destruction or devaluation of constant capital as part of the build-up of a war economy, which certainly does play a role in stimulating economic activity and technological development, and accelerates the concentration and centralisation of capital. Wars in decadent capitalism can also have the effect of eliminating competitor nations or blocs, creating the possibility of expansion for the winners who can take over their markets.

---

12   See the chapter by E. Maito in G. Carchedi & M. Roberts, *World in Crisis: A Global Analysis of Marx's Law of Profitability* (Haymarket, 2008). The core capitalist countries are defined as Germany, the United States, the Netherlands, Japan, the United Kingdom, and Sweden.

We are led to conclude that wars in capitalism's descent are the product, not of an objective economic process, but of the aggravation of all of capitalism's antagonisms. Whereas wars in capitalism's ascending curve represented an indispensable means to strengthen and enlarge the system and thus ripen the conditions for its revolutionary overthrow, in its decadence wars are fundamentally an expression of its increasing destructiveness and a growing factor in the acceleration of its descent into barbarism.

This also leads us to be sceptical of monocausal explanations of the economic roots of capitalism's descent, and to avoid rigid schemas when trying to understand its phenomena of growth; the idea that the dynamic of the entire span of capitalism's descent could be defined as a cycle of crisis-war-reconstruction was a hypothetical model that appeared valid to revolutionaries in the conditions they confronted in the 1930s, but it was always subject to review and revision in the light of changed reality.

Our starting point then, within the general framework of capitalism's descending curve, is the need to analyse each phenomenon of growth as the product of a unique conjuncture of factors within the exacerbation of capitalism's contradictions. Above all, we need to examine the evolution of the class struggle and the balance of power between the classes, recognising that capitalism is ultimately a social relation between human beings, and that all of its objective economic laws must ultimately resolve themselves into the class struggle. This approach will be tested and developed in the following section.

2. World war, world revolution and economic crisis: the development of state capitalism and the war economy

If we base ourselves on the concept of the descending curve, then by definition this begins at capitalism's highest point. Certainly, the period between c1890 and 1914 – the so-called 'Belle Époque' or 'Gilded Age' – is one where the social formation as a whole appears at its most confident and optimistic, with continued geographical expansion and economic growth that created fertile conditions for scientific developments (e.g. Freud's theory of the unconscious, and quantum and relativity theories). But beneath this, we can see the aggravation of its contradictions that signalled the end of its ascent.

At the economic level, the 'long depression' of 1873-1896 heralded a change from capital's previous ten-year cycle of periodic crises to a more generalised crisis of overproduction, whose roots, as Engels identified, lay in the insufficiency of the world market to absorb the growth of the productive output of the major capitalist powers:

> ...if there are three countries (say England, America and Germany) competing on comparatively equal terms for the possession of the Weltmarkt, there is no chance but chronic overproduction, one of the three being capable of supplying the whole quantity required.[13]

At the level of imperialist conflicts, territorial disputes in Africa between Britain and France (Fashoda 1898), and Germany and France (Agadir 1911) showed the sharpening of imperialist tensions and the growing threat of war, while in the Far East the US conquest of the Philippines was significant as the moment when European imperialist expansion eastwards met US expansion to the west; arguably the first war of capital's descent was fought between Russia and Japan (1904-05) contending for control of Korea and access to Chinese markets, which in turn precipitated an intense arms race among the Great Powers.

At the level of the class struggle, from the turn of the 20th century we can see a conscious response by the working class to the changing conditions of the class struggle in capitalism, with an international wave of struggles from 1900 throughout Europe and America (the 'mass strike' described by Rosa Luxemburg[14]), reaching its high point in the 1905 revolutionary uprising in Russia with the emergence of the soviets or workers' councils as embryo organs of proletarian power, and continuing right up until the eve of the First World War.

In response, from the late 19th century we see a growing tendency of capitalism towards greater state control of society. The development of state capitalism and of a war economy are from the beginning a response by the capitalist class, not only to defend its interests against external threats from competitors but also to protect its domination as a ruling class against the threat of unrest and disintegration that inevitably grows with the prolongation of the obsolete relations of production.

---

13 Engels, Letter to Wischnewetzky, 3 February 1886, <https://www.marxists.org/archive/marx/works/1886/letters/86_02_03.htm>

14 R Luxemburg, 'The Mass Strike, the Political Party and the Trade Unions' (1906), in *Rosa Luxemburg Speaks* (Pathfinder, 1970), pp.153-218.

From 1914 to 1929:
war, revolution and crisis

We don't intend to try to deal with the events of this period in any detail here, they have been described and analysed many times before. Instead, we want to focus on the development of state capitalism and the war economy, as the main mechanisms adopted by capital for its survival, in order to understand growth in decadence, highlighting what seem to us to be key trends or developments. Just as imperialist war becomes the permanent way of life of decadent capitalism, so state capitalism is inseparable from the development of a permanent war economy. Above all, these developments can only be understood by relating them to the evolution of the class struggle and the balance of power between the classes in this period.

The significance of the First World War – which the most advanced elements of the revolutionary movement had expected for some time – was that it demonstrated:

- that, as Rosa Luxemburg observed, capitalism's contradictions had returned to the very centre of the system, bringing 'catastrophe as a mode of existence back from the periphery of capitalist development to its point of departure';[15]

- that by decimating the most experienced fractions of the world proletariat on the battlefields, capitalism was now destroying the most important productive force of all; the revolutionary class, ultimately threatening to destroy the material conditions for a transition to communism;

- that, far from being a unique event, a whole period of wars had opened up, the final result of which could only be either the victory of socialism or 'the triumph of imperialism and the collapse of all civilization as in ancient Rome, depopulation, desolation, degeneration – a great cemetery'.[16]

The war was the clear, practical proof that capitalism had begun its descent into barbarism, as the Third International declared in 1919:

> The contradictions of the capitalist world system, which lay concealed within its womb, broke out with colossal force in a gigantic explosion, in the great imperialist world war...[17]

---

15   *The Accumulation of Capital – An Anti-Critique* (Monthly Review Press, 1972), p147

16   'The Junius Pamphlet: The Crisis in the German Social Democracy' (1915), in *Rosa Luxemburg Speaks*, p.269.

As we know, the war provoked a revolutionary response from the working class, which, despite its political disorientation in 1914, had not suffered a decisive defeat. Although with hindsight we can see all too clearly its weaknesses and political failures, the revolutionary wave from 1917 to 1921 – whose high point was the seizure of political power by the soviets in Russia, and which forced the main belligerents to end the war to deal with the class struggle in the centres of the system – remains today the closest the proletariat has ever come to overthrowing capitalism.

The needs of the war effort clearly demanded an even greater role for the state and a planned war economy. To finance it, the belligerents were forced to resort to massive manipulation of the economy by floating loans and creating a mountain of debt, thus preserving the system and protecting it against the threat of revolution, but at the cost of undermining its foundations. But at the war's end, the immediate priority of the bourgeoisie was to quarantine the proletarian bastion in Russia and to crush the revolutionary attempts of the workers in central Europe; the sudden, explosive nature of both the war and its revolutionary ending meant that the implications of the change in period were not yet clearly understood by either the bourgeoisie or the proletariat, and many wartime measures were dismantled in a futile attempt to return to the pre-war status quo; a process that was even more rapid and thorough in the US where there had been far less development of a war economy.

Far from creating new opportunities for expansion, the war weakened the system at the global level, which was most apparent in its original centre in Europe, where it resulted in stagnation, depression and crisis among both victors and vanquished alike. The effect of the class struggle was to worsen the capitalist crisis and accelerate the decline of the European capitalist powers, with the loss of Russia as an important pre-war market and source of raw materials.

The notable exception of course was the United States, which had suffered no physical destruction and few losses itself, and had prospered by supplying the Allied powers. The US now experienced an economic boom that continued throughout the 1920s, due to the development of new consumer industries, the introduction of Fordist assembly-line techniques into production of cars and consumer durables etc, and an enormous expansion of credit.

An effect of the destruction of the war and the revolutionary wave of workers' struggles, within the context of the decline of the system as a whole, was

---

17   J Degras (ed.), *The Communist International 1919-1943: Documents* (Frank Cass, 1971), pp17-19

thus to facilitate a shift in global capitalism and the emergence of the US as the world's leading industrial and imperialist power; a factor that is vital to an understanding of subsequent economic growth in capitalism's descent.

From 1929 to World War II:
crisis, counter-revolution and war

While the causes of the First World War were firmly rooted at the economic level in the looming crisis of overproduction – the insufficiency of the world market to absorb the growth of the productive output of the existing capitalist powers, and the sharpening of imperialist rivalries that this provoked – it was only in 1929 that this crisis was openly expressed at the global level of the system. The unprecedented worldwide depression that followed was the first generalised economic crisis of the system and a further qualitative step in its descent into barbarism.

Significantly the United States, as the world's leading economic power, was this time at the centre of the storm; essentially, America's exceptional growth after World War I came up against the limits of the available market, resulting in a situation of chronic overproduction, in which the foundations of the system were already undermined by the effects of war and militarism, debt and fictitious capital, exacerbated by protectionism. In short, as we know, the effects were truly catastrophic: world production (excluding the USSR) fell by a third, but in the US and Germany it fell by half; world trade, which before World War I had consistently increased, dropped further and more rapidly than in any previous economic crisis since the 1840s (see Figure 6).[18]

The crisis finally forced the bourgeoisie to realise that, unlike the periodic crises of the 19th century, the 'hidden hand' of the market was now no longer sufficient to restart production; in the absence of sufficient new external markets, strong state intervention in the economy was essential, both to regulate production and consumption and to control foreign trade and labour markets, so that from the early 1930s we see a qualitative change in the role of the state, taking different forms in each national capital: the New Deal in Roosevelt's USA, the Popular Front in France, fascism in Germany and Italy, and of course Stalinism in Russia.

Integral to this development of state capitalism is the build-up of a planned war economy; confronted by the aggravation of capitalism's contradictions, each national state is forced to defend its strategic and economic interests against its imperialist rivals, not only through protectionist measures but above

---

18   Sternberg, *Capitalism and Socialism on Trial*, p.277.

113

Figure 6: World trade 1827-2014

E Ortiz-Ospina et al (2018) - 'Trade and Globalization' in *Our World in Data*, <https://ourworldindata.org/trade-and-globalization>

all militarily. From a purely economic point of view, the war economy creates an outlet for capital, in which the state plays a direct role in organising the demand for armaments and other high technology goods, which also stimulates wider economic activity and technological development, and accelerates the centralisation and concentration of capital. Significantly, in the period from 1929 to World War II, it is only Germany, Japan and the USSR that were able to demonstrate any economic growth; all are prime examples of a war economy, with centralised state planning and enormously increased armaments production, and, especially in the case of Germany and Japan, imperialist expansion.

The 1929 crisis was also a final turning point for the development of state capitalism in the USA, but there was as yet no significant development of a war economy or a drive to increase exports, with production primarily still for the vast home market; military spending increased from the start of World War II but was still very low compared to other major powers up until Pearl Harbor.

If imperialist war is inherent in capitalism in its phase of decline, and the development of state capitalism and a war economy are firmly rooted in the capitalist crisis of overproduction, the growth of state control and a planned war economy in the 1930s can only be fully understood in the context of the physical defeat of the working class. It was this defeat – crowned by the victory of Hitler in Germany and the triumph of the Stalinist regime in the USSR – which opened the road to a new world war as a 'solution' to capitalism's crisis.

Even more than the last, the Second World War would be a total war for domination of the world market and the elimination of competitors, and this demanded not only centralised planning and greatly increased armaments production, but also the full mobilisation of all the economic, political and social resources of the national capital; above all of the proletariat, to fight on the battlefields and maintain the necessary level of production.

It is the defeat of the working class that is therefore the vital factor that enabled the capitalist class to complete the necessary development of state capitalism and a planned war economy in order to launch World War II.

3. The post-war boom

World War II reflected the growth of capitalism in its descending curve and its domination of the planet: this was the first truly global war, fought for domination of the world's resources and access to markets, and a total war waged by the major industrial and imperialist powers, who mobilised all of their military, economic and political resources. The war permanently transformed capitalism, increasing its destructive power and deepening and accelerating its descent into barbarism.

It is in this context that we need to understand the phenomenon of the post-war economic boom; let us just briefly remind ourselves that between 1950 and 1970 world capitalism achieved higher growth rates than at any other time in its history; the rate of profit rose to its highest point since World War II, and real wages rose in line with the increase in labour productivity. This was the 'long boom' or 'Golden Age of Capitalism'; in French the *Trente Glorieuses* or 'Thirty Glorious Years' (although it was more like twenty), and at the time it contradicted the expectation of some surviving revolutionaries that the only possible outcomes of the capitalist crisis were either world war or world revolution.

The conditions for the post-war boom

As we have already argued, this phenomenon cannot simply be explained as the result of the scale of destruction in World War II and the consequent need for reconstruction. Nor can it be understood in purely economic terms.

We can identify three main factors that explain why capitalism could give the appearance of overcoming its contradictions in the post-war period:

1. The division of the world into two military blocs

From 1945 we see an unprecedented phenomenon in the history of capitalism: the division of the world into two military blocs, with very few trading relationships between them.

Due to its economic weakness, and the specific conditions of the defeat of the Russian revolution, the Stalinist regime in the USSR could only survive by partially cutting itself off from the rest of the world market and imposing this autarkic economic policy on its eastern European satellites. China from 1949 under the Maoist bourgeoisie was also a relatively weak, militarised economy, which could to some extent be considered as being part of the USSR's trading bloc, while India, economically backward due to the effects of colonialism, militarism and wars, also pursued a semi-autarkic economic policy, while maintaining close military and economic links with the USSR. This was a complete reversal of the tendency in ascendant capitalism for trade barriers to be destroyed as the cheap products of the industrialised European powers battered down the 'Chinese walls' of undeveloped nations.

2. The emergence of the US as the world's most powerful capitalist economy

In a further demonstration of the economic irrationality of wars in capitalist decadence, the Second World War, like the First but with an even greater scale of destruction, resulted in the ruin and exhaustion of both victors and vanquished – with the highly significant exception of the USA, the only belligerent power to avoid destruction on its own territory.

Between 1939 and 1945, the US economy doubled in size. Mass production techniques were applied to existing industries like shipbuilding and to whole new industries: aircraft, electronics and computing, pharmaceuticals, plastics, etc, which involved a massive destruction and devaluation of constant capital:

> The result of all this was a phenomenon for which there is no parallel in world history – namely that **at the end of the Second World War, which brought unexampled destruction to many countries, the world as a whole produced more than it did before that war.**[19]

Not only that, but the US was able to use its involvement in the war to eliminate its main competitors; either through direct military victory, in the case

---

19   Sternberg, *Capitalism and Socialism on Trial*, p.465, emphasis in the text.

of Germany and Japan, or by bankrupting them through arms orders and stealing their markets, in the case of the British and French empires.

3. The defeat of the working class

The working class entered the Second World War having already suffered the physical defeat of its revolutionary wave of struggles, which had opened the road to war. Despite the fact that workers' struggles continued during World War II, the bourgeoisie had learned the lessons of the revolutionary wave of 1917-21 and ruthlessly crushed the few major uprisings, like that in Italy in 1943. This meant that, once the eventual defeat of the Axis powers became clear, the US and its democratic allies were able to begin consciously planning for the post-war reorganisation of capitalist society, to ensure social peace.

Table 1: Global GNP per capita annual growth rates	
1800-30	0.1
1830-70	0.4
1870-80	0.5
1880-90	0.8
1890-1900	1.2
1900-13	1.5
1913-20	-0.8
1920-29	2.4
1929-39	0.8
1939-50	0.8
1950-60	2.5
1960-70	3.5
1970-80	2.0
1980-90	0.9

P Bairoch, *Economics and World History: Myths and Paradoxes*, University of Chicago, 1993, p.7

Despite its overwhelming superiority – in fact because of it – US capitalism faced several key related problems:

- where to find outlets for its greatly expanded industrial output, which now accounted for half of the world's production,
- how to defend its national interests – for the first time truly global – against the threat of Soviet expansionism, and
- how to avoid social instability that could be exploited by the rival bloc, especially any threat from the working class.

Understanding how it set about attempting to resolve these problems is the key to understanding the post-war boom – and its limits.

The strategy adopted by the US bourgeoisie was to use its overwhelming military and economic power to tear down tariff walls that had constrained its economic growth before the war and in effect create a unified single market at the level of its imperialist bloc. This was backed by an international finance system whose rules could be imposed by US-controlled institutions, and by replacement of the gold standard with recognition of the dollar as the globally accepted currency (the 'Bretton Woods system', see also below).

These unprecedented state capitalist measures, based on the lessons learned by the most intelligent factions of the bourgeoisie from the generalised economic crisis of the 1930s, served to consolidate the US's position as the world's most powerful capitalist state and enabled it to 'kick-start' the post-war economy, by expanding credit to create demand and serving as a 'market of last resort' for its European and Asian allies, financed by gold reserves acquired during World War II and the dominance of the dollar backed by US military superiority.

All this meant that when post-war reconstruction was threatened by the inability of the devastated European economies to continue paying for American imports, the US was able to pump in massive amounts of capital. But even more importantly, the US was able to use the Marshall Plan, and its equivalent in Asia, to exert pressure on its allies to adopt American production methods to increase productivity; in other words, the US bourgeoisie deliberately strengthened its own competitors, with the closely linked aims of:

- ensuring a solvent market for advanced US machinery and manufactured goods,
- enabling the economies of its allies to export competitively to the rest of the bloc,
- facilitating the rearmament of the bloc against the Soviet threat,
- enabling wage rises and lowering prices to boost the consumption of the working class, strengthening the social stability of the bloc.

Total military expenditure divided by GDP. Figures correspond to current-prices estimates combining data from several sources.

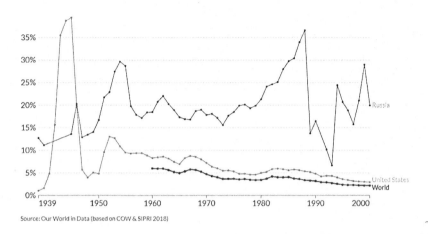

Source: Our World In Data (based on COW & SIPRI 2018)

Figure 7: Military expenditure, 1939-2000

M Roser et al, 'Military Spending (2013), *Our World In Data*, <https://ourworldindata.org/military-spending>

As a result of all these measures, between 1950 and 1970 capitalism was able to achieve higher growth rates than at any other time in its history (Table 1). For two decades, real wages rose in line with the increase in labour productivity and profit rates rose (although they did not regain the levels achieved during the two world wars – see Figure 8).

This entire period of economic growth is also characterised by the proliferation of imperialist conflicts and proxy wars between the blocs (Korea, Vietnam, Middle East, Africa, etc), and an extremely high level of military spending. Before World War I, Germany – considered the epitome of a militaristic nation – spent 4 percent of its GDP on its military budget; after World War II the USA's military spending dipped briefly to 4 percent before rising to about 14 percent during the Korean War and remained above 7 percent until 1970. In the same period the USSR's military spending was twice as high (see Figure 7).

This extremely high level of military spending indicates the consolidation of a permanent war economy. The extent to which this was able to create an outlet for US capital can be judged by the fact that, at its peak in 1968, the Pentagon controlled the production of $44 billion of goods and services, exceeding the combined net sales of General Motors, General Electric, US Steel, and DuPont.[20] Throughout the post-war period the US military also employed between 2-4 million troops and civilian personnel, all of whom had to be fed, clothed, housed, transported, their children educated, etc. Moreover, official figures for military spending do not include advanced research projects, foreign arms sales and military 'aid'.

Table 2 US debt as a percentage of GNP, 1946-74

	Public debt as % of GNP	Private indebtedness as % of GNP
1946	129.4	73.6
1950	84.0	97.2
1955	67.8	98.5
1960	59.7	112.4
1965	53.7	127.1
1969	40.8	133.8
1973	46.3	131.2
1974	50.0	140.0

E Mandel, *Late Capitalism* (NLB, 1975), p.418

The post-war boom contradicted the expectation of some revolutionaries at the time, like the Gauche Communiste de France, that the growth of a war economy inevitably meant the pauperisation of the working class. In fact, the specific conjunction of factors following World War II meant that the improvement of working class living standards was an integral part of its development.

---

20 S Milman, 'Ten propositions on the war economy', *American Economic Review* vol. 62, no. 1/2, 1972.

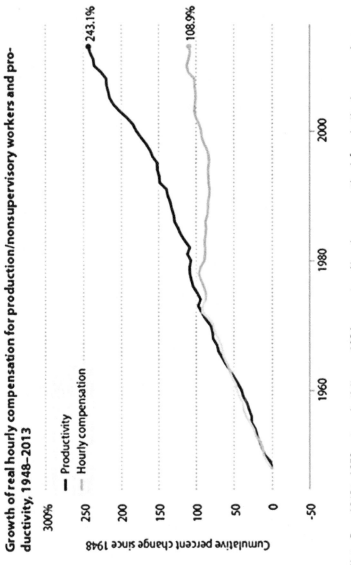

Figure 8: Growth of US real wages and productivity

L Mishel, 'The wedges between productivity and median compensation growth',
Economic Policy Institute Issue Brief no.330, 26 April 2012,
<https://files.epi.org/2012/ib330-productivity-vs-compensation.2012-04-26-
16:45:37.pdf>

Boosting the consumption of the working class was not only intended by the US to create an outlet for its production but also to strengthen the cohesion of the bloc against its rival; offering real wage rises and a social wage allocation enabled the bourgeoisie to offer the promise – at least for workers in the most advanced economies – of full employment and rising prosperity, which served as an important ideological weapon in the Cold War against the Soviet Union. This was only achieved by expanding consumer credit and increasing the rate of exploitation of the working class to ferocious levels. As a result, while US state debt fell between 1946 and 1969, private indebtedness rose from 73.6 percent of annual GNP to 140.0 percent (see Table 2).

The expansion of capital- and labour-intensive industries and the application of Fordist assembly line techniques to consumer goods, cars, etc, provided the basis for a rise in labour productivity and real wages, which kept pace from the end of World War II until the end of the 1970s (see Figure 8). This parallel development of productivity and wages is an exception in the history of capitalism.

The limits of the post-war boom

This unique and unrepeatable conjunction of factors, which made it possible, by a combination of state capitalist measures and an increase in exploitation, to raise wages and lower prices, despite the increased burden of military spending and armaments production, also defined the limits of the post-war boom:

1 The strategy adopted by the US bourgeoisie to deliberately strengthen its own competitors was dependent upon the US exporting more than it imported from Europe and Japan. When at the end of the 1960s for the first time the percentage of imports to the US exceeded its exports to Europe and Japan, this signalled the end of the post-war boom (see Figure 9).

Similarly, the post-war international finance system imposed by the USA, based on fixing currencies to the dollar which remained convertible into gold at a fixed price, only worked as long as the US had a trade surplus so that it could maintain its gold reserves. With the relative weakening of the US economy, worsened by the effects of the Vietnam war, this system was no longer viable and became a source of growing instability. Facing a looming gold run, rising inflation, slowing growth and unemployment, in 1971 the US bourgeoisie took the step of ending dollar convertibility ('The Nixon shock'), in effect scrapping the whole post-war 'Bretton Woods system'. In its place, the US bourgeoisie increasingly relied on its position as the world's largest economy to export the effects of the growing crisis onto its allies and attract finance capital to underwrite its growing deficits.

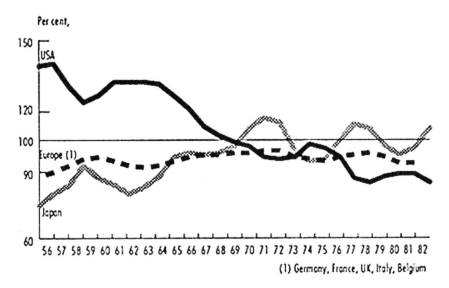

Fig 9: USA, Europe and Japan: exports as a percentage of imports, 1956-82

ICC, *The Decadence of Capitalism*, 2nd ed., 2006, p.iv

2 The high level of military spending that provided a temporary outlet for US industrial production in the longer term constituted an enormous burden of unproductive expenditure that weakened the competitiveness of the US economy. It is no accident that in the post-war boom Japan and West Germany, both unencumbered by high levels of military spending, achieved higher annual growth rates than the US (10 and 6.2 respectively, compared to 4 percent for the US).[21]

The permanent war economy (Eisenhower's 'military-industrial complex') not only grew to enormous proportions, but increasingly took on a life of its own, modifying the structure of the capitalist economy as a whole, its functioning in some respects running counter to the 'normal' functioning of capital described by Marx. Rather than the need to make a profit, many capitalist enterprises (including some of the largest) become dependent on winning and maintaining government contracts, resulting in costs that would lead to bankruptcy in any normal enterprise together with enormous amounts of waste and corruption, while the costs of wars themselves became ruinous, further weakening economic competitivity since they were paid for either by very high levels of

---

21   <https://www.statista.com/statistics/1234645/gdp-growth-us-japan-europe-1950-1987/>

taxation or by increased debt. The cost of the Vietnam War for the United States was a major contributory factor in the worsening of the economic crisis in the early 1970s.

3 The post-war boom was dependent on a defeated working class, exhausted by war and hunger, accepting increased exploitation in return for rising real wages and a social wage allocation.

But the very forms imposed by the bourgeoisie to manage the class struggle provoked potentially dangerous forms of resistance:

- the growth of capital- and labour-intensive industries based on mass production and assembly-line techniques created strong concentrations of working class militancy (Detroit, Renault-Billancourt, Fiat Turin, the Ruhr, etc), where workers could exercise a degree of control over the production process, encouraging strikes and stoppages in support of wage demands;

- the incorporation of the social-democratic parties and trade unions into the state apparatus to ensure social stability and the cohesion of the bloc, with the role of negotiating and distributing the products of the increase in exploitation, threatened to undermine their ability to control the working class.

The mid-1960s saw a revival of the class struggle, with an international wave of social unrest, political protests and workers' strikes, reaching a high point with the May '68 movement in France (10 million workers on strike). This was partly driven by the first effects of the economic crisis, with a fall in production and the rise of unemployment and inflation, but a key factor was a new generation of proletarians who had not directly experienced either the counter-revolution that followed the defeat of the 1917-21 revolutionary wave or the war itself, and who were prepared to challenge, not only the exploitation and the alienation of production line work but also the stultifying and repressive values of bourgeois society. Faced with this wave, the ruling class – not only in the Stalinist eastern bloc but also the 'democratic' West – did not hesitate to use state repression, but clearly this was not a long-term solution, while the continued ceding of wage rises above the growth of productivity and increased social spending in the major economies of the US bloc only encouraged more struggles – further reducing profits, increasing debt and deepening the crisis.

4. Understanding Globalisation

The convergence of the deepening of capitalism's crisis at the economic level with the resurgence of class struggle signified not only the end of the post-war boom but also a significant change in the balance of power between the classes since World War II: the continued resistance of the working class to the effects of the crisis and the attacks necessary to ensure continued accumulation meant that, unlike in the 1930s, the road towards a new world war as a 'solution' to the crisis was effectively blocked, while the conditions for the development of the proletariat's struggles into a political offensive against capitalism were more favourable than at any time since the 1917-21 revolutionary wave.

But, without analysing the development of this post-'68 wave of struggles or its strengths and weaknesses, we must note that despite continued struggles throughout the 1970s – including important struggles in the US, Britain, Poland and France, and the extension of the wave to include major struggles by Iranian oil workers (1978) and Brazilian steelworkers (1979) – the working class was unable to develop these struggles at the political level to give them an explicitly anti-capitalist perspective.

The late 1970s turned out to be a critical turning point, not only in the evolution of the crisis and the class struggle, but also in terms of the bourgeoisie's response:

1 **At the level of imperialist antagonisms**, there was a real escalation of tensions between the blocs, with the USSR's 1979 invasion of Afghanistan – which in hindsight we can see as a last desperate throw by the Stalinist regime to strengthen its position in a strategically vital region – provoking a warlike ideological campaign by the US bloc as part of a new aggressive strategy, which was essentially intended to escalate the arms race in order to bankrupt its weaker rival and to 'win' the Cold War, achieving US global hegemony.

2 **At the economic level,** in 1978 the failure of the US 'locomotive' to stimulate growth, which led to a crisis of confidence in the dollar, convinced the US bourgeoisie that the structures and policies of the post-war Keynesian order were now only making the crisis worse. In the name of a 'war against inflation' it acted to restrict the money supply to banks, in effect turning off the supply of credit that had financed the post-war boom, and launched a new aggressive strategy to restore profitability and ensure continued accumulation.

3 **At the level of the class struggle**, the 1980 mass strike in Poland marked a watershed in the post-'68 wave; only with the assistance of the western bloc was the Stalinist bourgeoisie able to isolate the Polish workers' struggles and prevent them spreading to the rest of the bloc – and even more dangerously to the west. Once order was restored, with the vital help of western banks, governments and unions, the way was clear for massive attacks on the working class in the west, using the threat of unemployment to reassert the power of capital and reinforce bourgeois domination.

The response of the US-led bourgeoisie to both the crisis and the class struggle resulted in a decisive defeat for the working class and a limited recovery of profit rates. It also accelerated the collapse of the Stalinist regimes and the breakdown of attempts at national autarky, thus creating the conditions for the phenomenon of 'globalisation' and the rapid economic growth of China, India and the Southeast Asian economies. At the same time it led to the collapse of the two-bloc system of the Cold War and the proliferation of regional wars (the two Gulf Wars, ethnic and nationalist conflicts in the ex-USSR and Yugoslavia, Afghanistan); clearly, we need to be able to offer a coherent explanation for these highly contradictory developments in capital's descent.

The bourgeois counter-offensive against the working class

From the beginning of the 1980s, the bourgeoisie of the western bloc, led by the US and its close British ally, launched a massive frontal attack on the working class to force down real wages, cut social spending and increase the rate of exploitation. The immediate effect was to raise interest rates to a record high, leading to the deepest recession since the 1930s, forcing bloc members to launch similar attacks, which resulted in a wave of factory closures and job losses spreading from the US to Europe and Japan; unemployment in the US rose to the highest level since the Great Depression. This was a deliberate 'shock and awe' tactic intended not only as a brutal reassertion of the power of the US over its own bloc but also of the power of capital over a working class that continued to resist the attacks necessary to ensure accumulation and restore profitability.

This period saw major workers' struggles in the US and western Europe; many, like the UK miners' strike (1984-5), showed enormous combativity, and some, like the strikes in Italy (1987), displayed a real capacity for self-organisation. But all these struggles took place in the context of a conscious and co-ordinated capitalist strategy at the level of the US bloc, not only to close factories and cut jobs to reduce productive capacity but above all to reinforce the domination of capital and achieve a decisive shift in the balance of class forces. After a final surge of workers' struggles at the beginning of the 1990s, it was clear that the bourgeoisie had been successful in consolidating the defeats experienced by key sectors of workers; the level of workers' demonstrations and strikes globally fell to the lowest since the Second World War, effectively marking the end of the wave of workers' struggles that had erupted in the 1960s to threaten bourgeois class rule (see Figure 10).

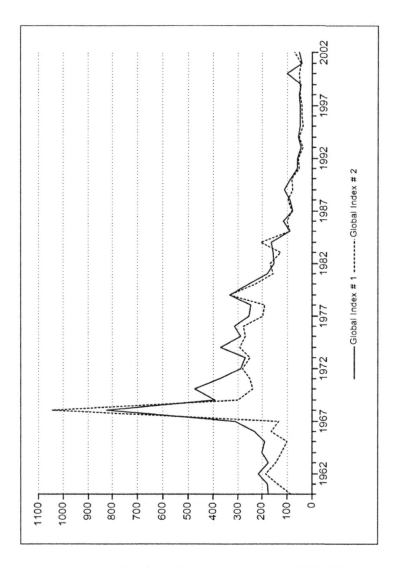

Figure 10: Global trends in work stoppages, 1960-2002

L Perry & P Wilson, *Trends in Work Stoppages: A Global Perspective* (ILO, 2004).
Number of days not worked due to work stoppages per thousand members of the
labour force. Global index # 1 = data for a collection of 38 countries; Global index #
2 = excluding May-June '68 France. Due to lack of data, China, the Russian
Federation, Brazil, Mexico and Indonesia are excluded.

The global restructuring of capitalist production

Under the political banner of 'Reaganism', 'Thatcherism' or 'neoliberalism', the massive frontal attacks on the working class formed part of a longer-term capitalist strategy to restructure capitalist production, whose main features were:

- the breaking up of traditional centres of working class militancy in the capitalist heartlands, accompanied by a management offensive against militant workers and the introduction of short-term contracts, temporary and part-time working, etc;

- a huge development of computing and communications technology driven by the development of the microprocessor, which enabled the reorganisation and automation of existing work processes;

- the shift of production to parts of the world with low labour costs, accelerating the flow of capital from unprofitable industries in the traditional capitalist heartlands.

At the economic level, by drastically cutting productive capacity, reducing the workforce and increasing the rate of exploitation this strategy enabled a limited recovery of profit rates – although not to the level achieved in the postwar boom (see Figure 11).

Restructuring also involved the massive destruction and devaluation of constant capital (through the privatisation of state assets, consolidation of existing capital through mergers, writing off capital, etc); first in the traditional capitalist heartlands, especially the USA and Britain, and later, after the collapse of the Stalinist regimes, in eastern Europe and the ex-USSR. This had a similar effect to the two world wars, stimulating technological development and wider changes in production, and accelerating the concentration and centralisation of capital.

Arguably, the destruction involved was not sufficient given the depth of the capitalist crisis: as the scale of accumulation grows, and the rate of profit continues to fall, so the amount of capital to be destroyed must grow if profitability is to be restored. But we cannot understand the global restructuring of capitalist production in the 1980s and '90s purely in economic terms; despite the depth of the crisis, the bourgeoisie was able to provide the system with a temporary breathing space and reinforce its class domination. resort to the unrestrained growth of debt.

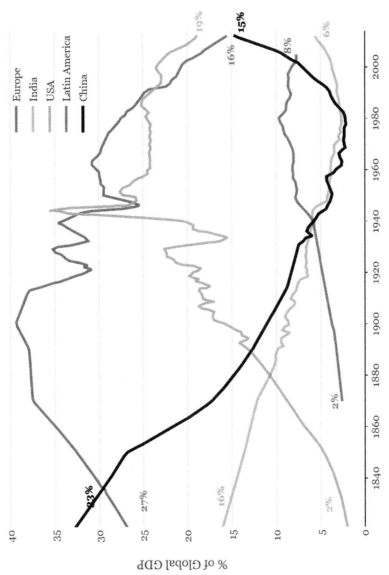

Figure 11: percentage of global GDP, 1820-2020

Data Source: A Maddison, *Contours of the World Economy I-2030 AD* (Oxford University Press, 2007)

At the same time, the depth of the capitalist crisis forced the bourgeoisie to resort to the unrestrained growth of debt. The importance of finance capital generally had been growing since the 1950s, but the turning point was the end of dollar convertibility in 1971, which opened an era in which money was allowed to circulate without any equivalent in gold or silver. When the US bourgeoisie turned off the state supply of credit at the start of the '80s, it opened the floodgates to private capital in order to finance its own growing state debt. As the world's largest economy, the US stood to gain most from this 'liberalisation' of global financial markets, using the dominance of the dollar to suck in vast amounts of foreign capital, while forcing its weaker allies to follow suit to try to stay competitive. Financial capital, highly mobile and freed from state control, became vital to the process of 'globalisation' and the restructuring of capitalist production, by facilitating the growth of trade, investing in new regions with low wage costs and in the new technologies central to restructuring (microprocessors, etc) – but at the price of increasing the instability of the system and further undermining its foundations.

In the absence of sufficient outlets for profitable investment in production, and in a desperate search for new sources of short-term profit, capital increasingly flowed into the financial sector, leading to a huge growth of 'fictitious capital' (i.e. investment and speculation in stocks and bonds, derivatives, etc, which had no material basis in commodities or production). Increasingly, debt was repaid by taking out more debt, and the huge growth of speculation became the only means to finance economic 'recovery'. The USA, which since 1914 had been the world's main creditor, in 1985 became its largest debtor. There was also rapid growth of personal indebtedness as households were offered ever cheaper debt in order to maintain demand, generating unsustainable levels of consumer debt and a growing series of enormous speculative bubbles, which eventually burst in 2007 – the most severe crisis of capitalism since 1929.

Far from representing the withdrawal of states from the economy as neoliberal ideology claimed, in reality, as the 2007 crisis showed, the role of the state became vital in bailing out financial institutions to prevent a collapse of the global financial system, with the American state acting as the lender of last resort.

The collapse of the Stalinist regimes

The collapse of the Stalinist regimes in the USSR and eastern Europe between 1989 and 1991 was fundamentally a product of the aggravation of capital's contradictions at all levels, and the effects of the prolongation of capitalism's crisis onto weaker national capitals, but it was shaped and accelerated by:

- the resurgence of the class struggle and the difficulties of the Stalinist regimes in managing the threat from the working class without undermining their own economic and political foundations;
- the new aggressive strategy adopted by the US bourgeoisie from the beginning of the 1980s, which set itself the explicit goal of winning the Cold War by destroying the threat from its imperialist rival, and
- the political and economic offensive against the working class in the west.

The deepening of the capitalist crisis faced the Stalinist regimes with a growing dilemma: either to increase their borrowing and dependence on western creditors; or retreat further into autarky and introduce even greater austerity that risked provoking an even greater and more dangerous reaction from the working class and exacerbating the political crisis of the regimes.

The rise in interest rates at the start of the 1980s and the ensuing global recession precipitated a debt crisis that left the eastern bloc economies tottering

Table 3: The growing debt burden of the eastern bloc ($ billions)

	1985	1986	1987	1988	1989	2000
Bulgaria	1.6	3.6	5.1	6.1	8.0	9.8
Czechoslovakia	3.6	4.3	5.1	5.6	5.7	6.3
Hungary	11.5	14.7	18.1	18.2	19.4	20.3
Poland	28.2	31.9	35.8	34.1	37.5	41.8
Romania	6.5	6.3	5.1	2.0	-1.3	1.3
USSR	15.8	16.6	25.1	27.7	39.3	43.4
Total	67.3	77.5	94.3	93.8	108.9	122.9

OECD data, in A Fabry, 'End of the liberal dream: Hungary since 1989', *International Socialism* no. 124, 2009

on the brink of bankruptcy; first Poland, then Romania, Hungary and East Germany (and Yugoslavia) had to be bailed out by western banks and governments. Their debt burden grew steadily during the decade (Table 3).

With this came pressure for political and economic 'reform' from the western bourgeoisie, whose strategy, in effect, was to use loans and financial support to 'batter down all Chinese walls' (*Communist Manifesto*) that prevented the free movement of western capital and commodities, tearing open the economies of the weaker bloc to provide access to new, previously unavailable markets, sources of raw materials and cheap labour.

This was complemented by the US bourgeoisie's new aggressive strategy towards its imperialist rival. From 1981 there was a dramatic increase in US military spending, funded by a growth of debt, and a heavy investment in high-tech weapons that the USSR could not possibly hope to match, including the announcement of the 'Star Wars' programme in 1983, which was not so much a proposed space-based missile defence system (its feasibility was questionable) as a clear statement of intent to escalate the nuclear arms race until it bankrupted its rival.

The Stalinist bourgeoisie in the USSR was confronted with a similar dilemma to its eastern European satellites: retreat into autarky, boost military spending and risk an explosion of class struggle, or give up the arms race, carry out fundamental political and economic reforms to attract western investment and integrate itself fully into the world market. But opening up to the west threatened not only the loss of the USSR's status as a world power together with its eastern European empire, but also the dismantling of the USSR itself, along with the power and privileges of its ruling class. The 'reformist' policy pursued by the Gorbachev faction from 1985 was deliberately intended to avoid this outcome, but the depth of the economic crisis in the USSR and the decomposition of the regime made it inevitable.

The collapse of Stalinism typically resulted in the coming to power of new democratic regimes – often factions of the existing Stalinist ruling class enthusiastically supported by the 'democratic opposition' – who, in return for western bailouts, played on workers' illusions in western democracy and trade unionism to implement the same kind of attacks on the working class as their western counterparts. But due to the bankruptcy of the eastern bloc economies the necessary 'liberal shock therapy' was even more sudden and devastating; in the former eastern European satellites 'market reforms' typically led to a sharp drop in production and a rapid rise of unemployment, with a major decline in living standards and wages and a rise in poverty and inequalities, while in the ex-USSR industrial production fell by half and inflation rose above 200 percent; average life expectancy, especially for working-age men, dropped to 'Third

World' levels. In some parts of the former Stalinist empire workers also found themselves mobilised to fight in bloody ethnic and nationalist wars backed by the imperialist powers.

The collapse of the Stalinist regimes was the most significant event in capitalism's descent since the Second World War: never had an entire imperialist bloc collapsed outside of revolution or war. But this was only the most dramatic manifestation of a wider phenomenon in this phase of capitalism's descent: the breakdown of attempts at national autarky.

Globalisation and the growth of China and India

The same conjunction of factors that precipitated the collapse of the Stalinist regimes also created the conditions for the phenomenon of 'globalisation' and the rapid economic growth of China, India and the Southeast Asian economies: from 1980 to 2005 India's GDP grew by a factor of 4 and China's increased ten-fold, compared to 2.5 globally.[22]

Both China and India of course were large and enormously wealthy precapitalist economies until the 19th century, between them accounting for something like 50 percent of the world's wealth (see Figure 11). Their story in the ascending curve of capital's development is one of unavailing resistance to the ruthless campaign of the major capitalist powers, led by Britain, to open up their pre-capitalist economies as outlets for capitalist production, and gain access to their raw materials and supplies of labour power, in a violent process vividly described by Rosa Luxemburg in her *Accumulation of Capital*. The aim and effect of this was to destroy the basis for the emergence of any indigenous capitalist development, apparently dooming them to underdevelopment in the phase of capital's descent, in which the emergence of new industrial powers became more difficult, due to the carving up of the world market between the existing major imperialist world powers in conditions of chronic overproduction.

Both countries entered the post-World War II period economically backward, because of the effects of colonialism, militarism and wars, and to different degrees cut off from the world market due to the political priorities of their ruling factions.

In the case of China we can identify three key developments that facilitated its economic growth from the 1980s onwards:

---

22   CMcL, 'The sources, contradictions and limitations of the growth in eastern Asia', *International Review* no. 133, 2008

1. In order to strengthen its own imperialist position against the USSR from the end of the 1960s the USA pursued a policy of rapprochement with China, which entered into an uneasy alliance with the stronger bloc in pursuit of its own military and economic interests, while avoiding absorption by it.

2. Following Mao Zedong's death in 1976 the faction around Deng Xiaoping was able to begin a process of 'liberalisation' to open up the Chinese economy to the world market, which proceeded in three main waves from the late 1970s to the early 1990s. As a result, foreign investment in China grew steadily from the start of the 1980s and more rapidly from the early 1990s.

3. By moving towards the US bloc and beginning to open up to the world market, Chinese capitalism was therefore already well placed to benefit from the new economic and political strategy of the US-led bourgeoisie, which was dependent on the shift of capital and jobs to parts of the world with low labour costs.

By comparison, India's move towards the US bloc was more gradual; despite limited steps towards 'liberalisation' it continued to have a close military and economic relationship with the USSR bloc right up until the latter's collapse. This precipitated a debt crisis which was ruthlessly exploited by the US bourgeoisie to force the Indian economy to open up, with World Bank and IMF support made conditional on the dismantling of all autarkic barriers. Foreign investment rose from 1991 and economic growth accelerated in the 2000s.

Both China and India possessed vast reserves of cheap rural labour, which enabled the bourgeoisie to keep wages at near subsistence levels while imposing very high rates of exploitation.

In summary, the aggravation of capitalism's contradictions undermined the attempts of weaker capitals to cut themselves off from the rest of the world market; the effects of this, and the conscious and coordinated response of the US-led bourgeoisie to both the economic crisis and the class struggle, created a conjunction in capitalism's descent that facilitated the growth of China and India. Despite this belated development, however – which has only been possible due to the shift of certain kinds of production from the US and western Europe – neither economy has been able to regain its previous importance in terms of share of global wealth (Figure 11).

A temporary reprieve for a system in its decline

In this section we set out to offer a coherent explanation for the most significant developments in capitalism's descent from the 1970s. We have explored the connections between these developments and attempted to show that there is a direct link between the economic and political offensive of the US-led bourgeoisie from the start of the 1980s and the breakdown of attempts at national autarky, which not only precipitated the collapse of the Stalinist regimes but created the conditions for 'globalisation' and the rapid economic transformation of China and India. The cumulative effect of these developments was to shift the balance of power between the classes significantly in favour of the bourgeoisie and provide the system with a temporary 'breathing space'.

The more the life of a mode of production in its descending curve is prolonged, the more the continued growth of the productive forces strains against the now obsolete relations of production and the system is put under increasing pressure to remove anything not strictly necessary in order to ensure its survival; in previous modes of production we can point to measures to free the slaves in the late Roman Empire and the serfs at the end of the Middle Ages. Hence the final phase of the system's descent can give the appearance of its most progressive development; as in the curbing of the power of the nobility and the partial liberties granted to the bourgeoisie in the last gasp of feudalism.

One of capitalism's central contradictions is that its tendency towards unlimited growth drives it to become a global system of production, but it is constrained by its organisation at the level of the nation state. The global restructuring of capitalist production from the 1980s – which was both a product of, and an active factor in, the breakdown of attempts at national autarky by weaker capitals – had the effect of creating much-needed outlets in a situation of chronic overproduction, and fundamentally represented capitalism's attempt to overcome this contradiction. While this remains impossible due to the very nature of capitalism as a system based on competition between capitals, it unquestionably gave the system a certain lease of life, as shown in the growth of world trade from the 1990s (see Figure 6 above), which was accompanied by the strengthening of international organisation at the economic level – symbolised by China's admission into the World Trade Organisation in 2001.

However, the bourgeoisie's attempts to prolong the life of the system only caused a further explosion of the system's contradictions, with the USA now at its epicentre. Without examining this in any depth we can highlight the following:

– At the level of imperialist conflicts, while the US bourgeoisie achieved its strategic goal of winning the Cold War and becoming the world's only superpower, the process facilitated the rise of a new and potentially more powerful competitor: China.

– At the same time, the collapse of Stalinism inevitably undermined the rationale for the existence of the USA's own bloc, encouraging the ambitions of secondary powers and the proliferation of increasingly uncontrollable imperialist conflicts as the USA tried to reassert its hegemony.

– The increase in global economic connectivity, and the rapid economic growth of China and India, led directly to the qualitative worsening of all the destructive consequences of capitalism's continued accumulation for both human beings and for the planet.

This final point will be explored in more depth in the final section.

5. The acceleration of capitalism's descent and the 'planetary boundaries' of capitalist accumulation

It has been estimated that, at current rates, capitalism needs 1.75 planets to sustain its consumption of the Earth's resources and absorb its waste. This alone indicates that capitalism has already passed the point where its continued survival threatens the sustainability of human life on Earth.[23]

Our starting point for understanding the consequences of capitalism's survival in its descending curve is its dynamism; its drive to continually expand production without any regard for the satisfaction of human needs. The longer that capitalism survives, even after it has created the conditions for a new, classless society based on human needs not profit, the more this blind drive to expand itself comes up violently against the restriction imposed by its own relations of production, with ever more destructive consequences for human beings and for the Earth.

The prolongation of capitalism's death agony has inevitably led to the aggravation of its contradictions at all levels; while in the last seventy years it has not – yet – led to a new world war, we have seen countless signs that capitalism's descent into barbarism is accelerating: disasters and convulsions, catastrophes and crises, as well as a proliferation of imperialist conflicts that reveal the increasing lack of an economic rationale even in capitalist terms, along with massacres, famines and other entirely avoidable man-made disasters.

Within this acceleration we can identify key phases, in which there was a qualitative worsening of the destructive consequences of capitalism's continued attempt to expand against the constraints of its obsolete relations of produc-

---

23   See the website of the Global Footprint Network, <https:// data.footprintnetwork.org/#/countryTrends?cn=5001&type=earth>

tion, to the point where it now threatens to destroy the basis for sustainable human life on Earth. It is no accident that both of these phases correspond to the two main phenomena of economic growth in the last seventy years:

- the post-war boom, and
- 'globalisation' from the 1980s onwards and the rapid growth of China and India.

The post-war boom and the 'Great Acceleration'

Some scientists have proposed the 1950s as a start date for the beginning of the 'Anthropocene'; the geological epoch where human activity begins to have a significant impact on the Earth's geology and environment, key indicators of which include:

- the release of radioactive debris from the first atomic bomb detonations,
- a rapidly rising world population,
- accelerated industrial production and carbon dioxide emissions,
- increased use of fertilisers, and
- man-made climate change.

Some scientists designate the first age of this new epoch as 'The Great Acceleration', in which changes in socio-economic and earth systems point to 'the synchronous acceleration of trends from the 1950s to the present day – over a single human lifetime – with little sign of abatement.'[24]

Bourgeois ideology of course presents this as a problem of the impact of 'human activity', but the empirical evidence shows clearly that the problems begin with the birth of industrial capitalism around 1750 and start to worsen from the beginning of the 20th century (see Figure 18).

The post-war boom was, as we have seen, the result of a conjunction of factors in the acceleration of capitalism's descent, driven specifically by the USA's need for outlets for its greatly expanded industrial production in a world divided into rival imperialist blocs, which demanded an extremely high level of military spending, the development of a permanent arms economy, and the expansion of the consumption of the working class.

24 See the Future Earth website, <https://futureearth.org/2015/01/16/the-great-acceleration/>. This contains the full set of indicators used. Earth systems = geosphere, biosphere, hydrosphere, atmosphere and cryosphere: i.e. the interior and surface of Earth; the limited part of the planet that can support living things; the areas of Earth covered with water; the envelope of gas that keeps the planet warm and provides oxygen for breathing and carbon dioxide for photosynthesis, and the ice at the poles and elsewhere.

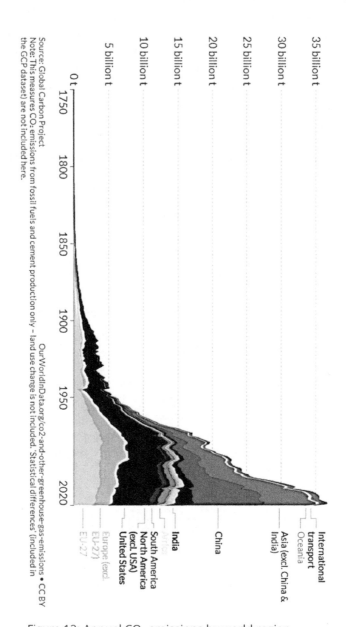

Figure 12: Annual CO$_2$ emissions by world region

Hannah Ritchie, Max Roser and Pablo Rosado (2020), 'CO$_2$ and Greenhouse Gas Emissions' in Our World in Data, <https://ourworldindata.org/co2-and-other-greenhouse-gas-emissions>

The economic growth that resulted was itself a key driver of the rapid rise in the world's population, while the expansion of industrial production – much of it a part of the arms economy – inevitably involved an increase in the pillaging of natural resources, burning of fossil fuels and the resulting acceleration of CO_2 emissions (see Figure 12), accompanied by increased pollution and waste. We can also highlight the effects of the industrialisation of agriculture and food processing in this period, which only achieved an enormous increase in productivity through the massive use of chemical fertilisers and pesticides.

The irrationality of 'globalisation' and the destructive effects of growth

From the point of view of a capitalism deeply mired in a long drawn-out crisis, the shift of production from the traditional heartlands of the USA and western Europe to low cost, low wage regions like China and India, may have appeared as perfectly rational 'human activity', leading to a growth of trade and increased economic connectivity.

But as we have seen, 'globalisation' was the product of a conjuncture of factors in the deepening of capitalism's crisis; the product of, and an active factor in, a strategy to ensure continued accumulation and reinforce capitalist domination of the main concentrations of the working class in the west. From the point of view of human needs it was deeply irrational, involving the shift of production to areas even more heavily dependent on fossil fuels, and then transporting finished goods back to the markets of the US and Europe, significantly contributing to increased greenhouse gas emissions (transport is almost totally dependent on oil), pollution, ocean acidification and reduced biodiversity.

The rapid economic growth of China and India – together now responsible for a third of the world's CO_2 emissions from fossil fuels – clearly demonstrates the destructive nature of capitalist accumulation in its phase of descent:

- pillaging of natural resources, burning of fossil fuels and carbon dioxide emissions,
- intensive use of fertilisers and pesticides, soil erosion and desertification,
- loss of forest and grassland, and loss of species and habitat,
- overfishing, reduced fish populations and oceanic pollution,
- air and water pollution, industrial waste and sewage, with high infant mortality rates and excess deaths, and
- the growth of an urban slum-dwelling population.

A specific effect of globalisation has been to increase the threat of zoonotic, animal to human infectious diseases like Covid-19, SARS, Ebola and MERS, which began to grow in the 1950s. Scientific studies highlight increased risks in regions where tropical rain forests rich in mammal species are being increasingly cleared to meet the needs of a growing human population. The mapping of risk factors for the emergence of zoonotic diseases identifies almost the whole of South and East Asia as a global 'hotspot'.[25] The increasing appearance of pandemics generally, and more importantly their ability to spread rapidly across the world, is of course partly due to the greater level of economic connectivity, as shown by the fact that in 1970 there were only 310 million air passengers, compared to 4.5 billion in 2019.[26]

The 'planetary boundaries' of capitalist accumulation

The longer that capitalist accumulation continues, the more destructive consequences it has for human beings and for the Earth; clearly it cannot continue indefinitely.

Scientists have proposed a set of 'planetary boundaries' beyond which the 'safe operating space for humanity' is at risk, crossing one or more of which could have catastrophic consequences for the planet.[27] By 2015 it was concluded that four of these boundaries had already been crossed:

- climate change,
- biodiversity loss and extinctions,
- conversion of tropical forests, grasslands, wetlands etc for agriculture,
- changes in the flows of nitrogen and phosphorus to the biosphere and oceans as a result of industrial and agricultural processes (use of synthetic fertilisers, etc).

In January 2022, some scientists concluded that a fifth boundary – chemical pollution from heavy metals, radioactive materials, plastics, etc – had also been crossed.[28]

---

25   See T Allen et al, 'Global hotspots and correlates of emerging zoonotic diseases', in *Nature Communications* vol 8, October 2017

26   Air transport, passengers carried, <https://data.worldbank.org/indicator/IS.AIR-.PSGR>

27   J Rockström et al, 'A safe operating space for humanity', in *Nature* no. 461, 472–475 (2009)

28   The other four boundaries are: ocean acidification due to CO_2 emissions; stratospheric ozone depletion due to chemical pollutants; atmospheric aerosol pollution, and deple-

Man-made climate change, with biodiversity loss, is seen as the most important boundary, being connected to all the others. Although inevitably there are still many unknowns about the exact nature of the connections, and the extent to which the crossing of one boundary might impact on all the others, we do know that global warming is already causing extreme events such as heatwaves, heavy precipitation, droughts, and tropical cyclones, as well as reductions in glaciers, Arctic sea ice, snow cover and permafrost.

From all this we must conclude, first, that if there is such a thing as an 'external limit' to capitalist accumulation then it has already been exceeded; and second, that, if capitalism is allowed to continue, the second century of its descent into barbarism will be truly, almost unimaginably catastrophic for humanity and for the planet; almost unimaginable because, in fact, the implications are already clear. As early as 1988 it was recognised that the ultimate consequences of climate change could be second only to a global nuclear war; today scientists openly warn that catastrophic climate change could trigger systems failures that 'unravel societies across the globe'.[29] This would, in effect, complete capitalism's descent into full barbarism:

> ...billions of people will be subject to continuous temperatures of around 29°C or more which make life unsustainable. Crops will fail and billions will be forced to try and migrate to higher latitudes leading to starvation, wars and a breakdown of civilisation. All this will occur if the capitalist system of production remains the global system of production.[30]

Even this apocalyptic vision is not the worst case scenario; by the end of this century carbon emissions could surpass thresholds that triggered previous mass extinction events in Earth history.[31] Without making the mistake of trying to predict the end of capitalism, we must conclude from all the growing evidence that we are now definitely looking at its 'endgame': in the absence of a proletarian revolution, humanity and a habitable Earth cannot and will not survive beyond the end of the 21st century.

---

tion of freshwater supplies. See the website of the Stockholm Resilience Institute, <https://www.stockholmresilience.org>.

29 L Kemp et al, 'Climate Endgame: Exploring catastrophic climate change scenarios', *Proceedings of the National Academy of Sciences*, vol. 119, no. 34, August 2022

30 CP, 'Global Warming: IPCC Report AR6 - Writing a Death Warrant?', *Revolutionary Perspectives* no. 19, series 4, 2022

31 L Kemp et al, 'Climate Endgame', 2022. See the Wikipedia entry <https://en.wikipedia.org/wiki/Extinction_event > for a list of extinction events.

In conclusion

'All this economic shit resolves itself in the class struggle' (Marx)[32]

In 1945 the Gauche Communiste de France (GCF) described capitalism in its phase of descent as like a building where the materials to construct the upper floors are taken from the lower floors and foundations:

> The more frenetic the construction of the upper floors, the weaker the foundation supporting the whole edifice becomes. The greater the appearance of strength at the top, the more shaky and unsteady the building is in reality. Capitalism, forced to dig under its own foundations, works furiously to undermine the world economy, hurling human society towards catastrophe and the abyss.[33]

The GCF was referring specifically to the effects of imperialist war but from today's vantage point it appears as an exact description of the nature and consequences of economic growth in capitalism's descent. After a further seventy years of accumulation the obsolete mode of production has undermined its own foundations to the extent that it is visibly destroying the planet it depends upon for its own survival, leaving humanity staring into the abyss.

The aim of this text was to offer a coherent explanation of economic growth in capitalism's 'descending curve'. Taking capitalism's dynamism as our necessary starting point, and within the general framework of capitalism's descending curve, we have given a brief overview of the most significant developments in the crucial period of 1914 to 1945, and then examined the main phenomena of capitalist growth, approaching each as the product of a unique combination of factors within the aggravation of capitalism's contradictions.

We have identified some of the main mechanisms that capitalism, faced with the aggravation of its contradictions, has adopted to ensure its survival:

1. The inseparable development of state capitalism and a war economy, which are both necessary in order to hold capitalist society together,

---

32 The actual quote, which comes at the end of a letter to Engels following the publication of the first volume of *Capital* that sets out the proposed contents of the next two volumes, is: 'Finally, since those 3 items (wages, rent, profit (interest)) constitute the sources of income of the 3 classes of landowners, capitalists and wage labourers, we have the class struggle, as the conclusion in which the movement and disintegration of the whole shit resolves itself.' The reader will have to judge whether our *précis* accurately reflects Marx's general view! (Letter to Engels, 30 April 1868, <https://wikirouge.net/texts/en/Letter_to_Friedrich_Engels,_April_30,_1868>

33 'Report on the International Situation', July 1945, reprint in *International Review* no. 59, 1989, our translation.

and to a limited extent are able to provide an outlet for capital, but also constitute an enormous burden of unproductive expenditure.

2.   The destruction and devaluation of capital in wars and economic crises, which in Marx's words is not external to capitalism but a condition of its self-preservation, the need for which becomes greater the longer that capitalism's life is prolonged and the more the scale of accumulation grows.

3.   The systematic recourse to debt in order to create solvent demand in the absence of sufficient new external outlets, which prolongs the life of the system at the cost of increasing instability.

We can see that each of these is both a mechanism for capitalism's survival and at the same time serves to undermine the foundations of the system.

Above all, we have examined the evolution of the class struggle and the balance of power between the classes as a key factor in explaining the main phases of capitalism's descent, specifically:

1.   It was the revolutionary wave of 1917-21 that forced the major imperialist powers to bring the war to a premature end without any decisive result – despite the unprecedented destruction of capital – while the effective disappearance of Russia as a market only served to deepen the crisis of European capitalism and accelerated the shift of global capitalism towards the US.

2.   It was the defeat of this revolutionary wave that opened the road to a new world war as an 'exit' for capitalism from the generalised economic crisis of the 1930s, enabling the qualitative development of state capitalism and a war economy, which reached its highest expression in the United States in World War II and created the conditions for the ensuing post-war boom.

3.   It was the resurgence of the class struggle that contributed to the end of the post-war boom in the late 1960s, in which a key factor was the role of a new generation of proletarians who had not directly experienced defeat, and it was the continued resistance of the working class to the attacks necessary to restore profitability that determined the need for the economic and political offensive of the ruling class from the 1980s.

4.   Finally, the defeat of the working class in the traditional capitalist heartlands in the 1980s was both a product of, and an active factor in, the global restructuring of capitalist production in the 1990s onwards.

This leads us to the tentative conclusion that the defeat of the working class is an essential precondition for the main phenomena of growth in capitalism's descent.

The question is often asked: 'how can you say capitalism is decadent today when there has been such enormous growth in the capitalist system?' The short answer is: we have seen such enormous 'growth' in capitalism because the proletariat has so far been unable to destroy it. In the absence of the proletarian revolution, capitalism will persist, and as long as it is allowed to persist, capitalism must on pain of death find opportunities to accumulate. But the longer it is allowed to persist, the more destructive this 'growth' becomes.

The descent of capitalism makes the proletarian revolution both possible and increasingly necessary – but it is not inevitable. As the *Communist Manifesto* recognised, previous class societies have ended 'either in a revolutionary reconstitution of society at large, or in the common ruin of the contending classes' and the whole history of capitalism's descent shows the unprecedented difficulty of the proletariat's task.

So where are we today? Despite the aggravation of capitalism's contradictions at all levels, the defeat of the working class in the 1980s remains a defining factor in the balance of power between the classes today. A full consideration of the nature and consequences of this defeat is beyond the scope of this text – and is obviously still very much a topic of debate in the proletarian movement – but, in the context of our focus on understanding growth in capitalism's descent, we can highlight some of its key features:

- the effects of the break-up of traditional centres of militancy in the capitalist heartlands and the resulting change in the composition of the working class, in the context of the bourgeois counter-offensive against the working class;
- the disorienting effect of the global restructuring of production from the 1980s, that gave the impression of dynamic, revolutionary change in capitalist society;
- the ideological campaigns about the 'death of communism', and the promise of a 'new world order' opening a 'new era of peace and prosperity', reinforcing the message that 'there is no alternative' to neoliberalism and western-style democracy.

In the longer term, the breakdown of attempts at national autarky enabled the bourgeoisie to create what was in effect a 'global reserve army of labour'; a pool of disposable labour power that enabled it to keep wages low and reinforce its domination of the working class. This development is dealt with in more detail in the article on surplus populations and pauperisation.

144

The reprieve for the system provided by the cumulative effects of the bour-geois counter-offensive, the breakdown of autarky and the restructuring of pro-duction has only caused an explosion of the system's contradictions, with the USA at its epicentre. Today, in 2022, humanity truly faces an accumulation of catastrophe:

- the Covid-19 global pandemic, which came at a time when there was already a sharp slowdown in economic growth, has triggered a global recession and the largest surge in debt since World War II;

- the Russian invasion of Ukraine – in effect a proxy war between the US-led bloc and Russia and the largest war in Europe since World War II – contains the unpredictable threat of escalation into a major imper-ialist confrontation involving nuclear weapons;

- the last two years have seen innumerable signs of the worsening cli-mate crisis, with heatwaves, wildfires and flooding across different continents;

- the war, on top of the pandemic and the effects of the climate crisis, has disrupted global food and energy supplies, causing price rises and shortages and raising the spectre of starvation and social unrest, espe-cially in underdeveloped regions like Africa;

- all these and other interconnected factors have caused a worsening of the world's refugee crisis, with a sharp increase of 7 million people forcibly displaced in just 12 months; more than double the number a decade ago.

This can only underline the necessity for capitalism's revolutionary over-throw. But time is clearly not on the side of the proletariat. We have emphas-ised the determinant role of the class struggle and of the balance of power between the classes in understanding the history of capitalism's descending curve. But we must conclude by recognising that the accumulation of cata-strophe since the birth of capitalism – in particular its pillaging of natural re-sources and burning of fossil fuels, together with its destruction of the soil – has now reached the point where the destructiveness of capitalism's growth is itself a determining factor in the situation facing humanity.

It is important to remind ourselves that, for both human beings and for the planet, capitalist accumulation has always been a catastrophe: from the expro-priation of the peasantry and the extermination and enslavement of indigenous peoples to the destruction of the intimate living relationship between human beings and the earth. Capitalism is the last, most extreme expression of the sep-aration of human beings from the products of their own labour, from each other, and from nature. At the same time, by creating the material basis for production to meet human needs, and by bringing into existence a class of associated, exploited labour, it creates the practical conditions for its own abolition. But from its birth, capitalism's blind drive to expand itself and, the sheer destructiveness of its growth have contained the threat that, if the proletariat is unable to overthrow it in time, this uniquely dynamic mode of production could destroy not only the material conditions for its abolition but also the basis for human life on Earth. If we believe what scientists are now telling us, this threat is now real: as a result of the dynamism of this uniquely destructive mode of production, the 21st century is capitalism's 'endgame'.

Note on sources

This text is essentially an attempt to reconstruct the history of the last 120 years or so and is largely based on secondary sources and existing research, primarily by existing organisations of the Communist Left: the International Communist Current, which has written copiously on aspects of the decadence of capitalism since its formation in 1975, together with the Communist Workers' Organisation (British affiliate of the Internationalist Communist Tendency). Rather than tax the reader with a forest of footnote references in the text itself, below I list the main sources used, in addition to the references given above. For further reading, and some of the original posts used as the basis for this text, see also my blog 'Breath and Light': <https://markhayes9.wixsite.com/website> .

International Communist Current:

'Economic crisis: thirty years of the open crisis of capitalism', in *International Review* nos. 96, 97, 98, 1999.

'The sources, contradictions and limitations of the growth in Eastern Asia', *International Review* no. 133, 2008 (online only).

'Internal debate: The causes of the post-1945 economic boom', *International Review* nos. 133, 135, 136, 138, 141, 2008-2010

'The decadence of capitalism', *International Review* nos. 132, 134, 135, 137, 139, 141, 142, 143, 145, 146, 147, 148, 149, 2008-2012.

Communist Workers' Organisation / Internationalist Communist Tendency:

'Capitals against capitalism', *Internationalist Communist* no. 18, 1996

'Globalisation and imperialism', *Internationalist Communist* no. 16, 1997

'On Class Composition and Recomposition in the Globalisation of Capital', *Revolutionary Perspectives* no. 28, Series 3, 2003

'Is capitalism finished?', *Revolutionary Perspectives* no. 48, Series 3, 2008

Surplus populations and the pauperisation of the working class

(Mark Hayes)

Marx's general law of accumulation in capitalism's descent

'In this chapter we shall consider the influence of the growth of capital on the fate of the working class.'[1]

Introduction

Marx's 'general law of capitalist accumulation' has largely been ignored by the Left Communist political current. This may be because it has previously been misinterpreted as a prediction that real wages must inevitably fall in capitalism and that workers' conditions can therefore only worsen.[2] Also, when the surviving left communist fractions were attempting to deepen their understanding of capitalism's decadence in the 1920s and '30s, this period seemed to be characterised by a cycle of crisis-war-reconstruction and it may have been assumed that the 'general law' could no longer be valid, while the post-World War II economic boom, which saw a growth of workers' real wages, appeared to further contradict the idea of 'immiseration'.

The return of capitalism's crisis in the 1960s should perhaps, with hindsight, have provoked more interest in the Communist Left. Instead, more recently the general law has been taken up by those associated with 'communisation' theory, like the group publishing the *Endnotes* journal who have used it to support the argument that the working class as a whole is becoming superfluous to capitalist accumulation and is therefore no longer a revolutionary subject,[3] while re-

1   Marx, Chapter 25, *Capital*, Volume 1 (Penguin, 1976), p.762.

2   For a description of these views see J Bellamy Foster et al, 'The Global Reserve Army of Labor and the New Imperialism', *Monthly Review*, November 2011.

3   See for example 'Crisis in the Class Relation' and 'Misery and Debt' in *Endnotes* no. 2,

sponses to this argument from the Communist Left have tended to reassert that the working class is still numerically growing rather than address the issues raised by the law itself.[4]

We don't intend to deal with these arguments directly here. Rather our aim is to promote an informed discussion of the 'general law of capitalist accumulation' described by Marx, and of its potential contribution to our understanding of capitalism in its phase of descent.

We comment below on some of the problems we face in trying to use official data and identify key trends in capitalism, especially today when so much of what really happens in capitalist society is deliberately distorted and disguised by a cynical bourgeoisie. But as materialists we have no option but to try to ascertain the facts...

The general law of capitalist accumulation

In general, Marx argues, we might expect that the more rapidly capitalism accumulates, the more the demand for labour increases, causing wages to rise. But if the trend for wages to rise continued unchecked, profits would decline and eventually threaten the future of accumulation. What happens in reality is that the more rapidly capitalism accumulates, the more it tends to produce a surplus population of workers, which forms an 'industrial reserve army'; a pool of disposable labour power that becomes a means both to regulate wages and to ensure the domination of capital. As the proletariat grows in size, so this industrial reserve army also tends to grow, and the more this grows in proportion to the active, working section of the proletariat, the more it tends to become a consolidated surplus population, resulting, according to Marx, in the pauperisation of the working class.

At the same time, the more rapidly that capitalism accumulates, the more the productivity of labour grows, resulting in a tendency for the demand for labour to diminish in proportion to the growth of capital, even as the size of the working class increases:

April 2010.

4   For the Communist Workers' Organisation see CP, 'The Disappointed of 1968: Seeking Refuge in Utopia', *Revolutionary Perspectives* no. 16, Series 4, August 2020. The other main representative of the Communist Left, the International Communist Current, has so far made no attempt to respond to the specific arguments of the 'communisers'.

> The labouring population therefore produces, along with the accumulation of capital produced by it, the means by which it itself is made relatively superfluous, is turned into a relative surplus population; and it does this to an always increasing extent. This is a law of population peculiar to the capitalist mode of production... [5]

The more that capitalism accumulates, in other words, the more the condition of the working class as a whole must worsen, *whatever the level of wages*:

> The greater the social wealth, the functioning capital, the extent and energy of its growth, and therefore also the greater the absolute mass of the proletariat and the productivity of its labour, the greater is the industrial reserve army. The same causes which develop the expansive power of capital, also develop the labour power at its disposal. The relative mass of the industrial reserve army thus increases with the potential energy of wealth. But the greater this reserve army in proportion to the active labour army, the greater is the mass of a consolidated surplus population, whose misery is in inverse ratio to the amount of torture it has to undergo in the form of labour. The more extensive, finally, the pauperized sections of the working class, and the industrial reserve army, the greater is official pauperism. [6]

For Marx this was 'the absolute general law of capitalist accumulation', and he considered it important enough to devote a whole chapter to its workings in the first volume of *Capital*.

At one level, the law can be understood as a gauntlet thrown down to the bourgeois political economists, exposing the brutal reality of their utopia of a capitalist society based on free competition. But for Marx, the fact that the demand for labour tends to diminish the more labour productivity grows expresses an inherent contradiction of capitalism; labour time for this mode of production is the only determinant of value, and yet the more it develops the productive forces, it is driven to reduce this to a minimum. [7] The same contradiction that inexorably leads to the worsening of the condition of the working class also demonstrates that capitalism must in theory reach a point where it becomes a barrier to the further development of the productive forces. [8] So by ex-

---

5   *Capital* Volume 1, Chapter 25, p.783.

6   Ibid, p.798.

7   'Capital itself is the moving contradiction, [in] that it presses to reduce labour time to a minimum, while it posits labour time, on the other side, as sole measure and source of wealth' (*Grundrisse*, 'Chapter on Capital, Section Two' (Penguin, 1973), p.706).

8   'Beyond a certain point, the development of the powers of production becomes a barrier for capital; hence the capital relation a barrier for the development of the productive powers of labour. When it has reached this point, capital, i.e. wage labour, enters into the same relation towards the development of social wealth and of the forces of production as the guild system, serfdom, slavery, and is necessarily stripped off as a fet-

amining the extent to which the workings of this law are observable today, we are also exploring whether we can say this point has been reached.

Marx also gives a detailed breakdown of the relative surplus population in English capitalist society in the 1860s; while it changed according to the cycles of production, the 'industrial reserve army' always contained three elements:

> *floating*: industrial workers, even the best paid, who are partially or wholly unemployed during periodic crises;

> *latent*: agricultural workers, whose wages are reduced to the minimum due to the advance of capitalism into agriculture, 'with one foot already in the swamp of pauperism';

> *stagnant*: those existing in the most precarious conditions, with extremely irregular employment, long hours and low pay, including part-time and casual workers, domestic outworkers, etc, often women or children. This 'stagnant' population 'finally dwells in the sphere of pauperism'; constantly replenished by rapidly exhausted industrial workers and surplus agricultural labour, it grows out of proportion to the working class as a whole, providing capital with 'an inexhaustible reservoir of disposable labour power'.

From this picture we can see that the definition of the relative surplus population includes not only the unemployed but even high-paid, part-time workers as well as all those in precarious and low-paid work. But before we address the question of the extent to which we can observe such a surplus population today, we need to obtain a brief overview of the size and composition of the working class as a whole.

The size and growth
of the working class today

In general, we would expect the proletariat to be growing in size; the world's population has risen from 1 billion in 1800 to 8 billion in 2022 and is projected to grow to over 10 billion by 2100.[9] This has been driven fundamentally by the growth of capitalist accumulation, and the resulting advances in medical science and agricultural productivity, etc. This is despite the destructiveness of capitalism's growth in its descent; the world's population has in fact risen more rap-

---

ter.' (*Grundrisse*, 'The Chapter on Capital, Section Three', p749)

9   Our World in Data, <https://ourworldindata.org/world-population-growth> ; United Nations, *World Population Prospects 2022: Summary of Results*, p.i.

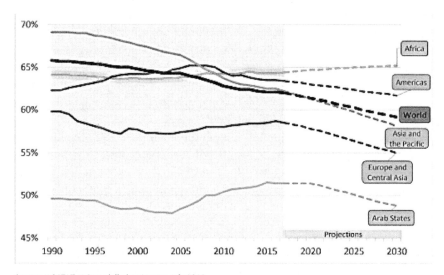

Source: ILOSTAT, ILO modelled estimates, July 2018.

Figure 13: Global and regional labour force participation rates, 1990-2030

ILO, Labour Force Estimates and Projections (LFEP) 2018 Key Trends, July 2018. The labour force participation rate measures the proportion of the working-age population that is either working or looking for work; i.e. it includes those officially unemployed

idly in this period, the growth rate reaching a peak during the post-World War II economic boom before starting to fall steadily.[10]

In relation to the 'general law', the key question is whether the surplus population is growing in proportion to the active, working section of the proletariat. There are of course all sorts of problems in trying to obtain an answer to this question using official data, which not surprisingly does not provide an accurate picture of the working class in 'classic' Marxist terms, i.e. as the class of wage labourers that produces surplus value for capital, but also as the class of associated, collective labour (and this is before we begin to consider the implications of changes in capitalism like the growth of unproductive labour, of the role of the state, the service sector). So we need to find proxy indicators and focus on key trends, accepting that what we find are approximations.

---

10   UN data shows that the world population's annual growth rate fell from a peak of 2.24 percent in 1963 to 0.83 percent in 2022 and is currently projected to fall to 0.11 percent in 2100 (<https://www.macrotrends.net/countries/WLD/world/population-growth-rate>)

According to official data, 3.3 billion people were in employment in 2019, of whom 1.7 billion were defined as wage and salaried employees. This will include senior managers, high-paid state functionaries and others who we would not consider part of the working class, and it will exclude some 'gig workers', freelancers, temp agency workers and others officially deemed to be 'self-employed', at least some of whom we would probably include. But it still gives us an approximation of the size of the working class. This 1.7 billion compares to 1.2 billion in 2000, so broadly the working class, as we might expect, is growing numerically.[11] It is also growing as a proportion of the total number of people in employment, from 45 percent in 2000 to 53 percent in 2019[12] – although there is some evidence that this proportion has remained relatively static since the start of the 20th century (see Appendix to this article).

However, the number of people in employment *as a proportion of the world's working-age population* is falling, and has been for at least three decades (see Figure 13).

There are some obvious reasons for this: life expectancy is rising and fertility rates are falling, so the working population is ageing. More people are retiring earlier and living longer, and there are also higher numbers in education, at least in the more advanced capitalist economies. Those people of working age (15 years and older) *not* in the labour force include full-time students and carers, as well as the retired and disabled. But they also include workers who have been marginalised to different degrees by the system – so-called 'discouraged' workers who fall into Marx's 'stagnant' population, the most pauperised portion of the proletariat – along with the criminal element, the 'lumpenproletariat'.

In summary, the working class is growing numerically, but it is not growing as a proportion of the world's working-age population. There also appears to be a growing population that is outside of the workforce, partly because of global demographic factors that did not exist in the period of capitalism's ascent when Marx was writing, but also because capitalism is producing a surplus population of workers.

Before examining this surplus population, we first want to quickly look at what for Marx is a key driver of the 'general law': the growth of labour productivity.

---

11   International Labor Organization, *World Employment Social Outlook, Trends*, 2020, p.90
12   Ibid, pp.84-5

The growth of labour productivity

Is there any empirical evidence for the tendency identified by Marx for the demand for labour to diminish in proportion to the growth of capital, even as the
size of the working class increases?

In fact the share of workers employed in manufacturing has been declining
at a global level for at least two decades. In the capitalist heartlands of western
Europe and North America this trend began in the 1960s and accelerated from
the 1970s (see Figure 14). But since the 1980s we can see that it has also been
falling rapidly in newly industrialising economies like Singapore, Korea and
Taiwan (see Figure 15).

From the 1990s China also saw a fall in the share of manufacturing employment; it recovered in the 2000s but started to fall again from 2013, when the
actual number of workers in manufacturing also began to fall (see Figure 16).

Globally, this trend does **not** imply a decline in manufacturing output,
which despite a slowdown due to the 2007-8 economic crisis has continued to
grow (see Figure 17).

The growth of the service sector

The decline in the share of workers employed in manufacturing must be seen in
the wider context of the increasing share of the service sector, which began to
grow in the capitalist heartlands in the 1960s and now accounts for over 70
percent of employment in the OECD countries.[13] While the growth of the service sector partly reflects an increase in low wage, precarious work, especially in
the weaker 'Third World' economies – a trend we will examine in more depth
below – it also performs functions that are vital to manufacturing, including
those that may have been previously carried out 'in-house', like design, catering,
transport, training, etc, together with functions vital to enabling capitalist accumulation as a whole, like health care and education, which are delivered in
some cases by very large, industrial-scale workforces; the UK's National Health
Service, for example, is one of the world's largest employers with 1.5 million
workers.

So we cannot simply conclude — as those associated with 'communisation'
theory tend to do – that the decline in manufacturing employment and the

---

13   *Growth in Services: Fostering Employment, Productivity and Innovation*, OECD Council, 2005,
     p.2.

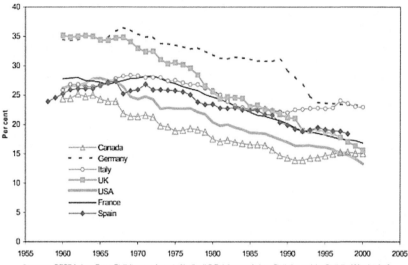

Fig. 14: Share of manufacturing employment in Europe and North America

Fig. 15: Share of manufacturing employment in selected Asian countries

R Rowthorn & K Coutts, 'De-industrialisation and the balance of payments in advanced economies', United Nations Conference on Trade and Development Discussion paper no. 170, May 2004

Share of manufacturing in total Chinese employment, 2000–17

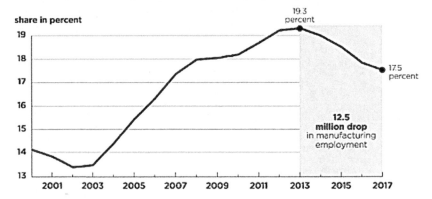

Sources: Conference Board Total Economy Database (TED) and International Labor Comparisons (ILC) Databases.

Fig. 16 Share of manufacturing in total Chinese employment, 2000-17

R S Lawrence, 'China, Like the US, Faces Challenges in Achieving Inclusive Growth Through Manufacturing', *Peterson Institute for International Economics Policy Briefing*, August 2019

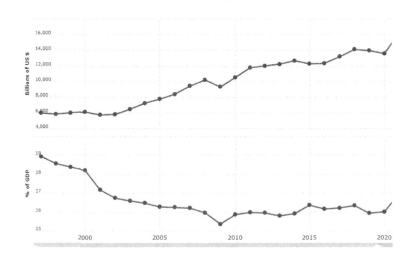

Figure 17: World Manufacturing Output 1997-2022

Output in current US dollars. See source for full definition.
https://www.macrotrends.net/countries/WLD/world/manufacturing-output

growth of the service sector in themselves prove that the working class as a whole is becoming superfluous to capitalist accumulation.[14]

The primary reason for the decline in manufacturing employment does indeed appear to be the growth of labour productivity, which has been led by the manufacturing sector, with newly industrialising economies tending to rapidly adopt the highest existing level of technical innovation. In the case of industrialising economies like China, whose rapid growth originally depended on very low wages, the growth of labour productivity has been spurred by the tendency for wages to rise in the long term, prompting the move of foreign exporting firms to other, even lower wage economies (like Vietnam, Bangladesh and Ethiopia), and a resulting push towards automation.[15]

To understand the full impact of these trends – the decline in manufacturing employment and the growth of the service sector – on the condition of the working class as a whole, we also need to examine changes in capitalism since the 1960s, which have resulted in the growth of precarious, low paid work and the creation of a global 'industrial reserve army'.

The growth of precarious, low paid work

Of the 3.3 billion people in employment, some two billion work 'informally'; that is, outside the formalities of state regulation, without contracts or benefits. In the weakest capitalist economies, informal jobs now account for up to 90 percent of employment, but they are also growing as a proportion in the traditional capitalist heartlands.

Informal workers are more likely to be working for low pay in poor conditions and to live in poverty.[16] The largest portion are self-employed, who in 'Third World' economies are likely to be street vendors, taxi drivers, market traders and others trying to survive in the absence of jobs in the 'formal' sector. The other main group of informal workers are those, mostly women in the 'Third World', working unpaid for family members.

---

14   See for example 'Crisis in the Class Relation' and 'Misery and Debt' in *Endnotes* no. 2, April 2010.

15   See for example S Rozelle et al, 'Moving beyond Lewis: Employment and Wage Trends in China's High- and Low-Skilled Industries and the Emergence of an Era of Polarization', *Comparative Economic Studies* no. 62 (2020), <https://link.springer.com/article/10.1057/s41294-020-00137-w>

16   ILO, *World Employment Social Outlook, Trends*, 2020, p.12; see also ILO, *Women and Men in the Informal Economy: A Statistical Picture*, 2018

But around 680 million wage and salaried workers also have 'informal' jobs – 40 percent of the total. Although some might be relatively well paid, this indicates that almost half of the global working class is now in precarious work.

A substantial portion of this informal workforce approximates to Marx's description of the 'stagnant' segment of the surplus population, while the emergence in the traditional capitalist heartlands of a supposedly new class – the 'precariat' – can more accurately be seen as the growth of the pauperised sector of the proletariat in the centres of the system.

A 'global reserve army of labour'

The breakdown of attempts at national autarky in the 1980s, which led to the collapse of the Stalinist regimes and the integration of China and India into global markets, in effect doubled the size of the pool of labour at the disposal of global capital, from around 1.4 billion workers to almost 3 billion.[17] This huge new supply of low wage labour enabled capital to shift production to lower cost areas, and to use the threat of doing so to cut workers' wages in the capitalist heartlands (these developments are dealt with in more depth in 'The accumulation of catastrophe'). It also enabled the bourgeoisie to create what is in effect a 'global reserve army of labour', the total size of which in 2011 was estimated at some 2.4 billion people.[18]

The 'global reserve army' includes the majority of the informal workforce described above, the officially unemployed (Marx's 'floating' surplus population), and a portion of the working-age population that is not in employment for a variety of reasons described above (the 'discouraged' etc.). Allowing for differences in definition, the total size of the global reserve army today is probably between 2.5 and 3 billion people, although it could be more.[19] As a reminder, this compares to 1.7 billion wage and salaried workers in the active workforce, 40 percent of whom are in precarious jobs. The largest part is as we

---

17   See R. Freeman, 'The great doubling: the challenge of the new global labor market', 2007, <https://eml.berkeley.edu/~webfac/eichengreen/e183_sp07/great_doub.pdf>. It should be emphasised here that Russia, China, India, etc., were already capitalist economies, the Stalinist regimes being essentially an extreme form of state capitalism, but their attempts to partially cut themselves off from the rest of the world market, in order to compensate for economic weakness, meant that their vast supplies of cheap labour were not available to global capital.

18   J Bellamy Foster et al, 'The Global Reserve Army of Labor and the New Imperialism', *Monthly Review*, November 2011

19   For the sake of consistency we have used ILO data for 2019, i.e. just before the Covid-19 pandemic.

would expect in the weaker capitalist economies, but it is also growing in the capitalist heartlands.

Marx envisaged that, as capitalism developed, it would acquire the ability to exploit cheap foreign labour or transfer production to low wage countries, toensure its dominationa ensure its domination.[20] The breakdown of autarky in the 1980s finally allowed capitalism to realise this objective at a global level.

* * *

Rather than attempting to provide an overall picture of the condition of the working class today, we want to highlight two phenomena that appear to illustrate the workings of this general law since the reappearance of capitalism's crisis in the 1960s:

— the growth of an urban slum-dwelling population, and
— capitalism's growing 'refugee crisis'.

Urban slums: dumping ground for capital's surplus population

Capitalism's surplus population must be housed somewhere and, as Marx put it over 150 years ago, 'the more rapidly flows the stream of exploitable human material, the more miserable are the improvised dwellings of the labourers'.[21]

The growth of slums was of course synonymous with the ascent of capitalism, to provide large-scale, low-cost accommodation for the proletariat in the rapidly growing industrial cities. Today, in capitalism's descent, more than half of the world's population live in cities, and this share is expected to grow to 70 percent by 2050. Of this total over one billion people today live in urban slums, and numbers could double by 2030 or 2040.[22]

Superficially the growth of an urban slum-dwelling population might appear to be the direct consequence of rapid industrialisation: China, for example, ad-

---

20   See his speech to the Lausanne Congress of the First International, 1867: '…a study of the struggle waged by the English working class reveals that, in order to oppose their workers, the employers either bring in workers from abroad or else transfer manufacture to countries where there is a cheap labour force. Given this state of affairs, if the working class wishes to continue its struggle with some chance of success, the national organisations must become international' <https://www.marxists.org/archive/marx/iwma/documents/1867/lausanne-call.htm>

21   *Capital* Volume 1, Chapter 25, p.815.

22   <https://unstats.un.org/sdgs/report/2022/goal-11/>. See also M Davis, *Planet of Slums*, (Verso, 2006), p.151

ded more city-dwellers in the 1980s than the whole of Europe did in the entire 19th century.[23] But the tendency has been for urbanisation to become increasingly disconnected from industrialisation, especially since the reappearance of the capitalist crisis in the 1960s, and has continued at a rapid pace in many parts of the world despite massive plant closures, falling real wages, rising prices and unemployment. Instead there has been a growth of precarious, low paid work and of surplus populations, with the rural poor driven into the cities by the effects of the mechanisation of agriculture, cheap food imports, and the impacts of civil war and drought, even as the crisis in the cities gets worse.

Urbanisation is increasingly being driven by the direct effects of the violent aggravation of capitalism's contradictions:

- Angola, which was only 14 percent urban in 1970, is now a majority urban nation as a result of the effects of a series of 'civil wars' (1975- 2002), in reality imperialist struggles between the USA and USSR, which forced 30 percent of the population to flee their homes;

- Gaza today contains over 2 million densely-packed people, the majority Palestinian refugees, in what is essentially an urbanised collection of refugee camps, with an economy devastated by the Israeli-imposed blockade and violent struggles between nationalist factions;

- in Colombia, which saw ceaseless struggles between armed bourgeois factions from the 1950s onwards, more than five million people were forced to flee their homes, more than 400,000 ending up in settlements around Bogota.[24]

The inevitable result is the rapid growth of slums, which outpaces urbanisation. As the authors of an official UN report conclude:

> Instead of being a focus for growth and prosperity, the cities have become a dumping ground for a surplus population working in unskilled, unprotected and low-wage informal service industries and trade.[25]

What does this mean for the poorest proletarians in these dumping grounds? Marx described the growth of the 'stagnant' element of the surplus population, in inverse proportion to the means of subsistence, as a 'law of capitalist society that [would] sound absurd to savages', calling to mind 'the boundless reproduction of animals individually weak and constantly hunted down'.[26] Today, in the slums around Bogota:

---

23   Ibid, pp.2,24.

24   Davis, *Planet of Slums*, pp.48-49.

25   UN Human Settlements Programme, *The Challenge of Slums*, 2003, p.46.

26   *Capital*, Volume 1, Chapter 25, p.797.

'Most displaced,' explains an aid NGO, 'are social outcasts, excluded from formal life and employment. Currently, 653,800 Bogotanos (2002) have no employment in the city and, even more shocking, half of them are under the age of 29.'

Without urban skills and frequently without access to schools, these young peasants and their children are ideal recruits for street gangs and paramilitaries. Local businessmen vandalised by urchins, in turn, form *grupos de limpiesa* ['clean-up squads'] with links to rightwing death squads, and the bodies of murdered children are dumped at the edge of town.

The same nightmare prevails on the outskirts of Cali, where anthropologist Michael Taussig invokes Dante's Inferno to describe the struggle for survival in two 'stupendously dangerous' peripheral slums. Navarro is a notorious 'garbage mountain' where hungry women and children pick through waste while youthful gunmen (*malo de malo*) are either hired or exterminated by local rightwing paramilitaries. The other settlement, Carlos Alfredo Dias, is full of 'kids running around with homemade shotguns and grenades.'[27]

In capitalism's descent, those 'constantly hunted down' as the result of the barbaric logic of its internal laws now include children armed with modern weapons, killing and being killed on the garbage dumps of its cities.

The 'refugee crisis' and the growth of an absolutely surplus population

Following the mass movements of millions of forcibly displaced people at the end of World War II there was a stabilisation of the refugee situation, partly because it was possible to integrate surplus labour into production as part of the US-led post-war reconstruction. But this temporary situation ended in the 1960s and the numbers of people 'forcibly displaced' – i.e. forced to flee their homes – began to rise steadily (see Figure 18).

By 2022 more than 100 million people were estimated to be forcibly displaced. This means 1 in every 80 people on the planet has now been forced to flee their homes. The majority are forcibly displaced in their 'own' country.[28]

Factors in this worsening crisis include:

— the spread and prolongation of imperialist conflicts (Syria, Myanmar, Yemen, Somalia, South Sudan, Afghanistan, etc, and now Ukraine);

---

27 Davis, *Planet of Slums,* p.49.

28 UNHCR, *Global Trends: Forced Displacement*, 2021, pp.5-7.

- the growing numbers of people unable to return to their homes due to the effects of wars and pogroms, poverty and food scarcity, environmental destruction and the closure of borders;

- the disintegration of once relatively strong industrialised economies like Venezuela, which now has one of the largest refugee crises in the world with 4.6 million people forced to flee the country.

A record-high share of the world's population is displaced from their homes

% of world population that is forcibly displaced

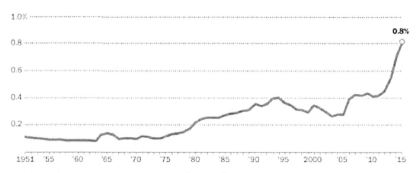

Note: Displaced includes internally displaced persons within their birth country, refugees and asylum seekers living in a different country who have yet to resettle permanently, and Palestinian refugees registered with the United Nations Relief and Works Agency (UNRWA) in Jordan, Lebanon and Syria.
Source: Pew Research Center analysis of United Nations data, accessed July 20, 2016.

PEW RESEARCH CENTER

Fig. 18: Share of the world's population displaced from their homes

(P Connor & J Krogstadt, 'Key facts about the world's refugees', Pew Research Centre, 2016)

These factors have been compounded by the effects of the Covid-19 pandemic.

The 'forcibly displaced' now form a growing section of capitalism's surplus population, falling into Marx's 'stagnant' reserve army; existing in the most precarious conditions and 'dwelling in the sphere of pauperism', but in many cases still providing capitalism with a reservoir of disposable labour power. Above all, the 'forcibly displaced' express the growing tendency of capitalism to give rise to a consolidated surplus population that is absolutely surplus to the needs of accumulation.

The general law of capitalist accumulation in the descent of capitalism

How has the descent or decline of capitalism since the start of the 20th century affected the operation of the general law of capitalist accumulation? We will restrict ourselves to setting out what seem to us to be some key points for further discussion.

As with all laws of capitalism identified by Marx – like the tendency for the rate of profit to fall – the 'general law' has counter-tendencies that modify its historical operation; production of existing commodities can be expanded and markets for new commodities created; but this of course depends on the capacity of society to consume, which is ultimately restricted by capitalism's own relations of production. In capitalism's ascending curve, when it is still progressively expanding across the globe, production can be expanded to meet the needs of new external markets; but this only leads to a further expansion of production, recreating the same problem at a higher level.

Capitalism's descent is precipitated by the insufficiency of new external outlets for its continued expansion creating a situation of chronic overproduction, and the hypothesis explored here is that in this period we see the progressive exhaustion of counter-tendencies to the operation of the general law. It is important to keep in mind, however, that according to the law, the surplus population is a necessary product of accumulation; 'indeed it becomes a condition for the existence of the capitalist mode of production'.[29] And since capitalism's descent is characterised by the accelerating growth of accumulation, we would logically expect to see a concomitant growth of the surplus population.

The lack of new outlets

One of the most obvious ways that capitalism's ascent provided an outlet to counteract the growth of the surplus population was emigration, at least for the first European capitalist powers: in Britain, for example, which had a population of 12 million in 1820, 16 million people emigrated – under varying degrees of duress – to the 'New World' and colonies between 1820 and 1915, while in the same period a total of 50 million people emigrated from Europe.[30]

---

29   *Capital* Volume 1, Chapter 25, p.784.
30   J Bellamy Foster et al, *Monthly Review*, 2011.

Except at some specific junctures described below, this outlet no longer exists to anything like the same extent in capitalism's descent; far from demanding large supplies of surplus labour from external sources, newly industrialising countries like China and India in the 1990s, for example, were able to do so precisely because they possessed their own vast supplies of cheap rural labour.

The destruction of the peasantry

In the 19th century, a portion of the population periodically expelled from production could return to the land to rejoin the peasantry. But, as Marx vividly described in the first volume of *Capital*, capitalism was only possible due to the expropriation of the agricultural population and their expulsion from the land, and its entire progress is characterised by the continuous destruction of the peasantry. This continued apace in the 20th century with the increasing industrialisation of agriculture, accelerating after World War II. According to one 'worst case scenario', if the logic of this process was followed to its conclusion, the remaining 3 billion or so peasants and poor farmers in Asia, Africa and Latin America would be replaced by 20 million capitalist farmers; if GDP grew at an unrealistic 7 percent annually for 50 years, capitalism could not integrate even a third of this total into production.[31]

The specificity of the post-war boom

The post-World War II boom (whose causes are explored in more depth in 'The accumulation of catastrophe'), depended among other things on the mass migration of agricultural labour into the new labour-intensive industries in the north and west of Europe, as well as migrations from former colonies and the 'Third World' into Europe and America. Even at the end of World War II large parts of Europe were still predominantly agricultural; in 1950 one working person in two was employed in agriculture in Spain, Portugal, Greece, Hungary and Poland; in Italy, two people in every five. Even in West Germany, 23 percent of the working population was still employed in agriculture. But by the 1970s this had dropped to 6.8 percent; only 16 percent of Italians worked on the land and 20 percent in Spain.[32] By definition, this could not be repeated.[33]

---

31   Ibid

32   Tony Judt, *Postwar. A history of Europe since 1945* (Penguin, 2005), p.327.

33   This is not to say migrant labour is no longer a significant factor today; in the capitalist heartlands of western Europe and North America migrant workers make up around 20 percent of the workforce (in the Arab states it is over 40 percent), with the majority concentrated in the service sector. Migrant labour tends to flow from the peripheries to the centre of the system, with the largest proportion from Asia; we can see this as the

The global restructuring of capitalist production from the 1980s

The effect of the global restructuring of capitalist production that began at the end of the 1970s was to replace labour-intensive industries in the traditional capitalist heartlands, which had become centres of working class militancy, with new capital-intensive industries that did not require large amounts of labour; to reorganise and where possible automate existing work processes, and shift production to parts of the world with low labour costs.

We can see this strategy – which took the form of a concerted bourgeois counter-offensive against the working class in the capitalist heartlands – as a demonstration of the general law in operation, in which the expulsion of labour, and the resulting growth of the 'industrial reserve army', was explicitly used, not only to reduce productive capacity and restore profitability, but above all to reinforce the domination of capital.

The breakdown of attempts at national autarky at the end of the 1980s, which was both a product of, and an active factor in, this bourgeois counter-offensive, in effect removed a barrier to the full operation of the general law at a global level, the resulting global reserve army becoming a definite 'lever' of capitalist accumulation, as Marx described.

From this we can conclude that there has definitely been a progressive exhaustion of counter-tendencies to the operation of the general law in capitalism's descent. But we still need to consider how more fundamental developments in this period have modified its operation.

State capitalism and the war economy

The general law was formulated by Marx partly to alert the working class to the brutal reality of a capitalist society based on free competition. But even in capitalism's ascent, free competition was more of an exception. The growth of state capitalism, which by its nature restricts free competition, is a clear sign that capitalism is becoming a barrier to its own further development.[34]

---

reserve army of labour in operation at a global level (ILO, *Global Estimates on International Migrant Workers, Results and Methodology, Third edition*, Executive Summary, 2020).

34 'As long as capital is weak, it still itself relies on the crutches of past modes of production, or of those which will pass with its rise. As soon as it feels strong, it throws away the crutches, and moves in accordance with its own laws. As soon as it begins to sense itself and become conscious of itself as a barrier to development, it seeks refuge in forms which, by restricting free competition, seem to make the rule of capital more perfect, but are at the same time the heralds of its dissolution and of the dissolution of

In the period of capitalism's descent or decline, state capitalism is in part a recognition by the capitalist class that the proletariat must increasingly be managed and controlled by the state, in the interest of ensuring continued accumulation and maintaining the domination of capital; the maintenance of the surplus population in this period becomes a necessary overhead and growing burden on capital, demanding increased state spending on social welfare and repressive measures to limit the dangerous political and social implications of the general law's workings.

State capitalism is from the beginning inseparable from a war economy, in a period characterised by sharpening imperialist antagonisms and wars, which also spells the end of the mass migration of labour that was essential to capitalism's rapid growth and expansion in the previous period; the overwhelming majority of the 50 million people who emigrated from Europe between 1820 and 1915, for example, went to the USA, where, with some exceptions (notably the explicitly racist 'Chinese Exclusion Act' of 1882), immigration was largely unrestricted up until World War I.

The irrationality of an obsolete system

The increasingly violent convulsions and crises of the system in this new period tend to cause explosive growth of the industrial reserve army, as in the catastrophic economic crisis of the 1930s. At the same time, in a period in which imperialist war becomes its permanent way of life, and having defeated the revolutionary struggles of the working class, capitalism is able to absorb this enlarged reserve army into the needs of the war economy, as part of the mobilisation of the working class for a new world war.

This was of course a preliminary to the slaughter of some 70 to 85 million people in World War II, which, far from performing some 'rational' function for the capitalist accumulation process, only confirms the irrationality of a system that, having become a barrier to its own further development, is now in an inexorable descent into barbarism. We are clearly no longer talking about the operation of a 'law' of capitalist accumulation in this situation, but fundamentally about the destruction of increasing numbers of human beings simply in order to prolong the death agony of an obsolete and increasingly destructive mode of production.

The resurgence of the class struggle in the 1960s and continued workers' resistance to the attacks of capital meant that, despite the deepening of the eco-

the mode of production resting on it.' (Marx, *Grundrisse*, Chapter on Capital, Section Two, Theories of Surplus Value (Penguin, 1973), p651

nomic crisis and intensified conflicts between the two rival imperialist blocs, unlike in the 1930s it was not possible for the bourgeoisie to mobilise the working class for a new world war, and therefore to absorb the growth of the surplus population into war production, ultimately to be massacred on the battlefields.

In the barbaric logic of its descent, capitalism could not destroy sufficient numbers of human beings to counteract the tendency of accumulation to create a growing population surplus to its own needs.

Conclusions

We set out to consider first of all whether Marx's 'general law of capitalist accumulation' was relevant in the period of capitalism's descent or decline. The growth of a surplus population in capitalism's decline has undoubtedly become complicated by demographic factors not observable at the time Marx was writing, namely falling fertility rates and rising life expectancy, which are resulting in an ageing working population. Inevitably it is also difficult in this period to separate the working of the general law from the specific effects of the return of the capitalist crisis in the 1960s and of the aggravation of capitalism's contradictions as a whole since the start of its descent. We have also identified some of the ways in which the evolution of capitalism has potentially modified the general law's operation in this period, specifically the development of state capitalism and a war economy, although we have far from exhausted this topic.

Nevertheless, empirical data on the size and composition of the working class today appears to give support to Marx's thesis that the more rapidly capitalism accumulates, the more it tends to produce a surplus population of workers, which forms an 'industrial reserve army of labour'. We also see supporting evidence for the growth of a consolidated surplus population, and of the pauperisation of the working class, in the trend towards precarious, low paid work, and the increase in the numbers of people living in urban slums, and those forced to flee their homes.

The creation of a 'global reserve army of labour', as a consequence of the breakdown of attempts at autarky in the 1980s, is perhaps the most powerful evidence we have for the relevance of the general law to our understanding of capitalism's period of descent or decline. In Marx's phrase, this acts as a 'lever' of accumulation, providing a pool of disposable labour power that enables global capital to keep wages low and ensure its domination of the working class. As Rosa Luxemburg argued, 'Capital [...] must be able to mobilise world labour power without restriction in order to utilise all productive forces of the globe – up to the limits imposed by a system of producing surplus value.'[35] The creation of a global reserve army, made possible by the breakdown of autarky in the 1980s, represents capitalism's final achievement of this goal, in the context of its descent into barbarism.

Far from being due to periodic crises or external factors, the creation of a global reserve army and the growth of a consolidated surplus population today are the products of the laws of capitalist accumulation themselves, which in the phase of capitalism's descent lead to the acceleration and qualitative deepening of capital's contradictions at all levels. Specifically, we have seen the progressive exhaustion of counter-tendencies to the operation of the 'general law': the lack of new external outlets, the accelerated destruction of the peasantry, and the unique and unrepeatable nature of periods of economic growth. As a result, the growth of capitalist accumulation in its descent is not only generating a numerically larger proletariat, and a surplus population of workers, but also a growing population absolutely surplus to the needs of accumulation, inexorably tending to reduce the working class as a whole to poverty and precariousness.

While there are no fixed limits to capitalist accumulation, the fact that a growing proportion of the world's population is becoming surplus to the requirements of capitalism, condemning billions of human beings to live in slums, extreme poverty and degradation, confirms that this mode of production has become a barrier to the further development of the productive forces and is descending deeper into barbarism.

To put it another way, the definitive fettering of the productive forces by capitalist social relations expresses itself, in capitalist terms, in the **inexorable growth of the waste of labour power due to the laws of accumulation itself**; and in more fundamental terms in the waste of the potential of human beings to transform the world and themselves through the use of all their physical and mental powers. This colossal, growing waste of human labour – a totally unnecessary waste given the development of science and human knowledge – demonstrates the historic bankruptcy of capital and the necessity for the revolutionary action of the proletariat to destroy it.

What better illustration of capital's bankruptcy than the fact that today, for a growing proportion of the world's population, it can no longer even offer the 'torment of labour' in the midst of chronic overproduction and unnecessary waste – only poverty and degradation:

> Thus the cities of the future, rather than being made out of glass and steel as envisioned by earlier generations of urbanists, are instead largely constructed out of crude brick, straw, recycled plastic, cement blocks, and scrap wood. Instead of cities of light soaring toward heaven, much of the

---

35   Rosa Luxemburg, *The Accumulation of Capital*, Chapter 26 (Routledge, 1963), p.362.

twenty-first-century urban world squats in squalor, surrounded by pollution, excrement, and decay. Indeed, the one billion city-dwellers who inhabit postmodern slums might well look back with envy at the ruins of the sturdy mud homes of Çatal Hüyük in Anatolia, erected at the very dawn of city life nine thousand years ago.[36]

---

36   Davis, *Planet of Slums,* p.19.

Appendix

Is the working class growing as a proportion of the working population in capitalism's descent?

We have seen that since 2000 at least, the working class appears to be growing as a proportion of the total number of people in employment: from 45 percent to 53 percent in 2019.[37]

The ICC in its pamphlet *The Decadence of Capitalism*, originally published in 1975, argues that World War I marked the end of the percentage growth of the working class in society. According to the ICC 'It is estimated that the proportion of the world population engaged in capitalist production was 10 percent in 1850. This proportion reached nearly 30 percent in 1914. But since the beginning of [the 20th] century this expansion has greatly declined in the industrialised countries.'[38]

The ICC uses a graph in Fritz Sternberg's 1951 book *Capitalism and Socialism on Trial* to claim that 'The number of German workers rose from 8 million in 1882 to 14 million in 1925, but their proportion in the working population, after having reached 50 percent in 1895, fell to 45 percent in 1925.' It then quotes Sternberg who claims: 'What was true of Germany was also true on an international scale. The working class percentage stabilised itself at round about 50 percent; in England it was rather more, in France and Germany it was rather less.'[39]

In general, we would logically expect the proportion of the working class in the population to grow rapidly in the 19th century, because obviously it was starting from a very low base. If capitalism continued to progressively expand across the globe during the 20th century, we would surely expect this proportion to continue to increase with the growth of accumulation, as capitalism expanded into all the remaining non-capitalist regions of the world and progressively integrated the peasantry and other non-capitalist strata into productive wage labour.

If we jump forward to 2000, allowing for differences in definitions and data collection, the figure of 53 percent we have cited suggests that the global working class has not grown significantly over the last century as a proportion of the

---

37   ILO, *World Employment Social Outlook, Trends*, 2020, pp.84-5.

38   ICC, *The Decadence of Capitalism*, 2nd edition, 2006, p.16.

39   Fritz Sternberg, *Capitalism and Socialism on Trial* (Gollancz, 1951), pp.102,103

working population, but has instead remained relatively static. This would tend to support the argument that capitalism is no longer a progressive mode of production. However, the evidence cited by Sternberg and the ICC is in our view not sufficient to draw such a conclusion, and we lack the data on trends in the intervening century; to coin a phrase, further research is necessary.

Capitalism versus the Environment
(Phillip Sutton)

The Age of Stupid

Introduction

In 2009 a film starring Pete Postlethwaite was released in which an old man in a devastated future looks back at the early 21st century and asks why humanity didn't try to save itself when it still had a chance. *The Age of Stupid*[1] is the film and it uses video clips and data from capitalism from our recent period to demonstrate the problems we face. Despite the myriad warnings of environmental disaster, our ruling class defiantly maintains their system of capital accumulation, profit making and class power. We are all passengers on this juggernaut running out of control. Today is indeed the age of stupid!

Whilst later in this article we draw attention to meteorites and asteroids and their potential impact on both the Earth and capitalism, in fact, the Earth has in the past experienced five extinctions of which only one is understood to have been caused by a meteorite and the remainder by climate change produced by increases in atmospheric carbon dioxide (CO_2) and methane. Since World War II however, the amount of CO_2 in the atmosphere has increased faster than at any time in history,[2] a fact that highlights capitalism's role in the process. As we enter the third decade of the 21st century, it is becoming ever clearer that capitalist production is now posing a threat to our own existence and even to life itself. As discussed elsewhere in this book, we face a catastrophe of accumulation.

Indeed a scientific report from 2022 suggests that, based on the amount of global warming already present, sea levels will increase by 10 inches in the coming period simply because of the melting of the Greenland ice cap[3] alone. Pro-

---

1   *The Age of Stupid* (2009) <https://www.imdb.com/video/vi2332885785/?playlistId=tt1300563&ref_=tt_ov_vi> [accessed 29.12.22]

2   D Wallace-Wells, *The Uninhabitable Earth*, (London: Penguin 2019).

3   *The Guardian*, 'Major sea-level rise caused by melting of Greenland ice cap is "now inevitable"', 29.8.22 <https://www.theguardian.com/environment/2022/aug/29/major-sea-level-rise-caused-by-melting-of-greenland-ice-cap-is-now-inevitable-27cm-cli-

duction has grown to the point that it now comprises a destructive element in human society. And what is more, the danger we are facing today is not that the world is moving to a new normal, but that the ecosystem is being destabilised and there will be no normal from hereon in, just a deteriorating ecosystem!

Marxists have been inclined to focus on the historical development of the productive forces as a positive sign of the development of humanity throughout the centuries, however brutal the modes of production themselves have been. Each mode of production represents the exploitation of labour, whether the workers were called slaves, serfs or wage labourers, by the power of the ruling classes which enjoy the wealth created. Marx in fact saw capitalism as the culmination of a process because wage labour and the use of money mean this society is free of formalised or legalised roles for individuals.

This article therefore intends to draw out Marx's view of the relationship between production and nature, and by updating our understanding of how this relationship is developing, to provide at least the basis for understanding the only way forward for humanity.

As a result of the impact that the environmentalist movement has had on society we can find many, many books about ecology which address the problems that the planet and humanity are faced with. These books are important in the sense that it is all too easy for us to continue our merry lives without recognising that the dangers we face are multiplied across the planet and that what is happening in Africa, Asia, Antarctica and the Atlantic is going to have a greater and greater impact on all of us with a relatively short space of time, if it has not done so already.

These books, the TV programmes and newspaper articles have already played a part in educating public awareness, despite their tendency to believe that capitalism can provide solutions, so in this book we intend to bring out some key considerations of the decline of capitalism and to emphasise how badly capitalism is affecting the world. Filmmakers may call it the age of stupid but scientists call this the age of the anthropocene, that is the period when humanity is having a major impact on the earth's ecosystems; unfortunately this does not mean humanity is in control or managing the environment.

We do not propose to investigate the whole of human history, nor the totality of its impact on the planet. Most sources are clear that significant changes in the environment began with the start of the industrial revolution but what is particularly important is that since the 1950s the resulting problems have undergone a major escalation. It is on this period, the current period of the last 70

mate> [accessed 30.12.22]. The report itself is available at Box, J.E., Hubbard, A., Bahr, D.B. et al. Greenland ice sheet climate disequilibrium and committed sea-level rise. *Nat. Clim. Chang.* (2022). <https://doi.org/10.1038/s41558-022-01441-2>

years, that we wish to focus and it is in this period that we have seen an almost exponential growth of industry, population, and environmental crises. It is hard in the 2020s to be totally unaware of the environmental issues but for most of us the science is confusing and humanity is in danger of being overcome by 'environmental fatigue' because there have been warnings for decades about what might or what will happen. It is true, we are at a point where no major catastrophe has occurred despite the ongoing problems that are emerging and it may be true that technological improvements may alleviate some issues (e.g. green energies, carbon extraction, deflection of the sun's rays) however we need to face up to and recognise the seriousness of the overall ecological threats and identify that capitalism is the cause. The solution may not be short term but it can only involve a change of society to a society without money and without classes. This chapter therefore will try to put in perspective the effects of environmental issues that face humanity and to present a marxist framework for understanding what is happening and what the prospects for humanity are.

Finally, it must be said here that this article on the environment is grounded on ideas discussed in other parts of this book. The chapter on 'Historical Materialism and the Descent of Capitalism' discusses our views of Marx's theory of historical development, the chapter on 'The Accumulation of Catastrophe' illustrates the relationship of decadence to the economic contradictions of capitalism, including especially a section on the 'Great Acceleration' since World War II, while the chapter on 'Humanity in Nature' discusses the impact of class societies on agriculture and how capitalism has come to impact nature as a whole.

Marxism and Ecology

Ecology is perhaps still not a topic that is generally seen as central to Marx's analysis of capitalist society. Marx is seen as an economist, a philosopher, or a politician and we, as marxists, focused on waged labour, technology and surplus value as the drivers of the capitalist system. At the end of the 20th century however, authors like Paul Burkett and John Bellamy Foster began to highlight the ecological aspect of Marx's writing and indeed that of marxists like Bukharin.

The chapter on 'Historical Materialism and the Descent of Capitalism' explains Marx's view that the natural world is an external factor that is also essential to production, in fact a productive force with a special role to play. Whilst saying that man is part of nature, Marx also recognised that humanity has nature outside itself. This chapter develops this argument concerning the clash between the environment and capitalist society as well as humanity.

A little research reveals that Marx wrote a lot about the relationship of production and the environment even if he produced no major writings explicitly on the topic. As discussed in 'Humanity and Nature', he saw production as conducting robbery of the Earth's resources because no payment was made. There is no cost in obtaining these resources as the cost to industry is purely the cost of labour and the cost of machinery required to do the job and no reparations are paid to the planet in the form of replacement of resources. It is pure and simple robbery of the planet's resources.

Another author, Kohei Saito, recently presented a book on the same topic and explains:

> Modern discussions of ecology owe a great debt to Marx's deep insight into the fundamental nature of a society of generalised commodity production. He shows that value as the mediator of the transhistorical metabolism between humans and nature cannot generate the material conditions for sustainable production. Rather, it causes rifts in the process of material reproduction. When value becomes the dominant subject of social production as capital, it only strengthens the disturbances and disruptions of that metabolism, so that both humanity and nature suffer from various disharmonies. This includes overwork as well as physical and mental illness and deformations with regards to human beings; desertification, devastation of natural resources, and extinction of species with regards to nature. According to Marx, this disruption of the metabolism of human beings and nature ultimately poses material limits to the measureless drive to capital accumulation and demands that humans have a more conscious interaction with their environment.[4]

What is evident is that Marx and Engels included in their studies of the natural sciences a particular interest in agriculture, deforestation and water management and whether or not this led to the deterioration of the soil. They were influenced by scientists such as Leibig[5], Johnson[6] and Fraas[7]. Saito points out that:

> ...we have seen in Marx's pre-1867 notebooks how Liebig's *Agricultural Chemistry* and Johnson's *Notes on North America* contributed to his project on political economy in an ecological sense. In opposition to his earlier writings, Marx came to clearly recognize natural limits as such, parting

---

4   Kohei Saito, 'Conclusion' in *Capital, Nature and the Unfinished Critique of Political Economy* (2017) <https://libcom.org/library/karl-marx-s-ecosocialism-capital-nature-unfinished-critique-political-economy> [accessed 29.12.22]

5   Justus von Liebig (1803-1873), German scientist who made major contributions to agricultural and biological chemistry, and is considered one of the principal founders of organic chemistry.

6   Samuel Johnson (1830-1909), American agricultural chemist.

7   Karl Fraas (1810-1875), German botanist and agriculturist.

from a myth of an unlimited technologically driven increase in production. He also treated the exhaustion and deterioration of natural fertility and natural resources as a contradiction between nature and capital, which capital can never completely overcome, despite its endless endeavours to appropriate labour power and natural wealth. [8]

Marx talks of labour as the metabolism between production and nature which involves the use of plant and animal life and the extraction of raw materials supplied by nature and used by human society.

It's pretty obvious when you think about it. You cannot produce anything without the resources provided by the environment in which we live. This is something that Marx and indeed other revolutionaries[9] from the early 20th century recognised. It has however been mostly put aside in the attempts by left communists to recover a revolutionary framework during the long period of counter-revolution since the 1920s. Indeed it can be said that previously society has not needed to concern itself with its impact on the environment. It is only in the last few decades that the necessity of recovering this particular concept has become evident as the industrial world collides with the natural world and threatens the existence of both humanity and nature.

According to JB Foster, Engels argued that:

>...capitalism was 'squandering' the world's natural resources, including fossil fuels. He indicated that urban pollution, desertification, deforestation, exhaustion of the soil, and (regional) climate change were all the result of unplanned, uncontrolled, destructive forms of production, most evident in the capitalist commodity economy. In line with Marx, and Liebig, he pointed to London's enormous sewage problem as a manifestation of the metabolic rift, which removed the nutrients from the soil and shipped them one-way to the overcrowded cities where they became a source of pollution.[10] He underscored the class basis of the spread of the periodic epidemics of smallpox, cholera, typhus, typhoid, tuberculosis, scarlet fever, whooping cough, and other contagious diseases that were affecting the environmental conditions of the working class, along with poor nutrition, overwork, exposure to toxics at work, and workplace injuries of all kinds. He highlighted, based on the new science of thermodynamics, that historical ecological change was irreversible and that humanity's own survival was ultimately in question.[11] In terms of the current rela-

---

8 Kohei Saito, chapter 6, (2017) <https://libcom.org/library/karl-marx-s-ecosocialism-capital-nature-unfinished-critique-political-economy> [accessed 29.12.22]

9 See Bukharin's and Gorter's writings on Historical Materialism.

10 Engels, *The Housing Question* (Moscow: Progress Publishers. 1975), p.92

11 On Engels's approach to thermodynamics, see John Bellamy Foster and Paul Burkett, *Marx and the Earth* (Chicago: Haymarket, 2016), p.137–203.

tions of production and the environment, he wrote of a society faced with ruin or revolution.[12]

Bukharin in particular wrote an important chapter on nature in *Historical Materialism*[13] in which he not only discussed the growth of accumulation and of the population but also provided further support for Marx's recognition of the exchange between production and nature and consequently human society's absolute reliance on the external environment. Human society does not exist in empty space and if it does not adapt to its environment it will not last long.

This is particularly interesting in that whilst Bukharin is presumably commenting on past societies which failed to develop into new modes of production (e.g. Aztecs, Mayans, Bablyon, Egypt, China and so on), he is suggesting not that their failure is a denial of historical materialism but rather a proof of its validity. We should also see its application to the future because unless the working class intervenes, capitalism can only fail to solve environmental crises.

Bukharin drew the conclusion that alterations in modes of production (whether in terms of progress, stagnation, or destruction of the system) were to be found in their relationships with their environment. The clash of production growth and the environment in capitalism is clearly becoming more dangerous and is likely to be one, if not the major, issue determining the future of capitalist development today. It is becoming more likely to be at the root of any future wars and economic crises as it is just too impactful on everything in society today. Capitalism has been poisoning the earth,[14] but now key thresholds (melting of glaciers, global warming, diversity loss, deforestation) are being crossed and they will come to dominate the world's political and economic evolution.

> In the current mode of production the perennial drive to increase capital is a necessity, not one political option amongst many. Social reproduction itself is inextricably linked to the process of capital growth. Market logic therefore conditions every political choice, including the crucial environmental and climate issue: how costly might the energy transition path be? What would such a choice entail for a state's productive and competitive capacity? What are the geopolitical consequences?[15]

---

12   JB Foster, 'Engels's Dialectics of Nature in the Anthropocene' in *Monthly Review* Vol 72 No6 Chapter: 'Engels in the Anthropocene' (2020) <https://monthlyreview.org/2020/11/01/engelss-dialectics-of-nature-in-the-anthropocene/#en26backlink> [accessed 30.12.22] (references in the original)

13   Bukharin, *Historical Materialism*, Chapter 4.

14   CD Ward, 'Capitalism is poisoning the Earth' in ICC *International Review* no. 63, (2006) <https://en.internationalism.org/ir/63> [accessed 30.12.22]

15   *Battaglia Comunista*, 'Marginal Notes on COP26 in Glasgow', (2021) <http://www.leftcom.org/en/articles/2021-12-08/marginal-notes-on-cop26-in-glasgow> [accessed 30.12.22]

What Marx and Bukharin both identify is that the planet exists but is not created by human society. It is external to whatever the conjunctural mode of production is, but the various modes of production establish different relationships with it and impact upon it in different ways. So whilst we must identify the world market as the completion of capital's ascendant period, i.e. it has expanded geographically as far as it can go, the planet itself remains as a barrier, an external environment which humanity exploits in new and different ways as the technology and size of humanity and capitalism develops and expands.

> Labour is, in the first place, a process in which both man and Nature participate, and in which man of his own accord starts, regulates, and controls the material reactions between himself and Nature. He opposes himself to Nature as one of her own forces, setting in motion arms and legs, head and hands, the natural forces of his body, in order to appropriate Nature's productions in a form adapted to his own wants.[16]

The issue of ecology and the environment clearly poses a major limitation for capitalism as an external fetter on the growth of the productive forces themselves. This limitation is obviously not an internal contradiction (see 'Historical Materialism and the Descent of Capitalism'), it is not a product of decline or obsolescence, but it may well turn out to be the cause of the end of capitalism as it poses a very real contradiction between capitalism's growth and the ecological system in which we live.

The materials that humanity extracts from the world have no cost in themselves so capitalism derives a significant advantage from this contribution to the growth of the economy. However, as discussed in the Chapter on 'Humanity in Nature', there is a labour cost to their extraction so in that sense capital has a price to pay for these materials in terms of labour and machinery.

> All production is appropriation of nature on the part of an individual within and through a specific form of society. In this sense it is a tautology to say that property (appropriation) is a precondition of production.[17]

Even in his own time, Marx was aware that this metabolism between man and nature must have an overall negative effect on nature. The fertility of the soil and the environment was and is still dependent on how they are used but the capitalist system depends on continual growth to obtain profits and this profit also depends on the robbery of the planet's resources. Persuading capit-

16   Marx, *Capital* Volume 1 Chapter 7, (1867): <https://www.marxists.org/archive/marx/works/1867-c1/ch07.htm> [accessed 30.12.22]

17   Marx, *Grundrisse* Chapter 1 (1857) < https://www.marxists.org/archive/marx/works/1857/grundrisse/ch01.htm> [accessed 30.12.22]

alists to forego these free resources in favour of paying for and maintaining them is just not how capitalism works.[18]

Today, after a further 150 years of development, we can see that this approach to nature is having a massively negative impact on the world and is becoming critical to our survival. Large scale industry, industrial agriculture and industrial fishing are now affecting all aspects of the environment both above and below ground, and in the oceans. Worse still, many of these consequences will take a long time to cure even if major social changes were to happen straight away.

In recent years the importance of this analysis has been recognised by current Left Communist groups as they attempt to understand current trends and get to grips with what is happening to capitalism.

> In the same way that the workers' labour power is commodified, our most intimate needs and feelings are seen as potential markets, so capitalism sees nature as a vast warehouse that can be robbed and ransacked at will in order to fuel the juggernaut of accumulation. We are now seeing the ultimate consequences of the illusion of ruling over nature 'like a conqueror over a foreign people': it can only lead to 'nature taking its revenge…' on a scale far greater than in any previous civilisation, since this 'revenge' could culminate in the extinction of humanity itself.[19]

Marx's view that capitalism is production for profit and for exchange value rather than use value also presents the basic conundrum that we are facing now; continual growth in a finite world is impossible.

> The universal advent of production for the market and for profit means that the tendency for the results of production to escape the control of the producer has reached its ultimate point; moreover, the capitalist exploiter himself, though benefiting from the proceeds of exploitation, is also driven by the remorseless competition for profits, and is, in the final analysis, merely the personification of capital. We are thus confronted with a mode of production which is like a juggernaut that is running out of control and threatening to crush exploiter and exploited alike. Because capitalism is driven by the remorseless demands of accumulation (what it

---

18   While we accept that capitalism does take some measures such as pollution controls, wildlife reserves, carbon credits, banning of toxic substances and so forth, these are relatively minor actions compared to the major problems facing the environment today and to the behaviour of industry in defiance of global warming objectives. National divisions in policy also emphasise the 'nation as fetter' as discussed in 'Historical Materialism and the Decline of Capitalism'.

19   ICC, 'Supplement on Ecology' < https://en.internationalism.org/files/en/try_this_climate_supplement_.pdf> p4 [accessed 30.12.22]

calls 'economic growth'), it can never arrive at a rational, global control of the productive process, geared to the long-term interests of humanity.[20]

Capitalism from the 1950s Onwards and its Impact on the Environment

The chapter entitled 'The Accumulation of Catastrophe' introduces the concept of the 'Great Acceleration' and discusses the major growth of the economy[21] and social change in capitalist society following World War II. In this section we will focus more on the impact of this growth on the environment (see Figures 19 and 20) and indeed the lack of measures by capitalism to protect the planet's ecosystems.

> It is widely recognized in contemporary science (though not yet official) that the Holocene epoch in geological time, extending back almost twelve thousand years, has come to an end, beginning in the 1950s, displaced by the current Anthropocene epoch. The onset of the Anthropocene was brought about by a Great Acceleration in the anthropogenic impacts on the environment, such that the scale of the human economy has now come to rival the major biogeochemical cycles of the planet itself, resulting in rifts in the planetary boundaries that define the Earth System as a safe home for humanity.[22]

From the 1950s onwards, the expansion of industry and population, and the increase in productivity, have led to an enormous expansion in the need for mineral resources, energy and foodstuffs. Ever more mining, gas and oil extraction, overfishing[23] and intensive use of pesticides are leaving lasting sores on the earth. The technological developments of this period from a base of mech-

---

20 CD Ward, 'Capitalism is poisoning the Earth' in ICC *International Review* no.63 (1990) <https://en.internationalism.org/ir/63_pollution> [accessed 30.12.22]

21 The economic crises of the 1960s to the 2008 and even World War II appear as little more than passing setbacks, since it is apparent that both the growth of world GDP and world population has in the meantime continued apace. In fact only the pandemic of 2021 caused any significant drop in world production and even that was only in the region of 5%. See *Our World in Data* at <https://ourworldindata.org/grapher/world-gdp-over-the-last-two-millennia> [accessed 30.12.22]

22 JB Foster, 'Engels's Dialectics of Nature in the Anthropocene' in *Monthly Review* Vol 72 no.6 Chapter 'Engels in the Anthropocene' (2020) <https://monthlyreview.org/2020/11/01/engelss-dialectics-of-nature-in-the-anthropocene/#en26backlink> [accessed 30.12.22]

23 A recent report from the World Wildlife Fund indicates a nearly 50% decline in marine life populations between 1970 and 2012. <https://edition.cnn.com/2015/09/17/world/oceans-report/index.html> [accessed 30.12.22]

anical engineering have now transformed production, products and lifestyles with major developments in micro-electronics, digital communications, high technology materials, biotechnology, nuclear energy and so forth. This has led to the creation of many new industries and markets such as for electronic consumer goods, household goods, toys, computer equipment, stereos, LPs and CDs, plastics, retail parks as well as major services such as insurance and credit companies, personal banking, streaming services and employment bureaux.

A consequence of this expansion of industry and social need is that greenhouse gases are being produced in enormous quantities. The production of materials such as concrete, cement, steel, glass and plastic all generate significant carbon dioxide emissions, and to change this situation and reduce greenhouse gas emissions to zero will require therefore not only significant technological change but also substantial social change.

The major changes in this period are not just measured by industry but also by lifestyle changes. The 1950s was the era of Lowry's paintings of factories, chimneys and terraced houses, and of the street photographers Cartier-Bresson and Doisneau. There was a lack of telephone systems let alone mobile phones, no television, no instantaneous news reports or pictures from around the world, no central heating, no double glazing, no internet, no computers. There were still only simple but unreliable cars, steam trains, telegrams, manual typewriters, open coal fires, outside toilets, horses on the roads, newspapers that took days to report the news, rationing of food because of supply shortages. The 'consumer society' has led to centralised shopping malls and cafes becoming a leisure industry, local shops are dying off and there is a significant increase in the use of energy, in the availability of household and general consumer goods and in the expansion of the transport industry for both leisure and commercial purposes. Furthermore, the production of food has been particularly distorted by the profit motive and what agriculture perceives as customer needs has led to the destruction of forests, the elimination of wildlife and animal diversity, the production of plant and animal foodstuffs which requires more calories than the crop actually provides for humanity. Agriculture is now one of the primary producers of greenhouse gases.

Global Change and the Earth System - Executive Summary

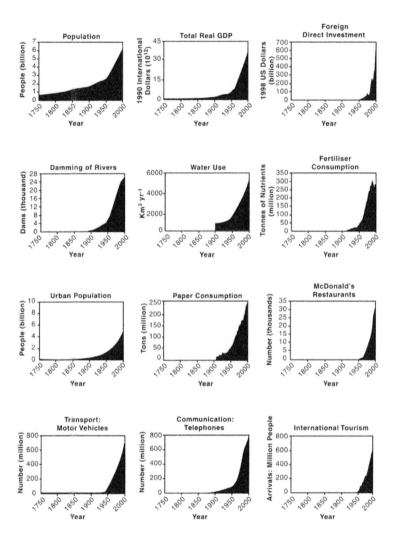

Figure 19: Global changes - 1

The Human Footprint, Global Change and the Earth System - Executive Summary, Chapter: The Anthropocene Era, (2004), <http://www.igbp.net/download/18.1b8ae20512db692f2a680007761/1376383137895/IGBP_ExecSummary_eng.pdf> [accessed 30.12.22] (See this text for the original sources of the individual graphs)

Global Change and the Earth System - Executive Summary

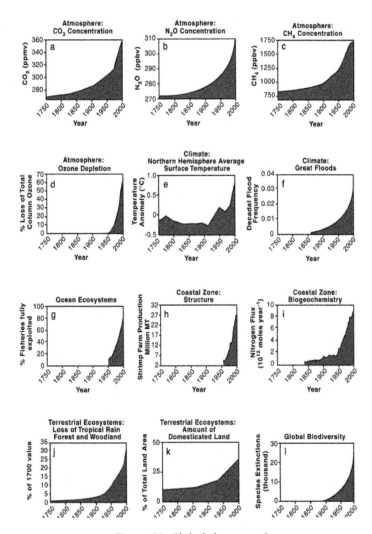

Figure 20: Global changes - 2

We tend to see this as progress and as enhancements to life and it is hard to argue against this in some cases, but it is all at a cost, and in ecological terms this progress demands excavating the planet for new and rarer materials and the disposal of increased waste material somewhere. In this process we have become totally adapted to a throwaway culture instead of a repair culture. Even the fact that we only build cars, buildings, household goods to last a relatively short period of time, means not only a high wastage of Earth's resources, but also the increased generation of climate warming gases. In this last period, plastics have conquered the earth and global warming has become a cata-strophe in waiting. The rapid changes since World War II have been enormous, yet at the cost of still greater impact on the planet's ecology.

A report written in 2019 for the Society for Environmental Sustainability provides a substantial summary of deteriorating conditions since the 1950s.

> Around 200,000 years ago, *Homo sapiens* evolved and started the great civilizations on the planet. Study suggests that the human population is only 0.01% of all the life forms on Earth. This shows how the existence of humans is just a miniscule part if we compare it with the existence of our planet or of the presence of life on earth. But if we go through the events particularly in the last 10,000 years (of recorded history of man-kind), it becomes clear that the presence of humans on earth brought sev-eral changes in both the biological and non-biological components. Most of the striking changes have appeared in the last 50 years or so. According to reports, humans have destroyed about 83% of wild mammals and half the species of plants to date. On the whole, humans have consumed 30% of the known resources resulting in scarcer ecosystem services for future generations. If these trends continue, the Earth will soon be experiencing mass extinctions and we will be left with an even more degraded planet. [24]

The graphs entitled 'Global Changes' (see Figures 19 and 20) provide a simple graphic illustrating a range of data about the changes during this period, giving a sense of the impact on our planet. Thereby they also demonstrate a clear correlation between the enormous expansion of production and popula-tion growth since the 1950s with the escalation of the environmental dangers facing us. See also the Appendix for a chart of temperature changes since the 19th century.

What is the significance of these changes?

At root, this is just the way capitalism works – an increasing scale of pro-duction, increasing populations and new technologies are the automatic con-sequence of competition and the need for profit. However what must be recog-

---

24   Arora, N. Earth: '50 years challenge'. *Environmental Sustainability* 2, 1–3, 2019, <https://doi.org/10.1007/s42398-019-00053-5> [accessed 30.12.22]

nised is that we have reached a stage where this growth of capitalist society is having a much greater and more destructive impact on our environment.

The scale of the development in the past seventy years is just too great for the planet to cope with and what is happening is that this rapid growth of humanity and of the economy is generating a conflict between that growth and the environment which calls into question the capacity of humanity, and the planet's ecology, to survive. What is worse is that it's already too late to solve all the problems with any ease, for example, capitalism did ban PCBs and CFCs back in the 1990s but they are still in the ecosystem and are still having an impact on us even now.

We have gone from recommending diesel cars instead of petrol driven cars and then back to preferring petrol cars despite their greater contributions to global warming. Now we are transferring to the use of electric cars but even when all cars are electric it will only reduce CO_2 emissions by about 10%. And what is the point of this, why because electricity is still profitable for capitalist industry. What will come next is the real question because electricity production and storage still remains as a destructive force against the environment. We need to look further forward than this.

What we have also to consider is that the ecological issues we face are not evidence of a decline in production by the capitalist system. It is evidence of the excessive growth of capitalism and, if anything, it is a cause of further decomposition of the capitalist system because this system of profit-making is not able to respond to the degradation of the planet. Some capitalists and politicians have certainly tried to change policies, and these attempts will no doubt continue, but for the most part the capitalist class will sit by twiddling its collective thumbs and worrying about profits as things go from bad to worse. Moreover, a particular issue currently is that the developed nations benefit from processes that are now having a negative impact upon the Third World countries and keep the people who live there in poverty as well as decimating vast areas. Desertification[25], droughts, flooding[26], storms[27], heatwaves[28] and the

---

25 Desertification does not seem important here in mainland Europe but it is a climate issue that is occurring or will occur on all continents including America, Europe and Australia. It affects more than half of Africa's land. For example, it is affecting about 80% of Kenya and a total of 7–10 million inhabitants residing in this area suffer from widespread acute poverty and other adverse effects of drought.

26 In Bangladesh, a low lying country, 20% of the land tends to flood every year and as a result rice paddies have been converted to crab and prawn nurseries. Bangladesh is one of the countries in danger of being submerged by sea level rises.

27 For example Madagascar in 2022 and the hurricanes of the Caribbean region over recent years.

28 For example in the USA and India during 2022.

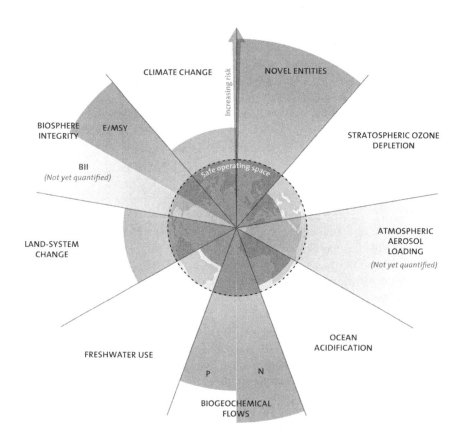

Figure 21: Planetary Boundaries

Stockholm Resilience Centre (see note 29)

loss of animal diversity affect primarily the underdeveloped regions of the world. Furthermore, because debt repayments to first world countries are increasing, many underdeveloped countries cannot afford to develop their health services let alone tackle global warming. Complaints by underdeveloped countries about the lack of support they receive to fight environmental issues, fall mostly on deaf ears. Africa for example represents 14% of the world population but issues only 5% of the greenhouse gas emissions and is suffering especially from the environmental changes.

It is true that marxist analysis focuses on the accumulation of capital in order to demonstrate the growth of the system, and that this accumulation is not the same as the figures for GDP provided by bourgeois economists. This is because GDP includes what are called unproductive industries which do not contribute to the future growth of capital. These industries include armaments, financial services, insurances, state administration, police and military spending which may be essential to the functioning of today's society but do not actually generate enlarged accumulation. However, since the 1950s, all of these activities have increased enormously along with actual capital accumulation and population increases, so what needs to be stressed is that it is the entirety of this economic activity that contributes to all the environmental threats that we are discussing in this book.

The escalation of industry's impact on the environment during the past decades will undoubtedly impact on workers' conditions across the world and will have to be a major concern of the working class movement if and when it tries to build a communist society.

Planetary Boundaries

Thresholds and tipping points are terms used to describe a point of no return where the environment cannot recover from the changes that have taken place in an ecosystem. The broader concept of 'planetary boundaries' was established by The Stockholm Resilience Centre (SRC) and these identified specific factors that affect the Earth's capacity to stay in ecological balance, which when broken will generate greater risks and impact the entire Earth system. It is important today to understand the threats posed by overstepping these thresholds. Figure 21 demonstrates graphically the nine planetary boundaries that were established and how some have already been overstepped.[29]

In this context we must now face the fact that the environmental thresholds confronting us are real, dangerous and imminent. Of these planetary boundaries, four are now said to have surpassed the threshold and three are linked specifically to an underlying condition, the excess of CO_2. These boundaries are not totally discrete and do tend to interact with one other.

Climate change

The presence of carbon in the air increases heat retention in the atmosphere and hence for the planet itself too. The concentration of carbon dioxide (CO_2) in the air was 280 ppm (parts per million) in the pre-industrial era.[30] It was said

---

29 Stockholm Resilience Centre, *Planetary Boundaries*, (2022) <www.stockholmresilience.org/research/planetary-boundaries.html> [accessed 31.12.22]

30 EcoMatcher, 'What are planetary boundaries and why are they significant?', 2018, <https://www.ecomatcher.com/what-are-planetary-boundaries-and-why-are-they-signi-

that atmospheric carbon concentration should not breach 350 ppm if the climate is to remain stable but we crossed that boundary in 1990, and hit 415 ppm in 2020. The last time this measure hit 500 ppm the world temperature was between 5 and 8 degrees hotter.

By the end of the 2020s, it will not be possible to hold back climate change to the levels that exist today and hence ocean levels are rising. The collapse of the Thwaites Glacier in Antarctica due to global warming is estimated to happen during the 2020s and will impact sea level significantly in the future.

We have reached a point at which the loss of summer polar sea-ice is almost certainly irreversible.

We are likely to cross the threshold for dangerous warming (+1.5°C) between 2027 and 2042[31] and it is generally accepted that we are unlikely to keep warming down to 2°C. It should be noted also that the levels of carbon in the atmosphere are cumulative so all new emissions make the problem of global warming worse: zero emissions as a target is no longer enough.

The Appendices contain an analysis of which industries contribute most to greenhouse gas emissions. One of the key elements to be noted is that energy production and usage is the largest source of global warming and it is therefore the development of new energy sources that will be key to our future – as long as it doesn't come too late.

Novel entities & Chemical pollution

Novel Entities are chemical products used in manufacturing that are unknown in nature and have generally unknown effects on the environment. It is estimated there are about 350,000 of these entities on the world market.[32] One group of these novel entities are PFAS (Perfluoroalkyl and Polyfluoroalkyl Substances) which are carbon-fluorine compounds used in products like teflon.[33] Used in many everyday products, they are highly persistent and find their way into the air, soil and water, and then inevitably into the whole life cycle.

---

ficant/> [accessed 31.12.22]

31 World Economic Forum, 'Earth could cross the global warming threshold as soon as 2027', 2021,<https://www.weforum.org/agenda/2021/01/global-warming-threshold-reached-by-2027> [accessed 31.12.22]

32 You Matter, 'Planetary boundaries: chemical pollution has now passed the safe limit for humanity' (2022) <https://youmatter.world/en/planetary-boundaries-chemical-pollution-novel-entities/> [accessed 31.12.22]

33 See the article on PFAS published by the US National Institute of Environmental Health Sciences: <https://www.niehs.nih.gov/health/topics/agents/pfc/index.cfm>

There has been a 50-fold increase in the production of chemicals since 1950. This is projected to triple again by 2050. Plastic production alone increased 79% between 2000 and 2015.[34]

Half of all plastics ever manufactured have been made in the last 15 years. Production increased exponentially, from 2.3 million tons in 1950 to 448 million tons by 2015. Production is expected to double by 2050. Not only is the production of plastic one of the most intensive in terms of greenhouse gas emissions, every year about 8 million tons of plastic waste escapes into the oceans from coastal nations.[35]

Biosphere Integrity (biodiversity loss)

Humanity's demands for water, mineral resources and land are having a major impact on animal life across the planet.

E/MSY[36] (see Figure 21) is the extinction rate and it is said it should not exceed ten species per million per year.

According to the World Wildlife Fund populations of mammals, birds, amphibians, reptiles and fish declined by 68% on average between 1970 and 2016 whilst humanity doubled (see Appendix 3). Furthermore, whilst humans account for 33% of animal life by weight, livestock amounts as high as 67% and wildlife is merely 1%.[37]

BII (see Figure 21) is the abbreviation for Biodiversity Intactness Index and is a measure of the reduction of world wildlife as opposed to the level of actual extinctions.

Ocean acidification

Ocean Acidificiation is a product of global warming because 25% of CO_2 emitted ends up in the seas. Also global warming means that ocean temperatures rise and this also increases acidity levels which impacts on coral, plankton and sea life in general and therefore threatens species diversity.[38] This process is not

---

34   Stockholm Resilience Centre, 'Planetary Boundaries', <https://www.stockholmresili-ence.org/research/research-news/2022-01-18-safe-planetary-boundary-for-pollut-ants-including-plastics-exceeded-say-researchers.html> [accessed 31.12.22]

35   *National Geographic*, 'The world's plastic pollution crisis explained' (2019) <https://www.nationalgeographic.com/environment/article/plastic-pollution> [accessed 31.12.22]

36   Extinctions per million species-years

37   *Population Matters*, 'Biodiversity' (2022), <https://populationmatters.org/biodiversity> [accessed 31.12.22]

38   'Highlighting that the ocean connects us all – Secretary-General Guterres said that be-

well understood but it appears that levels of ocean acidification have almost reached the planetary threshold and are therefore likely to impact humanity's diet. Furthermore, the availability of sea food has dramatically decreased due to overfishing by large fleets of industrial trawlers.

Land-use change

It is said that deforestation should not be allowed to exceed 25% of the Earth's land surface. Already, the expansion of agriculture is leading to serious reductions in biodiversity, and this also impacts on water flows.

Topsoil is vital for agriculture, since this is where 95% of food crops grow. It takes about 1000 years to build 3cm of topsoil, and yet it is being continually degraded by agricultural chemicals, deforestation and global warming.[39] It is effectively a non-renewable resource that is degrading rapidly. The UN even suggests this is a more serious problem than global warming as soil may now only last less than 60 years.[40]

It is also believed that rising levels of CO_2 may increase plant growth, but only at the cost of reduced nutritional value. It is also suggested that for each 1 degree of global warming, soil becomes 10% less fertile.

Globally, capitalism produces enough calories, i.e. food, to keep the whole world healthy and fed but it is wasted by unfair distribution, use of biofuels, household waste and, most absurdly, by using it to feed animals who produce less calories as foods for humanity than they eat[41]. Meats and dairy foods should be considered as luxuries and production reduced but there is no sign that capitalism can do that since these goods are highly profitable.

cause we have taken the ocean for granted, today, we face an "Ocean Emergency" and that the tide must be turned. Our failure to care for the ocean will have ripple effects across the entire 2030 Agenda' from a speech by Antonio Guterres to a UN Ocean Conference June 2022, <https://news.un.org/en/story/2022/06/112140>.

39   *Scientific American*, 'Only 60 Years of Farming Left If Soil Degradation Continues' (2014), <https://www.scientificamerican.com/article/only-60-years-of-farming-left-if-soil-degradation-continues/> [accessed 31.12.22]

40   United Nations Food and Agriculture Organisation, International Year of Soils 2015 <https://www.fao.org/soils-2015/events/detail/en/c/338738/> [accessed 31.12.22]

41   Mike Berners-Lee, *There is No Planet B*, (Cambridge University Press, 2019)

Biochemical pollution
(Nitrogen and phosphorus loading)

This is the accumulation of toxic, long term pollutants, heavy metals and radio-active substances which scientists are concerned may represent a risk to humanity as well as animal life. However at present no accurate thresholds have been determined.

Nitrogen and phosphorus are important agricultural chemicals which nevertheless, and along with animal waste, flow out into rivers and seas and have major consequences for sea life and soil content. Furthermore, their production contributes to global warming.

Freshwater usage

Freshwater is a limited resource and its availability is being reduced so it is estimated that half a billion people will be experiencing freshwater shortage by 2050.

> Only 3% of the Earth's water is freshwater, and two-thirds of that is stored in glaciers, leaving just 1% in rivers and streams or underground. The problem is that as humanity continues to grow (especially in arid urban environments like Los Angeles, Phoenix, or Tripoli), the sources of freshwater we use are being depleted faster than they can be replenished. Much of the water we use, 70%, is for agriculture; industry and consumer products account for another 20%.[42]

The loss of glaciers reduces the amount of freshwater available because it drains into the sea and contributes to an overall reduction in freshwater for humanity. The water bottling companies appear proud of providing healthy drinks but what they do is drain the aquifer[43] often for free and sell plastic bottled water at significant profits. Nestlé, the largest bottled water provider in the world, buys up cheap water resources in US, Canada, New Zealand, Africa, Pakistan

---

42 Mongabay, 'We've crossed four of nine planetary boundaries. What does this mean?' (2021) <https://news.mongabay.com/2021/09/weve-crossed-four-of-nine-planetary-boundaries-what-does-this-mean/> [accessed 31.12.22]

43 'The Ogallala Aquifer [in the USA], the vast underground reservoir that gives life to these [high plains] fields, is disappearing. In some places, the groundwater is already gone. This is the breadbasket of America – the region that supplies at least one fifth of the total annual U.S. agricultural harvest. If the aquifer goes dry, more than $20 billion worth of food and fiber will vanish from the world's markets. And scientists say it will take natural processes 6,000 years to refill the reservoir'. From *Scientific American*, 'The Ogallala Aquifer: Saving a Vital U.S. Water Source', (1.10.2009) <https://www.scientificamerican.com/article/the-ogallala-aquifer> [accessed 31.12.22]

etc and sells it worldwide but not necessarily to the residents of the locality where it is produced, as people in places like Africa and Pakistan cannot afford it. Nestlé believes water is a need not a right so people must buy it from them.[44]

It is estimated that by 2050 over 5 billion people could be living in 'water stressed areas' and even by 2030 there could be 700 million people living in extreme water scarcity.[45]

Atmospheric aerosol loading

This is not a reference to the dangers of aerosol cans but to the entirety of microscopic particles of solids and liquids that exist or are emitted into the atmosphere.

These particles are generated by natural phenomena such as water spray, volcanic activities, plant pollen, fungal spores, and dust raised by winds but also by human activities such as mining, use of explosives, burning fossil fuels and wood, agriculture, the wearing down of tyres, and of course the household products we use.

Aerosol particles can damage human health due to variations in air quality and also climate through their impact on water cycles i.e. any sort of particles in the air will tend to accumulate water droplets and therefore create clouds and ultimately impact on rain and snow levels.

Ozone depletion

The ozone layer in the atmosphere is damaged by use of chlorine based chemicals. It protects us from UV radiation so its depletion is a great risk to human health as well as animal and marine life. UV radiation can cause cancers and eye cataracts. However, it is believed levels are being relatively well controlled at present.

In short...

Overall then the nine planetary boundaries are linked particularly to global warming and confirm just how real the danger posed to humanity is. As we are

---

44   TMV, 'Here's how Nestle is leaving millions in Pakistan, Nigeria and Flint without clean water' (2018), <https://themuslimvibe.com/muslim-current-affairs-news/heres-how-nestle-is-leaving-millions-pakistan-nigeria-and-flint-without-clean-water> [accessed 31.12.22]

45   *Population Matters*, 'Food and Water' (2022) <https://populationmatters.org/food-water> [accessed 31.12.22]

likely to cross the climate warming threshold within 10 years, it is a short term threat too.

Climate warming is created by changes decades in the past, not when the temperature actually changes, so planning and implementation of new measures is very important.

A one-degree global change is significant because it takes a vast amount of heat to warm all of the oceans, the atmosphere, and the land masses by that much. In the past, a one- to two-degree drop was all it took to plunge the Earth into the Little Ice Age. A five-degree drop was enough to bury a large part of North America under a towering mass of ice 20,000 years ago.[46]

The thresholds that confront us mean that climate change cannot be held back to the levels that exist today in the early 2020s. Sea levels are already rising, the seas are already overfished and acidification continues, freshwater is continually being disrupted by floods, droughts and the disappearance of gla-ciers. Ice melting in the Arctic and Antarctica is threatening climate change and sea level rises, the Jet Stream is changing the balance of air temperatures and the Atlantic Meridional Overturning Circulation (AMOC) is changing the bal-ance of ocean temperatures. Climate warming is increasing the impact of wild-fires, droughts and floods across the world.

Crossing these boundaries doesn't mean that the Earth's systems will imme-diately shut down. But it does mean we are entering a danger zone where there could be irreversible changes and eventually, if nothing is done, outright col-lapse. This is what is happening right now. According to the most recent data, we have already shot past four of the planetary boundaries: climate change, biodiversity loss, deforestation and biogeochemical flows. And ocean acidifica-tion is nearing the boundary.

There is now no doubt that we are living in the Anthropocene era which means that humanity has a decisive impact on the climate. Yet humanity is not in control of changes taking place. As mentioned previously, this has been evid-ent since the 1950s, yet what does capitalism do? Scientists, environmentalists and even some politicians publicise the problem but little has changed. Interna-tional conferences turn out statements and set objectives and you should judge for yourself whether these are honest, naive or hypocritical, but capitalism goes on making profits out of fossil fuels, 'alien' chemicals, water resources, land, meat and seafood. The production of fossil fuels, plastics, meat-based agricul-ture keeps on increasing instead and there has been no serious effort to keep to the scientifically established thresholds.

46 NASA Earth Observatory, 'World of Change: Global Temperatures' (2022). <https://earthobservatory.nasa.gov/world-of-change/global-temperatures> [accessed 31.12.22]

Capitalism's Response
to the Threat of Global Warming

As marxists, we do not believe capitalism is capable of solving the environmental issues it creates. This is firstly because it obtains for free the earth's resources it needs for production (although obviously it has to pay for labour and equipment to obtain them). Secondly it is a system based on profit so for production to take place the capitalist must be making a profit out of the goods produced. These two factors are key.

We must nevertheless first investigate the truth of the statement because it is also clear that capitalists and capitalism in general do take measures to correct some of the issues we have identified, and various bodies, both governmental and non governmental, have taken up specific tasks in the realm of the protection of biodiversity, creation of wildlife protection areas, smoke-free zones and accessibility to clean water. New technologies have been developed such as renewable methods of generating electricity, some pollution controls have been imposed on manufacturing, land has been protected from flooding, techniques for controlling soil degradation are being developed, transportation efficiencies have been introduced, technologies that may be able to extract carbon from the air and so on and so forth. Many organisations, international, national and local have studied related issues and implemented actions and produced reports that demand and even get attention from the world at large. The new generation that has grown up in the 21st century are far more aware of the impact of environmental crises than any previous generation.

Certainly there is more to list here which could be considered as positive reactions. However these measures are primarily local and regional and remain too limited. They do not represent a concerted international effort to solve issues. We need to look at what capitalism overall actually does in practice to tackle the global issues.

One thing to bear in mind here when looking at what the world's politicians and industries actually do is that scientists have been warning of the dangers of climate change for over a century. The first of them was Swedish scientist Svante Arrhenius who as early as 1896 identified the link between carbon dioxide in the atmosphere and global warming.[47] It was not until the 1950s that scientists' understanding of the issues came to the fore however and in 1985, for example, Carl Sagan gave an extremely clear analysis of the greenhouse effect in

---

47   *Live Science*, 'When did scientists first warn humanity about climate change?' December 12, 2021 <https://www.livescience.com/humans-first-warned-about-climate-change> [accessed 31.12.22]

a speech to the American Congress.[48] From this period in the late 80s, the pressure from scientists for changes in environmental policies grew. However despite the clarity of the scientists, the responses of the politicians and industrialists have been at best totally insufficient and at worst totally detrimental to the environment.

What was the Significance of the Kyoto, Paris and COP26 Agreements?

Does the importance given to these conferences on global warming show that national leaders are taking the problems seriously?

The main significance of the Kyoto and Paris agreements was that they brought together almost all countries in agreements to set targets for limiting greenhouse gas emissions. In this respect, the Kyoto Protocol was the first of its kind. The Paris conference was meant to assess progress and set legally binding targets. The COP26 in 2022 (and yes it does mean there have been 26 annual meetings) was again due to assess progress but also to establish the Glasgow Climate Pact[49] which would agree to more specific steps to achieving targets.

The propaganda surrounding COP26 was indeed impressive as it was meant to achieve such a significant step in limiting global warming, but did it succeed in anything more than putting on a good show?

Well, first of all look at what the UN General Secretary said later in 2022 on the publication of the latest report by the Intergovernmental Panel on Climate Change (IPCC):

> UN secretary-general Antonio Guterres called investing in new infrastructure relating to fossil fuels, which are behind the continuing rise in planet-heating greenhouse gases, 'moral and economic madness'. 'Climate activists are sometimes depicted as dangerous radicals', he said. 'But the truly dangerous radicals are the countries that are increasing production of fossil fuels'. Mr Guterres called the latest IPCC report 'a litany of broken climate promises' [...] 'We are on a fast track to climate disaster: major

---

48 C Sagan, 'Speech on the Greenhouse Effect, to the US Senate', 1985 <https://www.c-span.org/video/?c4993366/carl-sagan-opening-statement> [accessed 31.12.22]. Sagan even recognised that capitalism cannot adapt to the needs of solving the problems because of its international nature and expresses the need for a new type of society without nations.

49 UK Government, 'COP26: The negotiations explained' (2022) https://ukcop26.org/wp-content/uploads/2021/11/COP26-Negotiations-Explained.pdf> [accessed 31.12.22]

cities under water, unprecedented heatwaves, terrifying storms, widespread water shortages, and the extinction of a million species of plants and animals,' he said. 'Some government and business leaders are saying one thing, but doing another. Simply put, they are lying. And the results will be catastrophic.'[50]

A genuinely revolutionary organisation could really not better that assessment – although the CWO/ICT's analysis of the overall situation is naturally much clearer:

> The irony of this situation is that sections of the bourgeoisie are aware of what needs to be done but as a global class they just cannot do it. The pathos of this predicament was illustrated by the UK president of the conference, Alok Sharma, who was choking back his tears as he read out what he clearly recognised was a completely inadequate final agreement... Of course, those in power will not acknowledge the conference was a failure; instead they claim it has kept alive the prospect of limiting warming to 1.5 degrees Celsius this century. Those holding the levers of power are doing very well out of the present system. It is calculated, for example, that the richest 1% of the global population are responsible for 15% of global GHG emissions, while the poorest 50% are responsible for only 6%, and hence have little incentive to change things. Instead they pretend, contrary to the science, that the slow minimal steps taken represent great strides towards a solution. They point to agreements such as those on halting deforestation, limiting methane emissions, new greenhouse gas (GHG) reduction pledges, and the zero carbon pledges. As a last resort they claim that another conference in 2022 will correct the glaring shortfalls.[51]

COP26 failed then because it could not agree to make a statement targeting the halt of carbon emissions preferring simply to state the need for a reduction of emissions.

Moreover, it is precisely during the period since COP1 that global warming has increased most rapidly. It is clear that as Guterres says, governments are lying. Despite the apparent commitments to change that Clinton, Bush and Obama made as they entered office, they were not genuinely committed to stopping climate change because they know that it will cost capitalism too much; they have been influenced far too much by the energy companies to achieve such a change and they are far too concerned about maintaining their country's imperial power. Fossil fuel energy consumption is eight times greater

50   *The Independent*, 'It's now or never: IPCC warns emissions must decline by 2025' 4.4.22 <https://www.independent.co.uk/climate-change/news/ipcc-report-un-global-warming-b2050474.html> [accessed 31.12.22]

51   CWO, 'The Historic Failure of COP-26' (2022) <https://www.leftcom.org/en/articles/2022-01-18/the-historic-failure-of-cop26> [accessed 31.12.22]

than in 1950 and is about double that of 1980.[52] The Mauna Loa Observatory in Hawaii has been continuously monitoring atmospheric change since the 1950s, and it revealed that carbon dioxide (CO_2) in the Earth's atmosphere reached levels in May 2022 not seen in millions of years.

Data from this Observatory reveals that:

> Prior to the Industrial Revolution, CO_2 levels were consistently around 280 ppm for almost 6,000 years of human civilization. Since then, humans have generated an estimated 1.5 trillion tons of CO_2 pollution, much of which will continue to warm the atmosphere for thousands of years. [...] CO_2 levels are now comparable to the Pliocene Climatic Optimum, between 4.1 and 4.5 million years ago, when they were close to, or above 400 ppm. During that time, sea levels were between 5 and 25 metres higher than today, high enough to drown many of the world's largest modern cities. Temperatures then averaged 7 degrees Fahrenheit higher than in pre-industrial times, and studies indicate that large forests occupied today's Arctic tundra.[53]

So it is clear that governments have either been ineffectual[54] or dishonest in their statements about environmental concerns. Even in 2022, after all the publicity given nationally to COP26, a UK government minister is still clueless enough to state:

> Producing [oil and gas] domestically [ie in the UK] creates only half the emissions around production and transportation than importing it from around the world, [...] In terms of the economy and the environment, domestic production is a good thing and we should all get behind it [...] it is good for the economy, good for jobs and stops us giving money to dubious regimes.[55]

---

52 'Global Fossil Fuel Consumption' in *Our World in Data*, <https://ourworldindata.org/fossil-fuels> [accessed 31.12.22]

53 US National Oceanic and Atmospheric Organisation, 'Carbon dioxide now more than 50% higher than pre-industrial levels' (3.6.2022) <https://www.noaa.gov/news-release/carbon-dioxide-now-more-than-50-higher-than-pre-industrial-levels> [accessed 31.12.22]

54 For example, Bush and Cheney came into office supporting caps on emissions but changed immediately the oil lobby got to them. Obama came into office with promises of major changes to environmental policies but soon fell into the grip of oil and gas firms. Only Trump can be said to have been honest in his policies dismissing climate change issues.

55 *The Guardian* 'UK fracking and oil drilling good for environment, claims climate minister' 12.10.22 <https://www.theguardian.com/environment/2022/oct/12/uk-fracking-and-oil-drilling-good-for-environment-says-climate-minister-graham-stuart> [accessed 31.12.22]

We need also to look more specifically at what industry and the industrialists have been doing to recognise what is really happening in the world today. Capitalists need to make profits and put this as a priority over any real response

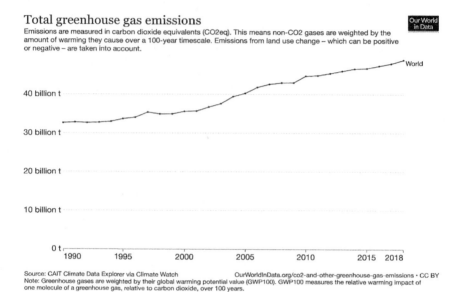

Total greenhouse gas emissions

Emissions are measured in carbon dioxide equivalents (CO2eq). This means non-CO2 gases are weighted by the amount of warming they cause over a 100-year timescale. Emissions from land use change – which can be positive or negative – are taken into account.

Source: CAIT Climate Data Explorer via Climate Watch   OurWorldInData.org/co2-and-other-greenhouse-gas-emissions · CC BY
Note: Greenhouse gases are weighted by their global warming potential value (GWP100). GWP100 measures the relative warming impact of one molecule of a greenhouse gas, relative to carbon dioxide, over 100 years.

Figure 22: Total Greenhouse Gas Emissions

'Greenhouse Gas Emissions' in *Our World in Data*,
<https://ourworldindata.org/greenhouse-gas-emissions> [accessed 31.12.22]

to environmental crises. We can be sure that this is true by looking at the practice which lies behind what the liars in capitalist industries have had to say particularly during the last couple of decades when these meetings were taking place.

What has Industry's Response been to the Global Warming Crisis and Pollution?

We need also to look more specifically at what industry and the industrialists have been doing to recognise what is really happening in the world today. Capitalists need to make profits and put this as a priority over any real response to environmental crises. We can be sure that this is true by looking at the practice which lies behind what the liars in capitalist industries have had to say particularly during the last couple of decades when these meetings were taking place.

The global warming crisis appears to be having the most significant impact on our environment at present so just what has industry been doing to combat its effects?

To answer this question we need to ask if there is evidence of serious steps forward by industry to tackle global warming. Firstly if we look at fossil fuel industries, one thing is completely obvious – as soon as any government, such as Trump did in recent years, opens up permission to search for resources, whether by mining, drilling or fracking, these companies just jump at the chance no matter where it is: Alaska, Northumberland, or the North Sea. Also in recent years they have been investigating more deep sea drilling sites.

Secondly let us look at the scale of the problem shown in Figure 22. This shows that the situation has continued to worsen during the 30 years of the COP conferences.

How has this happened despite the warnings of scientists and at least some politicians? IPCC2 in 1995 for example contained the following statement: 'The balance of evidence suggests a discernible human influence on global climate [...] Climate is expected to continue to change in the future'.[56] This report had some impact on the world and did lead to the conferences mentioned previously and some policy changes.

Yet what was industry doing during this time?

To assess this, it is constructive to start further back in time and look at the oil and gas industry and in particular Exxon. This was a highly profitable firm during the 1970s and 1980s, and the largest oil company in the world. At that time it was doing major scientific research into the possible impact of global warming on its core oil and gas industries as well as undertaking significant research into solar energy and other renewables. Indeed it claims to have been the first oil company to do such research. As early as 1978 and 1979, its own scientists produced internal reports on climate change for the company.[57] The summary of a 1978 internal report states:

> In the first place, there is general scientific agreement that the most likely manner in which mankind is influencing the global climate is through car-

---

56 'IPCC Second Assessment Report 1995' <https://www.ipcc.ch/site/assets/uploads/2018/03/TAR-12.pdf> [accessed 31.12.22]

57 Note also that Shell was later on to follow a similar policy of hiding the warnings of its own scientists. See *The Guardian*, 'Shell and Exxon's secret 1980s climate change warnings' (19.9.2018) <https://www.theguardian.com/environment/climate-consensus-97-per-cent/2018/sep/19/shell-and-exxons-secret-1980s-climate-change-warnings> [accessed 31.12.22]

bon dioxide release from the burning of fossil fuels. A doubling of carbon dioxide is estimated to be capable of increasing the average global temperature from 1° to 3°C with a 10°C rise predicted at the poles. More research is needed however to establish the validity of predictions with response to the Greenhouse Effect. It is currently estimated that mankind has a 5-10 year time window to obtain the necessary information. A major research effort in this area is being considered by the US Department of Energy.[58]

The covering letter to a 1979 internal report by Exxon's research scientists states:

> The major conclusion from this report is that, should it be deemed necessary to maintain atmospheric CO_2 levels to prevent significant climatic change, dramatic changes in patterns of energy use would be required.[59]

What did Exxon do? Did it change tack and try to develop strategies to lessen the impact of global warming on the world. No, of course not, it kept these findings hidden and initiated campaigns denying the science that showed the dangers of global warming; in other words, it lied to protect its profits. Instead of new research, it spent vast amounts of money protecting the lie that climate change was not a threat.

In the early 1990s, the Exxon group closed down much of the research it was doing on the basis that only oil and gas could be profitable. In fact, Lee Raymond, the CEO, was suggesting almost 20 years later in 1996 that CO_2 came from natural source emissions and that human produced CO_2 emissions were only a small proportion of the total: therefore no action was necessary.[60] Indeed in a speech to the World Petroleum Congress in 1997 he stated that:

> A recent study at Princeton University found 'no evidence that environmental quality deteriorates steadily with economic growth'. Instead, it found that after an initial decline, a nation's environment improves as its economy grows. So the real secret to environmental improvement is economic growth.[61]

---

58   *Climate Files*, '1978 Exxon Memo on Greenhouse Effect for Exxon Corporation Management Committee', Summary p.10 <https://www.climatefiles.com/exxonmobil/1978-exxon-memo-on-greenhouse-effect-for-exxon-corporation-management-committee/> [accessed 31.12.22]

59   *Climate Files*, '1979 Exxon Memo on Potential Impact of Fossil Fuel Combustion' <https://www.climatefiles.com/exxonmobil/1979-exxon-memo-on-potential-impact-of-fossil-fuel-combustion/> [accessed 31.12.22]

60   Lee Raymond, 'Speech to American Petroleum Institute' (1996): <https://www.c-span.org/video/?c4888500/user-clip-lee-raymond-climate-change-1996-1>[accessed 31.12.22]

61   Lee Raymond, 'Speech to World Petroleum Congress' (1997) <https://www.documentcloud.org/documents/2840902-1997-Lee-Raymond-Speech-at-China-World-

CO2 emissions by fuel, World

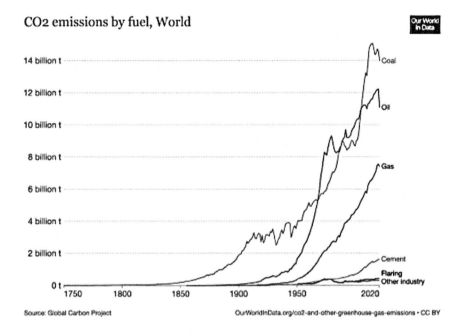

Source: Global Carbon Project

OurWorldInData.org/co2-and-other-greenhouse-gas-emissions • CC BY

Figure 23 Worldwide CO₂ Emissions by Fuel

'CO₂ Emissions by Fuel' in *Our World in Data*, <https://ourworldindata.org/emissions-by-fuel> [accessed 31.12.22]

He denied the need for action on climate change as the likelihood of any change in world temperature by 2050 was minimal despite his own scientists saying the opposite! Such is the activity of industry's leaders; defend profits at the expense of humanity.

Raymond was also instrumental in setting up the Global Climate Coalition (GCC),[62] an American lobby group existing from 1989 to 2001 which brought

Petroleum.html> [accessed 31.12.22]

62 The Wikipedia entry on this organisation says: 'The **Global Climate Coalition** (GCC) (1989–2001) was an international lobbyist group of businesses that opposed action to reduce greenhouse gas emissions and publicly challenged the science behind global warming. The GCC was the largest industry group active in climate policy and the most prominent industry advocate in international climate negotiations. The GCC was involved in opposition to the Kyoto Protocol, and played a role in blocking ratification by the United States. The coalition knew it could not deny the scientific consensus, but sought to sow doubt over the scientific consensus on climate change and create manufactured controversy. The GCC dissolved in 2001 after membership declined in the face of improved understanding of the role of greenhouse gases in climate change and of public criticism'. <https://en.wikipedia.org/wiki/Global_Climate_Coalition> [ac-

together many large international firms as well as industrial organisations representing industries such as rail, car manufacturers, chemical, mining and obviously fossil fuels. Its purpose was to spread the idea that global warming was a natural phenomenon and that human actions were not contributing to it. This group was incredibly influential not only in America but throughout the world in stimulating much of the climate change denialism at the end of the 20th century. It did this by funding the denial scientists, newspapers and political campaigns by a strategy of questioning the science and its accuracy, by picking on loopholes and irrelevant facts, by attacking the honesty of its proponents, and by simply denying there was a consensus. The GCC also funded economists who questioned the cost of environmentalism on jobs and income. Overall these strategies had a major worldwide influence on the public and politicians' opinions and hence on political decisions about environmental issues.

Former US Senator Chuck Hagel, who led the campaign in the US Senate against environmental policies in the 1990s, admitted in an interview in a recent documentary by the BBC:

> What we now know about some of these large oil companies' positions. They lied. Yes, I was misled and others were misled. When they had evidence in their own institutions which countered what they said publicly – they lied [...] It cost this country and it cost the world.[63]

Despite such admissions, we have to say in response so what! We should not be under any illusions that Hagel's admissions mean things have changed since then!

A major BBC documentary, *Big Oil vs the World*,[64] explains how the climate change denial campaigns became politicised and merged with right wing American campaigns during the early 2000s. Funded again by fossil fuel firms, Americans for Prosperity obfuscated the issues and perniciously attacked scientists and scientific data regarding climate change. It also campaigned to eliminate climate change activists from the US Republican Party which is even now still totally dominated by denial propaganda.

This documentary also demonstrates how the fracking industry has, during the 2010s, employed the same tactics of lies and obfuscation to present the natural gas industry as an environmentally safe bridge to the future. As it says, even the term used, 'natural gas' sounds like it should be... well, natural, and therefore good for us. Nothing could be further from the truth! So-called nat-

---

cessed 04.01.23]

63   Interview with Chuck Hagel in BBC *Big Oil vs The World* (2022) <https://www.bbc.co.uk/iplayer/episode/p0cgqlvk/big-oil-v-the-world-series-1-3-delay> [accessed 31.12.22]

64   Ibid

ural gas, whether obtained by fracking or drilling, is actually methane-based gas which leaks substantially during extraction. It produces a lot of heat but in being burnt releases carbon dioxide into the air (although less than oil). Methane is actually a far more dangerous greenhouse gas than carbon dioxide so all this industry does is release more dangerous emissions into the air and spend vast amounts of money on damaging technologies. All the investment in fossil fuel provision and campaign spending on greenwashing the industry prevents research and development of renewable clean energies.

Then came Trump. Unlike his predecessors in America he did not even pay lip service to environmental concerns. For him climate warming was a hoax and he spent his years rolling back such legislation as there was, and opening up new opportunities for the fossil fuel industry. Moreover he has not been alone amongst world leaders to take this view; over recent years, we can also point at least to Brazil's Bolsonaro, Turkey's Erdogan, Australia's Morrison, Russia's Putin, Canada's Trudeau and Britain's own Liz Truss. As of 2021, 432 new coal mines were planned with three-quarters of them in China, Australia, India and Russia.[65]

The Guardian produced a research report on the projects being planned by **oil and gas** companies after COP26 took place and in this quote summarises what the major firms in this industry were still planning:

> These plans include 195 carbon bombs, gigantic oil and gas projects that would each result in at least a billion tonnes of CO_2 emissions over their lifetimes, in total equivalent to about 18 years of current global CO_2 emissions. About 60% of these have already started pumping [...] The dozen biggest oil companies are on track to spend $103m a day for the rest of the decade exploiting new fields of oil and gas that cannot be burned if global heating is to be limited to well under 2°C.[66]

Nothing has changed! Capitalism looks after itself, not humanity, not the planet. So really the idea of 'The Age of Stupid' is not that accurate, perhaps this is the 'Age of the Malicious and Malevolent'!

It is also the case that in 2022, African nations are banding together to press at future COP meeting to be allowed to continue fossil fuel exploration and production and it's not hard to work out who is behind this movement.

---

65   Reuters, 'World's coal producers now planning more than 400 new mines' (3.6.21) <https://www.reuters.com/world/china/worlds-coal-producers-now-planning-more-than-400-new-mines-research-2021-06-03/> [accessed 3.1.23]

66   *The Guardian*, 'Revealed: the "carbon bombs" set to trigger catastrophic climate breakdown' 11.5.22, <https://www.theguardian.com/environment/ng-interactive/2022/may/11/fossil-fuel-carbon-bombs-climate-breakdown-oil-gas> [accessed 31.12.22]

Do not think we are being alarmist then! The environment is under threat from those companies and nations who put profits before humanity.

Let us see how *The Guardian* reports what the UN Secretary General had to say in early 2022 about the fossil fuel companies even before their profits and fuel prices rocketed:

> The oil and gas industry is extremely volatile but extraordinarily profitable, particularly when prices are high, as they are at present. ExxonMobil, Shell, BP and Chevron have made almost $2tn in profits in the past three decades, while recent price rises led BP's boss to describe the company as a 'cash machine' [...] The lure of colossal payouts in the years to come appears to be irresistible to the oil companies, despite the world's climate scientists stating in February that further delay in cutting fossil fuel use would mean missing our last chance 'to secure a liveable and sustainable future for all'. As the UN secretary general, António Guterres, warned world leaders in April: 'Our addiction to fossil fuels is killing us'.[67]

Despite small falls in emissions from coal and oil consumption in recent years, overall emissions appear to be still increasing especially through emissions from China and India. Note again the massive increase in emissions since 1950 supporting our view of specific changes taken place in this period of capitalism.

Coal consumption has shown a small drop worldwide since 2010 mostly through reductions in Europe and America and through an increased output from nuclear power stations in the same period. Nevertheless what has to be stressed is that overall usage has increased by 250% since 1965 and about 60% since 2000.[68] In addition, not just coal but all mining releases methane into the air.[69] Whilst it is true that energy use from non-carbon based sources has been increasing since 2010, this does include nuclear energy whose credibility as a clean energy source is not clear cut due to the problems of storage of radioactive byproducts.

Although year on year there has been a reduction in the number of new coal fired power stations being built or planned, the capacity of these power stations has increased.

---

67   Ibid

68   'Energy' in *Our World in Data*, <https://ourworldindata.org/global-energy-200-years> [accessed 31.12.22]

69   Remember, canaries were once used in the early days of mining to warn the miners about the presence of methane.

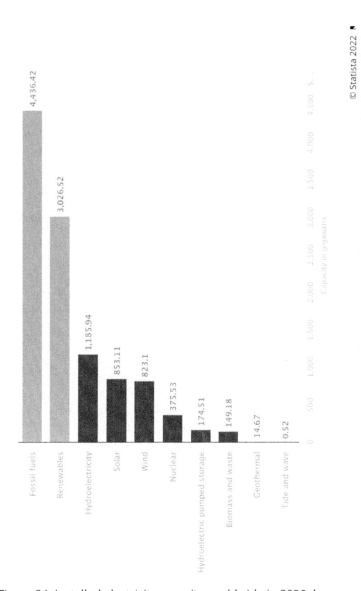

Figure 24: Installed electricity capacity worldwide in 2020, by source

Statista, 'Installed electricity capacity worldwide in 2020, by source',
<https://www.statista.com/statistics/267358/world-installed-power-capacity/>
[accessed 31.12.22]

Since 2000, the world has doubled its coal-fired power capacity to around 2,045 gigawatts (GW) after explosive growth in China and India. A further 200GW is being built and 300GW is planned. More recently, 268GW has closed due to a wave of retirements across the EU and US. Combined with a rapid slowdown in the number of new plants being built, this means the number of coal units operating around the world fell for the first time in 2018, Carbon Brief analysis suggests. Another 213GW is already set to retire and 19 of the world's 80 coal-powered countries plan a complete phaseout of the fuel, including the UK and Germany. Meanwhile, electricity generated from coal has plateaued since 2014, so the expanding fleet is running fewer hours. This erodes coal's bottom line, as does competition from other fuels. It would now be cheaper to build new wind and solar than to keep running half of existing coal plants. The way coal's next chapter unfolds is key to tackling climate change. Global unabated coal use must fall by around 80% this decade if warming is to be limited to less than 1.5°C above pre-industrial temperatures, according to recent Carbon Brief analysis.[70]

Regarding the issue of **deforestation** which impacts significantly on global warming, it is evident that since the start of the 21st century, the loss of tree cover continues to increase. It acts as a significant contributor to global warming despite the general awareness of this issue:

> The world has lost 437 million hectares (Mha) of tree cover since the turn of the century, equivalent to about 11 percent of global tree cover in 2000. Tree cover loss has been rising in recent history, from 13.4 Mha of tree cover loss in 2001 to 25.3 Mha in 2021.[71]

It is true that some countries are following policies of replanting trees but obviously this is not the general rule. One of the major contributors to deforestation has been Brazil where a populist leader, Bolsonaro, was positively encouraging the conversion of parts of the Amazon rain forest to agricultural use because of the profits that capitalism can make.

This leads us to another real problem for capitalism in that there is a clear division between the rich and underdeveloped countries. The former create most of the problems of global warming but the underdeveloped countries are unable to afford the measures to counter the rising impact of climate warming and are increasingly demanding support or recompense for the measures they need to take.

---

70   'Mapped: The world's coal power plants' in *Carbon Brief* 26.3.20 <https://www.carbon-brief.org/mapped-worlds-coal-power-plants/> [accessed 5.1.23]

71   WRI, 'Global Forest Review 2021', <https://research.wri.org/gfr/forest-extent-indicators/forest-loss#how-much-tree-cover-is-lost-globally-each-year> [accessed 31.12.22]

With regard to **chemical industries** and what are termed novel entities, i.e. chemical products unknown in nature, we can see that the global production of the materials is increasing rapidly.

> The chemical industry is the second largest manufacturing industry glob-ally. Global production increased 50-fold since 1950, and is projected to triple again by 2050 compared to 2010. Material extraction as feed stocks for novel entities was approximately 92 billion tonnes globally in 2017, and is projected to reach 190 billion tonnes by 2060. There are an estim-ated 350,000 chemicals (or mixtures of chemicals) on the global market. Nearly 70,000 have been registered in the past decade; many chemicals (nearly 30,000) have only been registered in emerging economies, where chemical production has increased rapidly, but chemicals management and disposal capacity often are limited.[72]

These companies are taking advantage of less developed countries to max-imise their profits and do not appear to care whether these countries have the facilities to manage waste disposal or not.

Concerning greenhouse gas emissions, the Chemical Industry suggests their emissions in 2010 were approx 25% less than in 2000 and approx 50% less than in 1990.[73] However it is the case that many chemical processes used in other industries (e.g. cement, iron and steel) themselves emit carbon dioxide into the air. Furthermore another product of chemical reactions, nitrous oxide, is a dangerous greenhouse gas and for an equal weight of carbon dioxide pro-duces a far greater impact on global warming. In the US, for example, agricul-ture is the source of over 70% of nitrous oxide in the air resulting from the ac-tion on nitrogen based chemicals added to the soil and the burning of waste materials by agriculture, yet:

> In 2020, nitrous oxide (N_2O) accounted for about 7% of all U.S. green-house gas emissions from human activities. Human activities such as agri-culture, fuel combustion, wastewater management, and industrial pro-cesses are increasing the amount of N_2O in the atmosphere. Nitrous oxide is also naturally present in the atmosphere as part of the Earth's nitrogen cycle and has a variety of natural sources. Nitrous oxide molecules stay in the atmosphere for an average of 114 years before being removed by a sink or destroyed through chemical reactions. The impact of 1 pound of N_2O on warming the atmosphere is almost 300 times that of 1 pound of carbon dioxide.[74]

---

72   ACS, 'Outside the Safe Operating Space of the Planetary Boundary for Novel Entities', 18.1 22 <https://pubs.acs.org/doi/10.1021/acs.est.1c04158> [accessed 31.12.22]

73   'Greenhouse Gas Emissions and the Chemical Industry 2022' in *Chemistry Views*, <ht-tps://www.chemistryviews.org/details/ezine/4382741/Greenhouse_Gas_Emissions_and_the_Chemical_Industry/> [accessed 31.12.22]

74   US Environmental Protection Agency, 'Overview of Greenhouse Gases' <https://

Buildings are not something we think of as dangerous to the climate, however the production of concrete, cement, brick, steel, glass and plastics are all significant contributors to greenhouse gases in the atmosphere. This is not just because of the energy used to heat and light buildings, nor just because of the waste generated by demolition and building anew, this is also because of the nature of the processes used to produce materials used in construction. Production of concrete, steel, and aluminium releases significant amounts of greenhouse gases into the air and 'The built environment generates 40% of annual global CO_2 emissions'[75], yet materials production is obviously an even larger contributor overall as not all these materials go into buildings. This obviously poses many challenges for reducing carbon emissions in future; in fact, it seems to pose the need for a whole new set of materials.

The melting of the arctic and antarctic ice and mountain glaciers has received a good deal of attention in the press in recent years. As a consequence of global warming, it is already too late to have any significant or immediate reduction in this process. Worse, it is also a factor in exacerbating global warming because the reduction of ice will increase the Earth's absorption of heat from the sun.[76]

> Scientists led by the University of Leeds found that the rate of ice loss from the Earth has increased markedly within the past three decades, from 0.8 trillion tonnes per year in the 1990s to 1.3 trillion tonnes per year by 2017...[77]

This is a 65% increase in the rate of ice loss in 23 years.

> Half of all losses were from ice on land – including 6.1 trillion tonnes from mountain glaciers, 3.8 trillion tonnes from the Greenland ice sheet, and 2.5 trillion tonnes from the Antarctic ice sheet. These losses have raised global sea levels by 35 millimetres.[78]

www.epa.gov/ghgemissions/overview-greenhouse-gases#nitrous-oxide> [accessed 31.12.22]

75 'Why the Building Sector?' in *Architecture 2030* <https://architecture2030.org/why-the-building-sector/> [accessed 31.12.22]

76 WWF, 'Six Ways Loss of Arctic Ice Impacts Everyone 2022', <https://www.worldwildlife.org/pages/six-ways-loss-of-arctic-ice-impacts-everyone> [accessed 31.12.22]

77 UK Research and Innovation, 'Global ice loss increases at record rate' 28.1.21, <https://www.ukri.org/news/global-ice-loss-increases-at-record-rate/> [accessed 31.12.22]

78 Ibid

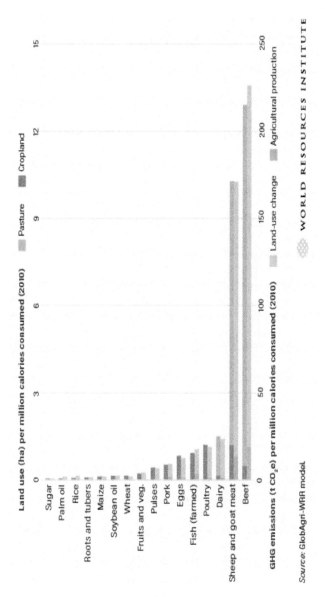

Figure 25: Animal-Based Foods are more resource intensive
than plant-based foods

WRI, 'How to Sustainably Feed 10 Billion People by 2050, in 21 Charts' (5.12.2018)
<https://www.wri.org/insights/how-sustainably-feed-10-billion-people-2050-21-charts >
[accessed 31.12.22]

Ice melt is a product of global warming that cannot be rectified in isolation, only measures to reduce the global temperature can have an impact but as we have seen above, there is no indication that this can happen within capitalism. In fact, there is little indication that the global temperature can be held at the present level let alone reduce it. In addition to actually increasing temperatures and the overall problems caused by this, the melting of ice is going to have a major impact on everybody living in coastal and low lying areas as well as on agricultural areas that depend on glacier melt; this will reduce food production and increase population migration significantly above today's levels. A related problem in this context is that methane is released from the ground by the melting of permafrost.

We must also include **food production** in this section on global warming in that it is a specific side effect of certain types of food production in agriculture. As mentioned previously capitalism produces enough calories to keep the whole world fed but it is wasted by unfair distribution, use of biofuels, household waste and, most absurdly, by using it to feed cattle who produce less calories in foods for humanity than they eat. Beef is a most inefficient product as each pound of beef requires 16 pounds of vegetation to be consumed and cattle require more than 20 times the amount of land that pigs and chicken require to thrive[79] yet produce more than 20 times the amount of greenhouse gas emissions. It also appears that producing the meat for one beefburger requires about 600 gallons of fresh water! As can be seen from Figure 25, there has to be a question raised over the value of producing specific foodstuffs, particularly meat and dairy, even if calories are not the only determinant in the value of foods.

From Figure 25 we can see that greenhouse gas emissions can be linked to specific foodstuffs and clearly the production of beef, mutton and goat meat is a major element of the carbon dioxide emissions from agriculture. Yet, the production of these meats increases significantly year on year in the developed countries of Europe and America. Worldwide, it is mostly poultry and to some extent pork consumption that has increased most. However meat and dairy production uses vast amounts of water, land, human edible foodstuffs, creates greenhouse gases and generates vast amounts of faecal matter polluting land and waterways. Meat production uses much higher values of calories than it provides as food for humanity and plant foodstuffs are a much more efficient way to feed humanity in this respect as well as in terms of land use.

---

79   'The 6 Worst Foods To Buy If You Care About Humanity', Chapter: Beef and Dairy, in *Global Citizen* 10.8.2016, <https://www.globalcitizen.org/en/content/deadliest-foods-produce-tomato-shrimp-chocolate-te/> [accessed 31.12.22]

This issue is no longer just affecting the developing world either. The Po Valley in Italy is one of Europe's major agricultural areas but it is being affected by the lack of water draining down from the glaciers in the Alps and as a result the water level of the river itself has dropped severely and this has brought regular droughts and declining crop yields. In America since 1970, the average temperature across the country has been increasing by more than the global average and the western states in particular are suffering not only from wildfires but also drought in many states all of which is reducing food production.[80]

Despite all this evidence, what is the interpretation? Well one set of results suggests the best way to reduce global warming is to have fewer children, in other words, blame people, not the system. This is clear evidence of the way statistics can be misused. Appendix 2 shows that only a few significant industries in the world produce the majority of such gases and Appendix 4 demonstrates how it is the super rich that generate the most gases. Then again we can point to the developed countries to show that they are the most damaging in this respect. However, it's better for capital to blame individuals isn't it!

Global warming is not the only way in which capitalism is damaging the world however.

The **plastics industry** only came into being after World War II and production has doubled in size to 400 million tonnes per year since the start of the 21st century despite the recognition that waste plastic does not fully decompose. As a result, our oceans and rivers accumulate plastic waste particularly in 'Third World' regions where little or no recycling systems are in place, and which moreover serve as a vast dumping ground for plastics that developed countries find too expensive to recycle (see below). Plastic does eventually break down into very small pieces, microplastics, and these particles are now to be found in almost all locations in the world as well as within the bodies of fish, animals and humans. The precise impact of microplastics is unknown but plastic pollution is well established as a killer of animal and sea-life.

> Since the 1950s, roughly 8.3 billion tonnes of plastic have been produced with more than 60 percent of that tossed into landfills, burned or dumped directly into rivers and oceans. Some 460 million tonnes of plastics were used in 2019, twice as much as 20 years earlier.[81]

---

80 MB Sauter, 27 Effects of Climate Change that cannot be stopped [in America] 7.11.2018 <https://247wallst.com/special-report/2018/11/07/27-effects-of-climate-change-that-cant-be-stopped/2/> [accessed 31.12.22]

81 Al Jazeera, 'Global plastic waste is projected to triple by 2060: OECD' 3.6.22, <https://www.aljazeera.com/news/2022/6/3/plastic-waste-can-triple-by-2060-if> [accessed 31.12.22]

Despite the impact and capitalism's inability to deal effectively with plastic waste, plastics production is expected to triple by 2060!

> 'Plastic pollution is one of the great environmental challenges of the 21st century, causing wide-ranging damage to ecosystems and human health,' OECD chief Mathias Cormann said.[82]

Agricultural pollution and soil degradation has also been an issue of significance since the 1950s when the use of pesticides and plant fertilisers escalated following WW2 (see 'Humanity in Nature').

Chemical pollution generally is especially related to waste disposal but with regard to planetary boundaries, it will be seen that there are a very large number of chemicals that are artificial in the sense that they do not exist in nature. Their impact is often unknown over an extended period of time and this may well be too late to prevent damage (the examples of PCBs and CFCs apply again).

In terms of foodstuffs, capitalism globally produces enough calories to keep the whole world healthy but it is wasted! Overall, we grow 5940 kcals pppd (kilocalories per person per day) but we only need 2350 kcals pppd to feed the whole world. Of the total produce, 1740 kcals pppd are fed to animals (in addition to the 3810 kcals of grass and pasture they consume) yet they contribute only 540 kcals pppd to our diet.[83] This really is an excellent demonstration of the anarchy of the market. Furthermore there are obvious variations in the food availability in different regions of the world which is linked to climate but is also a consequence of the inability of capitalism to fully develop all regions of the world. The World Wildlife Fund (WWF) estimates that currently the food industry is the single biggest contributor to global warming and uses 50% of the Earth's habitable land yet population growth could mean the need for 80% more food by 2100.[84]

Air pollution has in some ways been one of the areas where measures have been taken by governments to reduce pollution and some have been successful on a local basis. However, the problems keep changing with technological developments and air pollution generally remains an issue. Air pollution in urban environments is nothing new, but particularly from the 1950s the problem has been exacerbated by modern society and there has been a steady stream of problems such as smog (e.g. London and Los Angeles in the 1950s and then, more recently, in China, India, and many of the world's larger towns), acid rain, ozone layer changes, particulate matter emissions particularly from road transport. The release of gases such as sulphur dioxide (SO_2), Nitrous oxide (N_2O),

82   Ibid

83   Mike Berners-Lee, *There is No Planet B*

84   Population Matters, 'Food and Water' < https://populationmatters.org/food-water> [accessed 31.12.22]

ammonia (NH_3) and other organic compounds however remains high and can result in eutrophication (i.e. the transfer of nutrients into both sea and fresh water causing excessive growth of algae).

> It is therefore possible that the world has passed the point of maximum emissions of several major gaseous air pollutants as a combination of further controls in North America, Europe and East Asia drive down global totals. Climate change policies directed towards reduced use of coal and oil are expected to contribute further reductions in emissions of SO_2 and N_2O over coming decades. However, there are good reasons to be cautious, because emissions of ammonia, an important contributor to PM and eutrophication, continue to rise, and possible feedbacks between emissions of these gases and climate may drive overall emissions upwards. Global emissions of CH_4 [(methane)] and VOC [(volatile organic compounds)] also continue to rise, and in the case of biogenic emissions, it is possible that changes in climate and the widespread planting of new forests may accelerate global emissions of biogenic VOC.[85]

Another consequence of growth since World War II is **the proliferation of waste and the expansion of waste management** industries.

Waste is a major product of this society and waste management is an enormous industry. For developed countries, as well as being destructive, it's an enormous expense to deal with: 'The global waste management market size was valued at $1,612.0 billion in 2020, and is expected to reach $2,483.0 billion by 2030, registering a CAGR [Compound Annual Growth Rate] of 3.4% from 2021 to 2030'.[86]

So some of the waste is recycled, which is the constructive approach, but significant amounts are burnt which of course adversely affects global warming. What about the excess though? Well, it is sent to the underdeveloped countries of the world who get paid to dispose of it – except that by and large these countries do not have the technologies, the expertise or the money to be able to dispose of it properly. Mountains of scrap plastics are a feature of most countries and are a problem that no one can yet deal with, so they accumulate and plastic spreads throughout the planet as microplastics. Plastics and recycling industries say how wonderful they are but, in reality, recycling has failed (only 20% is recycled). Containers full of plastic waste are sold to the 'Third World' because only the Third World has the cheap labour that can be used to sort out the recyclable bits. Banning plastics may well be the only solution in

---

85   The Royal Society, 'A chronology of global air quality' (2020) <https://royalsociety-publishing.org/doi/10.1098/rsta.2019.0314> [accessed 31.12.22]

86   Allied Market Research, 'Waste Management Market 2021' <https://www.alliedmar-ketresearch.com/waste-management-market> [accessed 31.12.22]

communist society but, today, consumers have little choice; ending pollution by plastics has to start with the manufacturers and capitalism won't do that.

Even scrap shipping is sent to coastal areas of the Third World to be dismantled by hand in appalling conditions, thereby polluting coastal areas. In addition to the open cast mining, oil extraction and pollution from the multinationals that the ruling class in these countries is happy to profit from, we find the land being taken over by huge landfills, polluted regions and stocks in containers full of rotting waste. This is imperialism, importing the wealth and exporting the costs. This is a class issue, since the ruling class in the underdeveloped countries is complicit with those in the rich ones, and the poor and the workers in both suffer from the consequences.

Other waste is processed by burning and by dumping in landfills but just how much does this impact the climate? Industry still cannot operate in a way that creates zero waste and zero pollution but it is really only at the point of production that these issues can be solved. Retail still insists on over-packaging goods, maybe because of consumer legislations, but it is responsible for incredible amounts of waste. This needs to change, yes, through individual behaviour maybe, but primarily through the use of improved materials technologies and production systems and a profound change in the equilibrium between town and country.

Nuclear power is becoming more popular again in some countries[87] because it does not generate climate warming gases and is therefore supposedly climate friendly. For a communist society, it should only be a short term solution – except of course that new reactors will last for decades and will create yet more radioactive waste: something which is certainly not friendly to the Earth nor to future humans because it is buried away in bunkers for the thousands of years it will take to lose its radioactivity. Neither, of course, is the use of materials for buildings and supply let alone storage environmentally friendly.

Finally in this section, **human migration** should be addressed. From the 1950s onwards migration reversed and instead of pushing emigration into the undeveloped world, became a means for the developed world to draw in large numbers of workers to support its industries. This hindered the development of those underdeveloped countries who lagged behind economically. Since 1990 the number of displaced persons or refugees has doubled to nearly 90 million (in 2021), even before the outbreak of the war in Ukraine. Humanity is now approaching a new phase when climate change is going to lead to more and more displacement of people as a result of desertification and drought, fires, floods, storms and rising sea levels. The latter will impact coastal regions throughout the world and affect 200 million people by 2050 and maybe up to

---

87   Japan, unsurprisingly, not being among them.

600 million by 2100. Such changes will compound overpopulation in the remaining parts of the world and threaten living conditions generally.

> The World Bank's updated Groundswell[88] report [...] finds that climate change, an increasingly potent driver of migration, could force 216 million people across six world regions to move within their countries by 2050. Hotspots of internal climate migration could emerge as early as 2030 and continue to spread and intensify by 2050. The report also finds that immediate and concerted action to reduce global emissions, and support green, inclusive, and resilient development, could reduce the scale of climate migration by as much as 80 percent.[89]

While most of these issues have their origins in industrialisation and economic growth in Europe and America, they have been worsened catastrophically by the industrialisation of China, India, Brazil, Indonesia and other countries during the last thirty years. As always, it is the poorer parts of the world that suffer the worst negative effects in that they don't have the finance to protect themselves let alone start their own industries. A communist society will be confronted with the question, not just of resolving the problems of countries that are already industrialised, but of allowing all regions to develop on a new basis.

These selected issues dating from the 1950s onwards explain just how significantly humanity's relationship with the environment has changed in this period.

> Fifty years is just a very miniscule fraction of time if compared with the existence of life on Earth, but the changes brought in by anthropogenic activities in this period are very distinct and serious, endangering the sustainability of life on the planet.[90]

The environment presents an external limit to the continual accumulation of capital and as is apparent from this discussion, it now presents a factor that can only intensify the decay of the system.

---

88   See World Bank 'Groundswell' report, Part 2: <https://openknowledge.world-bank.org/handle/10986/36248> [accessed 05/01/23].

89   The World Bank, 'Climate Change Could Force 216 Million People to Migrate Within Their Own Countries by 2050', 13.9.2021, <https://www.worldbank.org/en/news/press-release/2021/09/13/climate-change-could-force-216-million-people-to-migrate-within-their-own-countries-by-2050> [accessed 31.12.22]

90   N. Arora, 'Earth: 50 years challenge'. Environmental Sustainability 2, 1–3 (2019). <https://doi.org/10.1007/s42398-019-00053-5> [accessed 31.12.22]

Can Technology save Capitalism?

Whilst we can recognise the immense contribution of fossil fuels to the development of humanity in the past centuries, we need to understand that the time for this type of energy source is past and that the time has come for change.

Hopefully this article has identified both the importance and the complexity of the issues regarding the ongoing ecological disaster. It is simply impossible to avoid the conclusion that the solution to these problems has to be undertaken on a global scale with a tremendous impact on everyday life. Bill Gates provides a simple summary of the sources of greenhouse gases and you will note that these figures demonstrate why the idea of reducing to zero emissions must inevitably involve a complete change in the way we live.

How much greenhouse gas is emitted by the things we do?[91]

Making things (cement steel plastic)	31%
Plugging in (electricity)	27%
Growing things (plants animals)	19%
Getting around (planes, trucks, cargo ships)	16%
Keeping warm and cool (heating cooling refrigeration)	7%

Individually, we can easily avoid eating beef or support the setting up of marine life reserves but this sort of activity will not solve the overall problem and capitalism, because of the way it works, will not do this either. This is why a working class world revolution is essential even to begin tackling the problem. 'The Age of Stupid' is simply 'The Age of Capitalism' and it will destroy us if we do not do something about it.

We can agree that capitalism is, on a local or limited level, capable of developing strategies to combat some of the environmental concerns. It is true that it is developing carbon capture technologies as well as solar energy, wind power and wave power. Even if they are developed to provide cleaner energy through the replacement of fossil fuels it is not at all certain that these energy sources can provide sufficient energy for current global needs, and the issue of battery storage that these sources would require is very far from being solved for usage on such a scale (already the disposal of used batteries has become a problem). There exists insufficient sources of clean energy for the world's needs therefore which raises a question as to the viability of electricity as the means of supplying energy. Bill Gates's ability to stimulate the development of sanitation systems for use in the Third World, and plans for safer, greener nuclear power sta-

---

91   Figures taken from Bill Gates, *How to Avoid Climate Disaster* (Allen Lane, 2021), p.55.

tions, may indeed all be very laudable in themselves, but they are merely individual projects that do not tackle the overall issues at stake today. It is essential for humanity to find ways of eliminating the fossil fuel industry, and of finding new materials for buildings and roads, new energy for transportation systems and new systems that prevent the usurping of the earth's free resources. Furthermore, preventing chemical pollution by industry and agriculture, preventing more global warming and the massive ice melts that is impacting on the arctic, the antarctic and the mountain glaciers[92]. Even then we still have the consideration that humanity should become vegan to solve the food supply difficulties that have been created. The problems of the Earth's ecology are just too interrelated and complex for green industries and philanthropy bound by the constraints of a money-based society, to be able to change the world.

What complicates the issue even further is that the so-called 'green technology' as it exists today is not only limited in its capacity to support the whole of society but also insufficiently developed to replace carbon emitting systems that humanity has used up until now. Worse still these industries also still cause the emission of significant levels of carbon-based gases and as we have seen all new emissions make the problem worse.

The banning of CFCs has held back global warming to some extent over the past few decades but obviously did not solve the problem. The banning of PCBs and DDT in fertilisers reduce pollution in the soil but the chemicals are still around, draining into the sea and killing sea-life.[93] PFAS, as we have noted earlier, are used extensively but their effects are still unknown and they remain permanently in the environment. These few examples demonstrate the problem we have with capitalism, there is little consideration given in planning to the impacts on soil, sea and air, and attempts to mitigate them come too late.

Capitalist technology may have the knowledge and skill to reverse many of the environmental issues, but does it have the mindset to do so? Undoubtedly not, because production is subservient to the needs of accumulation and because it would cost too much money and it would require the participation of the whole world, not just the occasional clever individual. What is noteworthy is that the likes of Carl Sagan, Mike Berners-Lee[94] have recognised this need for social change: these people are clearly not communists, but as idealistic scient-

92 This is another problem that can only get worse; the ice in Greenland is said to contain enough water to raise sea levels by 2 metres and it is melting rapidly.

93 Toxic-Free Future PCBs and DDT <https://toxicfreefuture.org/key-issues/chemicals-of-concern/pcbs-and-ddt/#aboutpcbs> [accessed 1.1.23]

94 We quoted Carl Sagan earlier on the need for social change but Mike Berners-Lee also says (in *There is no Planet B*) that to solve our environmental problems: 'We need thinking skills and habits that fit the 21st century context of enormous human power and technology on a now fragile planet'.

ists they can clearly see that stopping climate change will require a multi-disciplinary approach and a commitment for change from the whole of society. In industry in general, what we clearly see instead is the capitalists' lying and manipulative nature when it comes to maintaining profits and sales; even bourgeois politicians concede this on occasions.

There are two targets posed for levels of carbon emissions but both remain very problematic. Net zero emissions is presented as an achievable target by the environmental lobby but it needs to be questioned as to what it means and how it is to be achieved. There would be the need at least to virtually eliminate fossil fuel industries and their derivatives in particular plastics,[95] and totally restructure agriculture and the food industry generally. There would still remain the need to eliminate at least some carbon emissions that have already been made, because as we have seen, even at existing levels climate change must inevitably continue to worsen. This target would still depend on both the development of new technologies firstly of carbon capture, which just do not appear practical yet on the scale required, and secondly, whilst we continue to depend upon electricity, on new battery systems less dependent on mineral resources. Zero emissions sounds like a more acceptable target for the benefit of humanity and the environment, but it would be very hard to achieve, perhaps even impossible. The concern is that even if all fossil fuels stay in the ground, and this must be a target, this will not prevent all carbon emissions since every act of production (manufacturing and raw materials extraction), distribution and consumption appears to generate carbon emissions. Carbon capture would have to be developed to an extreme to achieve the result in the first place. Furthermore, it would therefore depend very heavily on a complete change in materials usage including for buildings, transportation systems, heating systems and so on.

Both targets are going to have such an impact on existing industry, the economy and everyday life that neither target is a task that capitalism can perform. They both will require such a total reorganisation of everyday life as well as a transformation of social relationships and values that only a communist society can bring to even start this process.

Because capitalism is driven by the remorseless demands of accumulation and profitability, it can never arrive at a rational, global control of the productive process, geared to the long-term interests of humanity. Capitalism tries to take the easy way out with half-baked solutions that either delay putting things right, or that do not cure anything because profits and growth need to be main-

---

95   Almost all plastics are produced from fossil fuels but so are many everyday items such as polyester for clothing, dentures, shampoo, toothpaste, lipstick, aspirin and even solar panels

tained. In a globalised economy, all nations and the large industries must compete to maintain their profits and their shares of the market which can only run counter to any attempt at cooperation to solve the environmental threat. Sustainability requires the maintenance or replacement of existing resources but can capitalism ever achieve this? No, it needs to make a profit from its production and replacing resources that it takes from the environment would minimise profits substantially.

When we consider the planet there are obviously limits to the resources available and limits to the ecological degradation that humanity can provoke and this means there is limited growth potential. Yet as we have seen, capital is committed to continual growth which undermines its own foundations. Today, the limitation of resources is having a more and more significant impact on production and on humanity.

Today it is the climate scientist and the environmentalist that are becoming mainstream viewing in the news media whilst the politicians talk but do little to respond.

All this means that we cannot see the ecological crisis as a product of an internal decay of the system but as a product of the system driven to unlimited growth, which it cannot materially achieve: this contradiction presents the prospect of the end of humanity. In fact we could argue it is the cause or at least a major stimulus to the further decomposition of capitalist society because it poses impossible questions. What has become a feature of decadence that threatens us all is the ongoing growth of capitalism!

We must also recognise that these warnings are no longer about the long term. UN scientists and IPCC reports are now delivering stark warnings about the impact of climate change on people and the planet saying that ecosystem collapse, species extinction, deadly heatwaves and floods are among the 'dangerous and widespread disruptions' the world will face over the next two decades due to global warming.

> 'This report is a dire warning about the consequences of inaction,' said Hoesung Lee, Chair of the IPCC. 'It shows that climate change is a grave and mounting threat to our wellbeing and a healthy planet. Our actions today will shape how people adapt and nature responds to increasing climate risks'... The world faces unavoidable multiple climate hazards over the next two decades with global warming of 1.5°C (2.7°F). Even temporarily exceeding this warming level will result in additional severe impacts, some of which will be irreversible. Risks for society will increase, including to infrastructure and low-lying coastal settlements.[96]

---

96   'IPCC Report 2022' <https://www.ipcc.ch/2022/02/28/pr-wgii-ar6/> [accessed 1.1.23]

We are facing ecosystem collapse and the world will face escalating problems over the next few decades due to global warming. Yet capitalism is clearly unable to prevent many of the most serious problems facing the earth today. It is too late already to prevent certain issues deteriorating further. Global warming, ice melt, sea level rise, desertification of certain areas, increased heatwaves and increasing rainstorms, loss of natural diversity, ocean acidification, soil degradation are all processes that are well underway and can only be halted or reversed in the long term.

The Twin Threats

Although this text has focused on the issue of ecological crisis, please do not think that the threat of world war has been or should be forgotten. From the early 1900s, communists have seen the threat that capitalist imperialism poses for humanity. Luxemburg talked of a period of wars and revolutions and as we saw the platform of the Communist International[97] directly links the intensification of competition and conflict between the great powers with the emergence of imperialist wars on an international scale.

The CWO expresses it in this way:

> In a system which has such an over-accumulation of capital that it needs some massive act of destruction in order to kick start its economy once again imperialist rivalries are rising. We are once again approaching a situation where 'new problems will have to be solved by the sword' which will have disastrous consequences for humanity.[98]

In other words after periods of accumulation and the intensification of imperialist competition, capitalism is forced down a path of war. The CWO praises both Lenin and Bukharin for presenting war 'as the ineluctable consequence of the development of the capitalist mode of production'.[99]

From 1945 to 1990, world war was seen as the one great threat for the destruction of humanity; every new local war raised fears of a USA-USSR confrontation as both were almost automatically involved on opposing sides. When the Russian bloc collapsed, this threat diminished while the threat of ecological catastrophe (and the recognition of this threat) continued to grow.

---

97 See 'Historical Materialism and the Descent of Capitalism'

98 CWO, 'Bukharin on State Capitalism and Imperialism', 2020, <https://www.leftcom.org/en/articles/2020-08-21/bukharin-on-state-capitalism-and-imperialism> [accessed 1.1.23]

99 CWO, 'The Real Cause of the Beginning and End of World War I', 2019, <https://www.leftcom.org/en/articles/2019-11-06/the-real-cause-of-the-beginning-and-end-of-wwi> [accessed 1.1.23]

Today China is clearly posing itself as a new power bloc and the threat of a China vs USA confrontation is growing with China to some extent in the position of Germany in 1914: it is clearly trying to expand its sphere of influence across the world but it nevertheless remains the weaker power and hence is likely to be the more aggressive. Russia also remains weaker than the West but the events in Ukraine in 2022 have changed the world situation and whatever the specific result of this war, there will be a heightened threat of conflict from here on in. Russia has shown its aggressiveness by its activities in Syria, Chechnya and in Ukraine and the USA has provoked the Ukraine war by stating beforehand that it would not interfere should Russia invade – but then supplying weapons and weaponising sanctions. Both Russia and the US continue to be threats to peace and the Ukraine will remain as a sore spot causing global tensions. Not only does this situation pose the possibility of World War III but the pollution, general destruction and the consequential need to rebuild resources caused in these wars all exacerbate long term environmental problems as well.[100]

Capitalism today poses a twin threat to humanity – world war and ecological disaster. These threats will not go away.

Whilst the increased threat of war, and indeed the actuality of a major confrontation, even a limited one, forces ecological crises to the background just as it has with the conflict in Ukraine, it must also exacerbate the environmental crises facing the world. Not only does the rebuilding of the destroyed cities, farms and general infrastructure call upon the use of the Earth's limited resources and generate new global warming gases and new pollutants, but also the act of destruction itself discharges volumes of land, air and sea pollutants and yet more global warming gases.

Guterres indeed suggests that: 'Fossil fuel interests are now cynically using the war in Ukraine to lock in a high-carbon future.'[101]

Furthermore it has to be suggested that because the environmental crises will be destroying resources and displacing populations, then nations will find themselves inevitably confronting each other to protect themselves against these losses and to make gains that limit these losses at the expense of others. Imperialist tensions will grow as the ecological crises develop.

In more recent years, the American military establishment has dominated this subgenre of climate projection. Extreme weather events, the Senate learned from the 2013 edition of the 'worldwide threat assessment' com-

---

100 For further discussion of these issues see 'The Accumulation of Catastrophe'

101 *The Guardian*, 'Revealed: the 'carbon bombs' set to trigger catastrophic climate breakdown' 11.5.22, <https://www.theguardian.com/environment/ng-interactive/2022/may/11/fossil-fuel-carbon-bombs-climate-breakdown-oil-gas> [accessed 31.12.22]

piled by the US intelligence community, will put food markets under serious strain, 'triggering riots, civil disobedience, and vandalism'. If the armed forces are firefighters tasked with suppressing outbreaks of rebellion, their workload will increase in a warming world. Pursuing its consistent and candid interest in the issue, in such stark contrast to the denialism of the American right, the Pentagon submitted a report to Congress in July 2015 detailing how all combatant commands are now integrating climate change into their planning. The 'threat multiplier' is already at work, undermining fragile governments, turning populations against rulers unable to meet their needs: and it will only get worse.[102]

This quote shows that the US military has been preparing for some time for global warming as a threat multiplier which will impact on social stability.

Climate change is a 'threat multiplier' [...] because it has the potential to exacerbate many of the challenges we already confront today – from infectious disease to armed insurgencies – and to produce new challenges in the future. The loss of glaciers will strain water supplies in several areas of our hemisphere. Destruction and devastation from hurricanes can sow the seeds for instability. Droughts and crop failures can leave millions of people without any lifeline, and trigger waves of mass migration. We have already seen these events unfold in other regions of the world, and there are worrying signs that climate change will create serious risks to stability in our own hemisphere. Two of the worst droughts in the Americas have occurred in the past ten years [...] droughts that used to occur once a century. In the Caribbean, sea level rise may claim 1,200 square miles of coastal land in the next 50 years, and some islands may have to be completely evacuated. According to some estimates, rising temperatures could melt entire glaciers in the Andes, which could have cascading economic and security consequences. These climate trends will clearly have implications for our militaries. A higher tempo and intensity of natural disasters could demand more support for our civil authorities, and more humanitarian assistance and relief. Our coastal installations could be vulnerable to rising shorelines and flooding, and extreme weather could impair our training ranges, supply chains, and critical equipment. Our militaries' readiness could be tested, and our capabilities could be stressed.[103]

Both these twin threats therefore are likely to interact and worsen the threat of war and ecological crisis; capitalism is moving these threats inexorably towards the destruction of humanity and the environment we depend on. Unless of course the working class intervenes.

---

102 Malm A, *Revolutionary Strategy in a Warming World*, 2018, <https://climateandcapitalism.com/2018/03/17/malm-revolutionary-strategy/> [accessed 1.1.23]

103 Hagel C, 'Speech to Conference of the Defence Ministers of the Americas', (13.10.2014) <https://www.defense.gov/News/Speeches/Speech/Article/605617/> [accessed 1.1.23]

Conclusion:
The Response of the Working Class

It should be emphasised that the issues raised in this article are not just problems facing capitalism even if it is capitalism that is making them worse; they will not disappear even if capitalism does. These issues are creating major problems which capitalism will leave for the working class to confront if it takes power before capitalism has destroyed us all. What will be needed then is radical change which draws everyone into the running of society and the only political system that can achieve this must be created by the working class. The working class offers the only answer because it is the only class in society that represents opposition to capitalism as a whole. It is the only class that can get rid of the capitalist system. What is also to be understood is that the working class will need the scientists to devote themselves to finding solutions and forgetting about the costs and governmental strategies that bind them today. As in other areas, they will need to be in tune not only with the working class but also the needs of the planet.

Only a world that does not use money and is based on production for need can hope to make manufacturing responsible for the lifetime costs of the materials they use in products. Only such a world can hope to make manufacturing responsible for cleaning up the side effects of production systems. Only such a world can stop spending vast amounts on stockpiles of arms instead of having stockpiles of health equipment in readiness for medical emergencies and pandemics:

> ...it is therefore a question of combining the denunciation of the effects of global warming with the battle against capitalism as a whole. In order to pursue this ambitious project, internationalists undertake to produce and circulate a critique of capitalism on the three levels of the environment, imperialism, and the economy. The climate question, as we have seen, is also a product of the relationship between classes: between a predatory bourgeoisie that strips the planet of all its resources, and a proletariat that must find within itself [...] the ability to combine the fight against exploitation, war and climate change and environmental devastation with the strategic elements of a revolutionary project.[104]

One of the big problems facing the working class both in power let alone in its struggles today against capitalism is how to accept the negative consequences of the reorganisation of industry and how to accept the elimination

---

104 *Battaglia Communista*, 'Climate-Production-Capital', (21.9.2021) <http://www.left-com.org/en/articles/2021-09-21/climate-production-capital > [accessed 1.1.23]

of dangerous industries. Will the working class fight against environmental damage when it means the loss of jobs in many of these industries discussed in this text or conversely will the working class fight against the deterioration of conditions caused by environmental damage? Furthermore, how would a socialist society manage these issues?

Not only are workers suffering restricted wages, price inflation and whatever other consequences the pandemic will lay at our door, but we will also be affected more and more by environmental issues that disrupt our daily lives and our capacity to support our families. As the quote above from *Battaglia Communista* suggests, there is no simple solution to ecological crises, but the politicisation of the working class in its struggles is an essential feature in humanity's capacity to face up to the horrors being created by capitalism.

What is true, is that whilst the working class has not recently posed a direct threat to capitalism, when it does, the focus of society and the struggle with existing conditions created by capital will have an enormous impact and will establish the possibility of a change to a society based on human needs and not on money and profit.

Not only do we need to emphasise the threat posed by the environment to humanity but it should also be clear by now that we also need to emphasise the huge size of the task facing the working class in power.

There will be the tasks of organising themselves to manage social and political affairs; there will be specialist decisions on technological and scientific issues that affect the environment; there will be very hard decisions about which industries and jobs will need elimination and which will need expanding; about how to improve conditions in the most poverty ridden areas of the world which may well, at the start of the process, mean taking resources from other regions. These will indeed be major tasks that will affect all workers personally as well as globally. Even the likes of Berners-Lee's proposals, based as they are on pure ecological considerations, may well be a contribution to these tasks.

The question posed by *Battaglia Communista* is important therefore, just how will future events combine the working class struggle and the need to save the environment?

Building a new world must be seen as not just the elimination of money, private property and wage slavery and the creation of a free society based on equality of all: it has become a question of creating new technologies, new transportation and building systems, new approaches to decision making about resources. This means nothing less than the qualitative redevelopment of productive forces as the primary concern rather than their quantitative development.

Appendices

Appendix 1 – speech by UN Secretary-General Antonio Guterres

Third[105] – we need to support real climate action in developing countries.

Emissions must fall, but they continue to rise.

Coal-fired power generation is surging towards a new all-time record.

Even if all developed countries kept their promises, very important promises, to drastically reduce emissions by 2030 – the problem is that with all developing countries achieving their present Nationally Determined Contribution, especially emerging economies – global emissions would still be too high to keep the 1.5 degree goal within reach.

We in fact would need a 45 per cent reduction in global emissions this decade.

Yet, with the present conditions, global emissions are set to increase by 14 per cent by 2030 – defying reason and ignoring the impacts on people, economies and our planet.

1.2 degrees of warming has already brought devastating consequences and soaring price tags measured in dollars and despair.

Over the last two decades, the economic toll from climate-related disasters skyrocketed by 82 per cent.

Extreme weather in 2021 caused $120 billion in insured losses, and killed 10,000 people.

Climate shocks forced 30 million people to flee their homes in 2020 alone – three times more than those displaced by war and violence.

And one billion children are at an extremely high risk of the impacts of climate change.

Turning this ship around will take immense willpower and ingenuity from governments and businesses alike, in every major-emitting nation.

A number of countries have pledged to make meaningful emissions reductions in the 2020s.

105 This is the third section of a speech by Antonio Guterres to the World Economic Forum in 2022. 'UN, Secretary-General's remarks to the World Economic Forum', 17.1.22, <https://www.un.org/sg/en/content/sg/speeches/2022-01-17/remarks-the-world-economic-forum%C2%A0> [accessed 1.1.23]

Other countries face enormous structural obstacles. They have an energy mix that relies on heavy dependence on coal. That stands in the way of progress for us all.

They need assistance. Let's not go into a blame and shame. Let's assist, help key emerging economies accelerate the transition, I'm calling for the creation of coalitions of countries, public and private financial institutions, investment funds, and companies that have the technological know-how to provide targeted financial and technical support for every country that needs assistance.

We have had the U.S. and China making an agreement that I hope will provide China with more adequate technologies in order to accelerate the transition from coal. India doesn't like the coalition but India has accepted several bilateral forms of support and I have been in close contact with the U.S., the UK and several other countries to make sure there is a strong project to support India, namely in their investment in 450 gigawatts of solar energy. Indonesia and VietNam already accepted the concept of a coalition supporting them to get rid of coal.

This must be a priority for us all – to phase out coal.

No new coal plants should be built.

As I said, the governments of Indonesia and Vietnam have just announced their intention to get out of coal and to have a transition to renewable energy but they need support for that.

South Africa now has in place a just energy transition with a partnership that involves a number of key countries and international financial institutions to support in accelerating, moving out, progressing, moving out from coal.

We see a clear role for businesses and investors in supporting our net-zero goal.

The Net-Zero Asset Owners Alliance has set the gold standard.

Last week, I took part in a meeting of the Glasgow Financial Alliance for Net Zero. That group represents more than $130 trillion of assets mobilised to the net-zero goal.

The entire financial system should follow their lead.

But these efforts must be complemented.

We need entire sectors on board.

Heavy industry, shipping and aviation and others must be on a trajectory for net-zero by 2050.

At COP26, I also announced the creation of a high-level expert group to evaluate the standards and criteria used to set, implement and monitor net-zero commitments by non-State actors – businesses, cities, financial institutions, and regions.

Over the course of this year, the group will propose new frameworks and develop recommendations.

It is encouraging to see the private sector take the lead, but it is essential to put pressure on governments to keep up and not be left behind.

The truth is that many of today's policies and regulatory frameworks are an obstacle for private sector engagement.

At the same time, international financial institutions are not doing enough to create forms of partnership that would allow to de-risk private investment in countries that need to speed up their transition.

All this needs to change.

Dear friends,

Across all three of these areas, we need the support, ideas, financing and voice of the global business community.

We cannot afford to replicate the inequalities and injustices that continue condemning tens of millions of people to lives of want, poverty and poor health.

We cannot continue building walls between the haves and have-nots. Or, building walls that undermine a global market that needs to work in a united way.

We need to come together – across countries and across sectors – to support those countries who need the most help.

Let's stand together to make 2022 a true moment of recovery.

I look forward to working with all of you to make this happen, and I look forward to the discussion that we are going to have.

Thank you very much

Appendix 2 – Global greenhouse gas emissions

Global greenhouse gas emissions by sector

This is shown for the year 2016 – global greenhouse gas emissions were 49.4 billion tonnes CO_2eq.

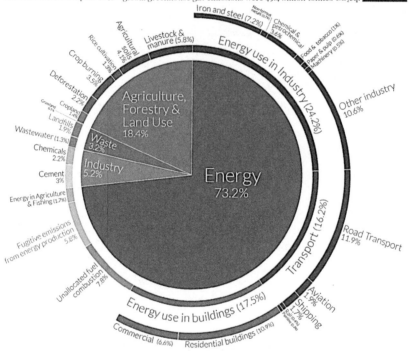

'Global Greenhouse Gas Emissions by Sector' in *Our World in Data*,
<https://ourworldindata.org/ghg-emissions-by-sector> [accessed 1.1.23]

Appendix 3 – Global temperature change

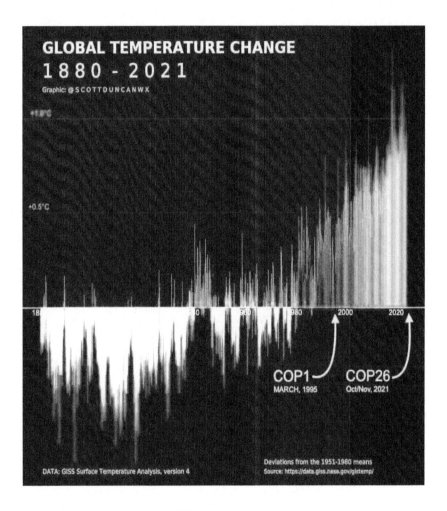

Scott Duncan Twitter @ScottDuncanWX's video tweet

Appendix 4 – Per capita emissions by wealth

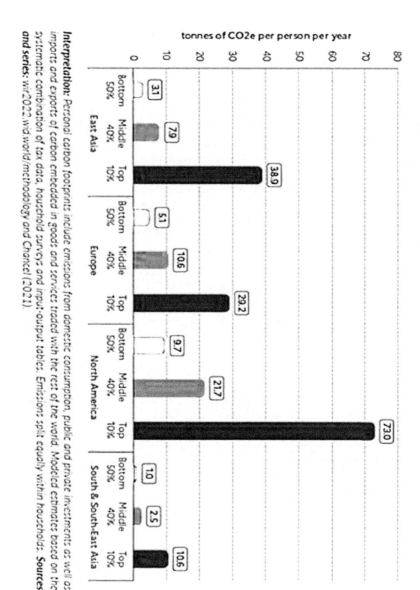

Per capita emissions across the world, 2019

tonnes of CO2e per person per year

East Asia — Bottom 50%: 3.1, Middle 40%: 7.9, Top 10%: 38.9
Europe — Bottom 50%: 5.1, Middle 40%: 10.6, Top 10%: 29.2
North America — Bottom 50%: 9.7, Middle 40%: 21.7, Top 10%: 73.0
South & South-East Asia — Bottom 50%: 1.0, Middle 40%: 2.5, Top 10%: 10.6

Interpretation: Personal carbon footprints include emissions from domestic consumption, public and private investments as well as imports and exports of carbon embedded in goods and services traded with the rest of the world. Modeled estimates based on the systematic combination of tax data, household surveys and input-output tables. Emissions split equally within households. **Sources and series:** wir2022.wid.world/methodology and Chancel (2021).

Roberts, World Inequality 16.12.21,<:https://mronline.org/2021/12/16/world-inequality/# >
[accessed 1.1.23]

Imagining the future

(Lars Torvaldsson)

Theory, my friend, is grey, but green is the eternal tree of life[1]

The function of communists is twofold: first, to make the past and the present, and their unfolding dynamics, comprehensible; second, to work toward the future. So far this book has been devoted to the former. This article is devoted to the future; it is intended to serve both as a conclusion to the articles that have preceded it here, and as an introduction to a proposed second volume on the nature and perspective of communism.

What it means, practically, for communists to 'work towards the future' is determined by the dynamics of the period in which they find themselves. In periods of open struggle, of social upheaval, they will be plunged in the thick of the action; in periods of reaction like today, their work will be largely confined to theoretical reflection – a form of struggle in itself – and debate, to 'prepare men's minds for the coming revolution' as Engels put it.[2] There is no dichotomy between the two: more than any other, the proletarian revolution depends on the consciousness of the revolutionary class and theoretical reflection is a vital element of that consciousness.

The importance of imagination

We have already seen[3] that imagination – the ability to envisage alternative future outcomes and to choose between them – is an essential component of human action in the world, and indeed a defining characteristic of the human species.

Paradoxically, it is easier today to project the imagination into a future beyond the revolutionary overthrow of capitalism, than to imagine the revolutionary process itself. Why is this? The most straightforward answer is that before preparing for a journey we need to have some idea of our destination: are we

---

1   From Goethe's *Faust*. Quoted by Lenin in 'Letters on tactics', written between April 8 and 13 (21 and 26), 1917. <https://www.marxists.org/archive/lenin/works/1917/apr/x01.htm> [accessed 13 January 2023]

2   In 'Socialism, Utopian and Scientific'. He was speaking in this case of the Enlightenment thinkers who prepared the way for the French Revolution.

3   In the article on 'Humanity in Nature'.

heading for the desert or the Arctic? More profoundly, it is a question of time scales, what is visible to us, and our theoretical heritage.

Although the revolutionary overthrow of bourgeois political power must precede in time the long construction of a new society, we are already, in a sense, engaged in the transitional period. The disaster of capitalism's continued domination is already here: we can see it clearly unfolding before us.[4] The technical, scientific, and above all the social chains that capitalism imposes on us are known and visible.[5] The disaster is thus something concrete, and this makes it possible to envisage concretely – albeit only in broad outline – the possible alternatives facing humanity as a whole: either continue with more of the same and face a long slide into an atrocious barbarism of which the war in Ukraine is a mere foretaste, or else the leap to social transformation and humanity's further development. Never have these words of Marx rung more true:

> proletarian revolutions [...] constantly engage in self-criticism, [...] with merciless thoroughness they mock the inadequate, weak, and wretched aspects of their first attempts; they seem to throw their opponent to the ground only to see him draw new strength from the earth and rise again before them again more gigantic than ever; they shrink back again and again before the indeterminate immensity of their own goals, until the situation is created in which any retreat is impossible, and the conditions themselves call out: *Hic Rhodus, hic salta!*[6]

The 'conditions call out' today, of that there is no doubt, yet fundamentally the working class can only 'mock its past weak, inadequate attempts' in action and the preconditions for that action are clearly absent from the present situation: we do not know when and how the working class will become aware of itself and capable of action on an international scale, which alone can open the way to social transformation.

We can envisage the material foundation of communist society on the basis of existing historical conditions, and we can call on the theoretical heritage of the workers' movement, and more generally on the artistic and philosophical heritage of humanity as a whole, to imagine its landscape; of the revolutionary overthrow of bourgeois power, and the creation of a world wide proletarian power we can say little more than that it will differ profoundly from our only

---

4   See the articles on 'Capitalism vs the Environment' and 'Surplus Populations'.

5   See the section on 'Types of fetters acting on the productive forces' in the article 'Historical materialism and the descent of capitalism'.

6   'The 18th Brumaire of Louis Bonaparte' in Marx, *Surveys from Exile* (Harmondsworth: Penguin Books, 1973), p.150. The Latin expression is taken from Aesop's fable 'The Boastful Athlete', in which an athlete vaunting his prowess claims to have made a remarkable jump on the island of Rhodes. At this, a bystander counters with the words: 'Let's say we're in Rhodes. Now then, make the same jump here!'.

historical experience to date, that of the October Revolution in Russia. To envisage the conditions and contours of humanity's future emancipation is therefore a call to our collective imagination, whereas any attempt to predict the shape of a future world revolution could be, in the present circumstances, no more than speculation. This may seem paradoxical, it is nonetheless true. Hence we do not propose to deal here with a number of questions which have exercised communists since the Revolution of 1917, such as the nature of the transitional state or the relationship between 'the' Party and the workers' councils.[7]

The working class must become aware of itself in action, but action in and of itself is not enough. To act without any sense of direction would be merely revolt, not revolution. Revolutionary action is only possible with a sense of perspective, of a possible future towards which action can tend. This possible – imagined – future will necessarily be inadequate, incomplete, but it is no less vital for all that.

The conscious imagination of communism

The creation of a new society to replace capitalism can only be a conscious act, or rather, a succession of increasingly conscious acts undertaken not by leaders or an enlightened minority but by the vast masses of the exploited. Its aim is a society rationally planned for the satisfaction of human needs, which is to say the fullest possible flowering of the human spirit.

While revolution depends on rational consciousness, it is not only a rational act, it is also an emotional and moral one. Revolution is therefore not a science but an art.

In his autobiography, Trotsky recounts his first revolutionary group and its efforts to agitate for socialist ideas among the workers during the 1890s. Meetings were held secretly in houses, in the woods, or on the river in the town of Nikolayev. According to Trotsky,

> The predominating element was composed of highly skilled workers who earned fairly good wages. They already had an eight-hour day at the Nikolayev ship-building yards; they were not interested in strikes; what

---

7   This last problem, which occupied a good deal of time during the International Conferences of the Communist Left at the end of the 1970s, rather begs the question of whether there will ever be, or could ever be, a single Party.

they wanted was justice in social relations [...] Many of the workers were so infected by the new ideas that they began to compose verses.[8]

It is this kind of activity, repeated many, many times, that developed the revolutionary imagination of the Russian workers and 'prepared their minds for the revolution' that was to come in 1905, then again, more decisively, in 1917. The revolution derived its emotional power – without which it could never have succeeded – from the workers' ability to imagine a future which would offer a way out of the terrible disaster of world war. Our situation today is different, in many ways much worse. If the only future we can imagine is one of disaster, then disaster is what we will have. However mistaken we may be in the details, we can only hope to have a future if we are able to imagine that it might exist. As Marx put it, 'The social revolution of the [21st] century cannot create its poetry from the past but only from the future'.[9]

How then, are we to imagine the future?

For the early socialist thinkers,[10] the solution was to be found in an appeal to human reason. First, it was necessary to lay out the ground-plan for the future society, quite literally: Charles Fourier set out detailed instructions for the construction and organisation of his phalansteries (today we might call them communes); Robert Owen even drew up the architectural plans for his ideal settlements. Once these were laid before humanity, they thought, it would be a straightforward matter of building the new settlements and setting them, so to speak, in motion.

By the time we get to Marx, it is clear that the problem cannot be posed like this. For the *Communist Manifesto*,

> The theoretical conclusions of the Communists are in no way based on ideas or principles that have been invented, or discovered, by this or that would-be universal reformer. They merely express, in general terms, actual relations springing from an existing class struggle, from a historical movement going on under our very eyes.[11]

Communism, then, is not the fruit of brilliant ideas or eternal reason, it is the continuation of a real historical movement, and as such its contours can be perceived in society as it has developed in the past, and as it continues to develop 'under our very eyes'. However, precisely because this is a movement, the transition from capitalist to communist society is not something that can happen instantaneously. The communist programme is not like a bourgeois party

---

8   Trotsky, *My Life* (Penguin Books, 1979), p.110-111.

9   Marx, 'The 18th Brumaire', p.149.

10   These are the thinkers to whom Engels paid tribute in his pamphlet *Socialism, Utopian and Scientific*.

11   Karl Marx and Friedrich Engels, *Selected Works* (Lawrence & Wishart, 1970), p.46.

political programme that can be enacted (or more usually not enacted) during a parliamentary term. It is an attempt to make visible those features of present society which point towards the future.

In his 'Critique of the Gotha Programme', Marx clearly distinguishes between what can be envisaged in the immediate future, and the ultimate goal of the workers' movement:[12]

> What we have to deal with here [(i.e., in the programme's proposals for the immediate future)] is a communist society, not as it has developed on its own foundations, but, on the contrary, just as it emerges from capitalist society; which is thus in every respect, economically, morally, and intellectually, still stamped with the birthmarks of the old society from whose womb it emerges. [...] In a higher phase of communist society, after the enslaving subordination of the individual to the division of labour, and therewith also the antithesis between mental and physical labour, has vanished; after labour has become not only a means of life but life's prime want; after the productive forces have also increased with the all-around development of the individual, and all the springs of co-operative wealth flow more abundantly – only then can the narrow horizon of bourgeois right be crossed in its entirety and society inscribe on its banners: From each according to his ability, to each according to his needs!

Thus there are two aspects to the emergence of a fully communist society. On the one hand there is the 'development of the productive forces', itself dependent in part on 'the all-around development of the individual'. On the other, and equally important, is the individual's liberation from the 'muck of ages', all the ideological dross with which the 'cash nexus', the capitalist relations of exchange, and even the previous millennia of class society, infect our thinking. Remember that not least of the productive forces are first, the productive class itself, and second the mode of social organisation; the 'development of the productive forces' thus necessarily means the self-transformation of the working class, and at the same time the transformation of the relations of production as the proletariat absorbs other classes into itself.

This cannot happen overnight. In another context, Marx once said that

> ... [it is] the real conditions [not] a mere effort of will [that is] the driving force of the revolution [...] You [the workers] will have to go through 15, 20, 50 years of civil wars and national struggles not only to bring about a change in society but also to change yourselves, and prepare yourselves for the exercise of political power.[13]

12   Marx & Engels *Selected Works*, pp.319-321.

13   'Revelations concerning the Communist trial in Cologne', in Karl Marx (ed. Rodney Livingstone), *The Cologne Communist Trial* (London: Lawrence & Wishart, 1971), p.62. The context here was the dissolution of the Communist League.

He was speaking here of the proletariat's struggle to forge itself as a class within capitalism, rather than to build a new society, but the same principle holds true: for the working class, the struggle to change society is also a struggle to change itself.

Necessity and freedom

The movement towards communism is also posited by Marx and Engels as one leading from 'the realm of necessity' to 'the realm of freedom'. Thus in *Capital*, Marx writes:[14]

> In fact, the realm of freedom actually begins only where labour which is determined by necessity and mundane considerations ceases; thus in the very nature of things it lies beyond the sphere of actual material production. [...]
>
> ...freedom in this field [of necessity] can only consist in socialised man, the associated producers, rationally regulating their interchange with Nature, bringing it under their common control, instead of being ruled by it as by the blind forces of Nature; and achieving this with the least expenditure of energy and under conditions most favourable to, and worthy of, their human nature. But it nonetheless still remains a realm of necessity. Beyond it begins that development of human energy, which is an end in itself, the true realm of freedom, which, however, can blossom forth only with this realm of necessity as its basis. The shortening of the working day is its fundamental prerequisite.[15]

It is important here to realise that the 'true realm of freedom' is not some blissful state to be attained in the distant future when the 'realm of necessity' has been left behind. On the contrary, the 'realm of necessity' will always exist, because humans will always be material beings dependent on their interchange with nature. The 'realm of freedom' is thus dependent on the greatest possible reduction in the working day, or rather, in the amount of time devoted to the essentials of human civilisation.

The future, when communism is able to develop 'on its own foundations', is unknowable, not merely unpredictable, because it will itself be increasingly the product of free choice, both individual and social: 'the associated producers [will] regulate their interchange with nature rationally', that is to say consciously.

---

14   Note here that Marx is essentially talking about the end to the alienation of labour, stripped of the rather post-Hegelian language of the 1844 Manuscripts.

15   *Capital*, Volume III (London: Lawrence & Wishart, 1977), p.820, in the chapter 'Trinity Formula'. It is quoted (with a slightly different translation) in the chapter on 'Marx's concept of socialism' in Erich Fromm, *Marx's concept of man*.

There is, however, a fundamental difficulty at the heart of the whole notion of working class consciousness. On the one hand, for Marx the emergence of social consciousness is itself determined by social being, in other words it is an unconscious process which plays itself out 'in secret' or 'behind men's backs'. For the bourgeoisie, as for all exploiting classes, it is inevitably a false consciousness, since it cannot by definition grasp the contradictory process of capitalism which must lead, in one way or another, to its own dissolution. Inevitably, the dominant consciousness is that of the ruling strata in society.

And yet, the whole communist project is posited on the assumption that it will for the first time be a conscious overthrow of the existing state of things, that it will somehow be possible for the exploited class, the class which does not possess think tanks, universities, research laboratories and so on, to arrive at a level of awareness of the most complex society in human history both in its present and in terms of the future towards which it tends. This awareness begins with the consciousness of its own slavery, of its underlying unity of interest; it demands first and foremost that the modern proletariat become conscious of what it is potentially: as Engels put it, 'conscious of its own position and its needs, conscious of the conditions of its emancipation'.[16]

Not the least among the paradoxes of historical materialism is this: the world is not teleological, in the sense that there are no divinely ordained future goals for either the individual or society; yet the more humanity escapes from the realm of necessity, the more the individual and society are free in the choices that it is possible to make, and the more we are able to determine our own, collective, goals; the more also, the goals we set ourselves determine our present actions – the more, in short, the future will determine the present. As Erich Fromm puts it:

> Marx expected that by this new form of an unalienated society [i.e. communism] man would become independent, stand on his own feet, and would no longer be crippled by the alienated mode of production and consumption; that he would truly be the master and the creator of his life, and hence that he could begin to make living his main business, rather than producing the means for living. Socialism, for Marx, was never as such the fulfilment of life, but the condition for such fulfilment. When man has built a rational, non-alienated form of society, he will have the chance to begin with what is the aim of life: the 'development of human power, which is its own end, the true realm of freedom.' Marx, the man who every year read all the works of Aeschylus and Shakespeare, who brought to life in himself the greatest works of human thought, would never have dreamt that his idea of socialism could be interpreted as hav-

---

16   Engels speech at Marx's graveside, 1883. <https://www.marxists.org/archive/marx/works/1883/death/burial.htm>

ing as its aim the well-fed and well-clad 'welfare' or 'workers'' state. Man, in Marx's view, has created in the course of history a culture which he will be free to make his own when he is freed from the chains, not only of economic poverty, but of the spiritual poverty created by alienation. Marx's vision is based on his faith in man, in the inherent and real potentialities of the essence of man which have developed in history. He looked at socialism as the condition of human freedom and creativity, not as in itself constituting the goal of man's life.[17]

In this, Marx showed himself truly the heir to the best humanist tradition. Marx's vision of the 'development of human power' would surely not have been entirely foreign to Wilhelm von Humboldt, brother of the great naturalist Alexander von Humboldt, who wrote that 'the end of man, or that which is prescribed by the eternal or immutable dictates of reason, and not suggested by vague and transient desires, is the highest and most harmonious development of his powers to a complete and consistent whole'.[18] Marx's revolutionary originality lay in showing that this 'full development' was possible only on condition that the historical processes born in capitalism should develop into a new social form, and that it would then be possible for the whole of humanity not just a privileged few.

A historical movement going on under our very eyes

The 'historical movement' that abolishes the existing state of things can be nothing other than the development of capitalist society itself, and of the working class and its consciousness within that society.

The *Manifesto* not only lambasts capitalism's hypocrisy and brutal exploitation of labour, it also shows how capitalism, by developing humanity's productive forces and potentially uniting the whole of humanity in a single world wide social system, lays the basis for a transition to a new and higher social form which will resolve its own destructive contradictions.

When Marx and Engels wrote the *Manifesto*, the development of working class organisation and consciousness was visible and even measurable in the growing numbers of workers organised in trades unions, and in the develop-

---

17   'Marx's Concept of Socialism' in Eric Fromm *Marx's concept of man.* <https://www.-marxists.org/archive/fromm/works/1961/man/ch06.htm>, accessed 10/01/2023. This work by Fromm is essentially an extended commentary on the 1844 MS, which attacks, in particular, the attempt by Stalinist theoreticians like Louis Althusser to separate the 'young Marx' of 1844 from the 'mature Marx' of *Capital*.

18   Quoted in JS Mill, *On Liberty* (Random House, 2002), p.57.

ment of socialist political parties. That period ended in 1914, but – as we have seen in the articles collected here – even in its phase of decline/descent, capitalism continues to develop.

Since the first half of the 20th century, following two devastating world wars and a catastrophic economic crisis in between, capitalism has entered its endgame. But this turned out to be something very different from what the communists, from Marx onwards, had expected.

In one of his rare statements on the subject, here is how Marx, very succinctly, envisaged the possible outcome of capitalism's internal contradictions:

> Along with the constantly diminishing number of the magnates of capital, who usurp and monopolise all advantages of this process of transformation, grows the mass of misery, oppression, slavery, degradation, exploitation; but with this too grows the revolt of the working class, a class always increasing in numbers, and disciplined, united, organised by the very mechanism of the process of capitalist production itself. The monopoly of capital becomes a fetter upon the mode of production, which has sprung up and flourished along with, and under it. Centralisation of the means of production and socialisation of labour at last reach a point where they become incompatible with their capitalist integument. This integument is burst asunder. The knell of capitalist private property sounds. The expropriators are expropriated.[19]

Like Marx, the Left Communists of the 1970s expected capitalism to enter into a definitive, essentially economic crisis so great that the working class would be forced to revolt, overthrow the whole system, and in doing so establish the premises for a communist society. This was an entirely reasonable hypothesis at the time, and was largely common ground for both Luxemburgists who expected the crash to come as a result of the contraction of the market relative to capital's need to expand, and for those who looked to the tendential decline in the rate of profit to fall, to act as a catastrophic brake on capitalism's ability to accumulate.

---

19   *Capital*, Volume One (London: Everyman, 1972), p.846, in Chapter 32 'The Historical Tendency of Capitalist Accumulation'. It is worth noting that Marx also envisaged the possibility that the transition to socialism could be achieved by peaceful, democratic means: 'You know that the institutions, mores, and traditions of various countries must be taken into consideration, and we do not deny that there are countries – such as America, England, and if I were more familiar with your institutions, I would perhaps also add Holland – where the workers can attain their goal by peaceful means' (Speech following the 1872 Hague Congress of the International Workingmen's Association, delivered in Amsterdam on 8 September 1872, printed in *La Liberté* of 15 September; see <https://www.marxists.org/archive/marx/works/1872/09/08.htm> [accessed 10/01/2023].

However, as the figures for GDP growth show clearly, these expectations have not been borne out by reality since then. On the contrary, far from capitalism being in permanent crisis, even serious crises like the 1997 'Tigers and Dragons' crash in East Asia, or the Lehman Brothers financial collapse in 2007-8 appear as little more than blips in a constant upward movement of GDP. The equally constant and rapid increase in primary energy consumption is still more striking and arguably more significant, especially since the ever greater efficiency of energy use means that the number of megawatt-hours used per unit of GDP is decreasing.

While they disagreed on the details, all the Marxists of the Left Communist tradition were agreed that capitalism's decadence was fundamentally a matter of economic contradictions inherent to the system, that these economic contradictions would oblige the working class to react, and that through this reaction against the effects of a final devastating economic crisis a revolutionary overthrow of capitalism as a whole would become both possible and necessary.

But it turns out that this was wrong or at the very least, that it has not been validated by experience. The fundamental contradiction, it seems to us, is to be found in capitalism's 'universal nature' (to use Marx's expression) whereby production is driven by the purely abstract need for its own constant expansion. Far from declining since 1945, this production has increased monstrously to the point where it is now pushing up against, or has even gone beyond the physical boundaries imposed by the finite nature of the planet. Capitalism is universal, in short, but the planet is not.

This does not mean that the threat of imperialist war has receded, quite the reverse. Indeed it is precisely the planet's limit on the possibility of capitalist expansion that determines the never-ending threat and reality of generalised war between the great powers.

This, then, is part of the 'historical movement going on under our very eyes'. The consequences of this contradiction are already with us in the form of extreme weather events. It will certainly 'abolish the existing state of things';[20] it has serious consequences for the class struggle, both in terms of the immediate defence of living conditions and the necessary struggle for communism.

The enormous expansion of industry in countries once called 'under-developed' – China being the most significant – has increased the absolute numbers of workers by hundreds of millions. Yet the world's population has grown faster still, and capitalism has proven incapable of integrating this rising population into productive labour, condemning billions to endemic misery in its slums and refugee camps.

---

20   In Karl Marx and Friedrich Engels, *The German Ideology* (Moscow: Progress Publishers, 1976), p.57.

This phenomenal rise in world population (it has almost quadrupled since 1950), which risks overwhelming the planet's ability both to feed humanity and to absorb its waste production, is itself the product of a clash between the continuing development of the human understanding of nature in the form of spectacular advances in medical science and agricultural yields, and the continuing backwardness of highly patriarchal rural societies which for millennia have condemned women to an endless round of childbirth. This clash is rooted fundamentally in the persistence of obsolete relations of production which decadent capitalism has proven unable to absorb, and the contradictions this creates. In the past, the population was kept roughly stable by disease and malnutrition; today these populations survive in miserable conditions, but they do survive,[21] and the main factor limiting the birthrate is women's economic and social independence, resisted tooth and nail not just in backward societies but in the most advanced capitalist economy of them all: the United States.[22]

The rise in crop yields since World War II has indeed been extraordinary: the world's average cereal yields, for example, have increased from 1.35 tonnes per hectare in 1961 to 4.07 tonnes in 2020.[23] Yet this has been achieved at the expense of the land itself. The spread of industrialised farming has driven people from the land; since 2007 more than 50% of the world's population lives in urban centres, a figure that has risen above 80% in the United States, and even in a country like France that traditionally likes to think of itself as having rural roots.[24] Humanity's alienation from nature, expressed in the contradiction between town and country identified as long ago as the 16th century in Thomas More's *Utopia*, has reached a paroxysm.

Industrialised capitalist farming, on which all other human activity ultimately depends, has become one of the principle factors underlying the destruction of its own natural foundation.

21　It should not be forgotten that starvation conditions often were, and still are, created not by natural but by human disaster. The Irish potato famine reduced the population by half while Ireland continued to export wheat in order to maintain the profits of the Anglo-Irish aristocracy. The dreadful Bengal famine in 1942-43 was the result of Churchill's decision not to divert food for famine relief during World War II. The recurrent famines in Ethiopia and the Horn of Africa are the result of endemic warfare, and so on.

22　This is particularly evident in America's 'culture wars', and the continuing outsized influence of the most backward, reactionary fractions of the American population and ruling class, evidenced most recently in the striking down of Roe v Wade by the Supreme Court and the ensuing raft of anti-abortion legislation.

23　Hannah Ritchie, Max Roser and Pablo Rosado (2022), 'Crop Yields' in *Our World in Data* <https://ourworldindata.org/crop-yields> [accessed 10 January 2023]

24　Hannah Ritchie and Max Roser (2018) 'Urbanization', in *Our World in Data* <https://ourworldindata.org/urbanization> [accessed 10 January 2023]

Food production accounts for 26% of world greenhouse gas emissions,[25] the most immediately obvious looming disaster that confronts humanity. Since the beginning of capitalist industrialisation, carbon sequestered in the Earth's crust in the form of coal and oil over millions of years has been loaded into the biosphere in a matter of decades. As a result climate change is now unstoppable: the only question is how bad it will get. As things stand, the 'business as usual' scenario is likely to lead to temperature increases that will, by the end of the century, leave large swathes of the planet literally uninhabitable, and to sea level rises that will drown low-lying coastal areas and cities, including some of the world's most populated (Bangladesh, Shanghai, London, Florida, Holland...). The number of 'climate refugees' would be counted in the millions, perhaps even the billions, in poor and rich countries alike, making the present refugee crisis seem like a paradise by comparison.

Some sections of the ruling class itself are aware of the climate problem and are even trying to do something about it. We hear far less of other, concomitant problems which are potentially equally devastating, notably chemical pollution and the threat to biodiversity.[26] The first is a direct result of the phenomenal and unthinking expansion of the plastics and chemical industry, the second of the expansion of the human footprint. Production of plastics has increased exponentially, and is expected to double again by 2050; 8 million tons of plastic are released into the world's oceans every year. The chemical industry is estimated to have released 350,000 'novel entities' into the biosphere, whose effects on both the environment and human health are largely unknown. The reduction in biodiversity through the destruction of natural habitats and the spread of industrial monocultures concerns not just the loss of iconic animal species but a generalised impoverishment of the environment and the interactions between plant and animal species, rendering crop plants and livestock more susceptible to disease and threatening the natural basis of human existence.

The question posed for humanity today is not whether change is necessary; change is coming, inexorably.

Given the extreme gravity of the present situation, one could be forgiven for thinking that capitalism's destructive processes have already gone so far that there is no more room for hope, that capitalism in its death agony has definitively undermined the necessary material foundation for a communist society liberated from material want and able to aspire to the 'realm of freedom'.

---

25   Hannah Ritchie and Max Roser (2020) – 'Environmental Impacts of Food Production', in *Our World in Data* <https://ourworldindata.org/environmental-impacts-of-food> [accessed 10 January 2023]

26   See Phillip Sutton's piece on 'Capitalism versus the Environment'.

Whether or not this is the case, time alone will tell. One thing is certain, however: to envisage a radical, that is to say communist, reorganisation of society may seem utopian, but it is much less unrealistic than to think that capitalism can overcome its own contradictions. The much touted 'energy transition' from fossil fuels to green electricity and hydrogen, for example, is a fraud.[27] Recognising this, one current of thought around groups like Extinction Rebellion is starting to talk of 'post-capitalism', thus avoiding the 'C-word' (i.e. 'communism'), but when we look beneath the surface of their proposals they are merely capitalism-lite, no more realistic when push comes to shove than 'business as usual'.

The working class across the world showed during the 1970s that it was capable of massive struggle and highly creative organisation in defence of its immediate material interests. But even at its apogee in Poland 1980, the proletariat never succeeded in putting forward its own perspective. Despite some strong rear-guard actions, the bourgeois counter-offensive launched from 1980 onwards was to inflict on workers a serious defeat.[28]

Then in 1989 the USSR disintegrated. It was not just an imperial power that disappeared but, so it seemed, the very idea that something different from capitalism – however corrupted – could actually exist, that there could be some perspective of building a different and better society. Liberal capitalism, said ideologues like Francis Fukuyama, is the only game in town. Talk of communism is mere Utopia. Since then, 'liberal' capitalism has offered us wars without end and the perspective of planetary destruction. It is high time to set out for Utopia.

The realm of necessity

By Utopia, we mean the 'realm of freedom' that Marx envisaged emerging in a communism built on its own foundations. But human beings can only develop freely on the basis of their material social organisation through which they produce and reproduce their existence; the 'realm of freedom' can only be built on the material foundation of the 'realm of necessity'. This 'realm' is closest to us

---

27 A leader in *The Economist* of 30 September 2022 is subtitled 'Profit-seeking companies have too little incentive to save the planet', which says it all. But the suggested solution (government intervention to tax carbon) forgets that states, just as much as companies, are in competition amongst each other, including military competition. As the Ukraine war hots up and gas supplies run down, European governments envisage restarting mothballed coal-fired power stations.

28 See the article on 'Accumulation of Catastrophe'.

because the material foundation for freedom – for communism – can only emerge from the material conditions of production existing today.

To talk, today, of this material foundation, is only possible in terms of a transition away from the present capitalist society. It means thinking through a radical reorganisation of the whole productive process, in ways and confronted with problems that were only barely apparent, if at all, to our predecessors.

As we have seen throughout this short volume, capitalism has called into being the elements on which this material foundation can be built: the world market that has united all humanity in a single society, world wide associated labour, a scientific understanding of the natural world and the technology it underpins. Yet we have also seen how it is precisely the present capitalist organisation of society that not only prevents these productive forces from being applied for humanity's greater good, but worse still, fetters them or transforms them into active agents of destruction.

All the existential threats that we have considered – climate change, the impoverishment of the land, sea-level rises – have one thing in common: they concern the entire planet and respect no national boundaries. They cannot be solved by an economy based on private appropriation precisely because private appropriation is in fundamental contradiction to the associated labour which sets the productive forces in motion, but also because they concern the commons: the air we breathe, the land we walk on, the oceans and rivers on which life itself depends. They cannot be solved by the nation-state, which is the political-organisational framework of capitalist society, and has become one of the principal threats to human survival (nowhere more clearly, as we write, than in Ukraine), one of the heaviest shackles weighing on humanity's productive powers, one of the greatest barriers to humanity's free development. They can only be solved on a planetary basis, by a planetary class: the worldwide class of associated labour, a proletariat which has at last recognised itself for what it is.

When we envision the immediate measures of the proletarian power, we are therefore conducting a thought experiment in which we assume that such a power exists worldwide, ushering in a lengthy period of transition from a society still 'stamped with its birthmarks' in capitalism, to a communism which has 'developed on its own foundations'; this is a bold assumption indeed.[29]

---

29   In *The German Ideology* (Ibid, p.57) Marx had this to say: 'Empirically, communism is only possible as the act of the dominant peoples "all at once" and simultaneously, which presupposes the universal development of productive forces and the world intercourse bound up with communism. [...] The proletariat can thus only exist world-historically, just as communism, its activity, can only have a "world-historical" existence. World-historical existence of individuals means existence of individuals which is directly linked up with world history'.

Its first task will be to halt, then reverse, the destruction that capitalism has wreaked on the planet, to lay the foundations of the 'realm of necessity' on which the 'realm of freedom' can be built. It will be a job of immense complexity taking many generations, for everything is interlinked just as the natural world is one indivisible whole. Here we will go no further than summarise some of the main issues, and that with a very broad brush, which we hope to look at more closely in another volume.

Everything , in the final analysis, comes down to energy. All human societies prior to industrial capitalism depended on the muscle power of humans and animals, and on the combustion of biomass. Capitalism was able to multiply human labour power many times over, and to replace almost entirely animal power, only by adding a new primary energy source to the mix: fossil fuels, first coal, then oil and gas.

A communist society too, will depend on abundant energy; indeed it will in all likelihood demand yet more energy to raise the living standards of the impoverished masses in the Global South. In the short to medium term however, the most urgent need is to stop burning fossil fuels, and in the immediate this can only be done by reducing energy consumption, and therefore production in general, which in turn means that decisions will have to be taken as to which production is essential and what can be dispensed with.

This will inevitably involve some extremely difficult choices, with huge implications for parts of the world heavily dependent at present on fossil fuels, but it is by no means wholly negative. Today, the workers are alienated from their labour, condemned to work without any thought of, or control over, their final product. To reduce production also means to reduce labour time, which is itself a precondition for the fullest possible participation of all workers in the decision-making that affects everyone. More than that though, it raises the question: what is necessary? What is the necessary material foundation on which the 'realm of freedom' alone can be built? This is a vast issue which we intend to deal with in more depth later. For the moment, let us just say that it is a political question on a world scale, and perhaps even more profoundly a problem that philosophy has posed since it existed: what does it mean to be human? What is necessity and what is freedom? What is 'the good life'? Emerging from a capitalist society which can only survive by constantly creating new 'needs', knowing what it is that we truly need and what are 'false needs' imposed on us by ideology and advertising is by no means easy; it was a problem already posed by Marx:

> The increase in the quantity of objects is accompanied by an extension of the realm of the alien powers to which man is subjected [...] the extension

of products and needs falls into contriving and ever-calculating subservience to inhuman, unnatural, and imaginary appetites.[30]

Along with energy, the land is our most pressing problem. It is the basic source of human subsistence, yet it is under attack from multiple directions. 'Most assessments show that between 20-40% of the global land area is degraded or degrading to varying extents and degrees'.[31] Industrialised monocultures are inherently more vulnerable to disease than biodiverse farming; they are only sustainable with massive inputs of herbicides that sterilise the soil, in the long run rendering it lifeless and unfit for farming. In addition, industrialised agriculture is one of the main factors in producing CO_2, reducing the land's ability to act as a carbon sink and aggravating climate change. The ruthless exploitation of the world's remaining wild resources, and the desperation of poverty-stricken peasants, is destroying the last virgin forests, driving uncounted plant, animal, and insect species to extinction.

The vast monocultures, the pesticides and artificial fertilisers that characterise industrialised agriculture, must all be done away with. The earth must be nurtured not exploited, if we are to survive. Ending the contradiction between town and country – a Utopian dream ever since Thomas More – is no longer a distant objective but an urgent necessity.

But how is all this to be done?

It takes only a moment's thought to realise that the conversion of the world's electricity supply away from fossil fuels, and the provision of electricity to every community on the planet, will be a vast undertaking of immense technicity. The geographical constraints imposed on renewable energy sources (solar, wind, geothermal, wave and tidal, hydroelectric etc), and in most cases their intermittent nature, mean that general energy distribution can only be achieved through sophisticated smart grids on a continental, even an intercontinental scale, respecting no national frontiers. It is likely that, at least at first, some form of rationing will be necessary: not by price, as is the case today, but by need so that (for example) unlimited electricity is made available to hospitals and public transport, but not to private vehicles. There will be a constant search for greater efficiency in the generation and distribution of electricity, which in turn will demand a constant stream of research into new materials, batteries, solar panels, and so on.

The same holds true for agriculture. The conversion of industrialised monoculture, the elimination of toxic herbicides, pesticides, and fertilisers, cannot be achieved by returning to a bucolic idyll of peasant agriculture based on tradi-

---

30   Marx, 'The meaning of human requirements', in *The Economic and Philosophical Manuscripts of 1844*, p.147.

31   UN Convention to Combat Desertification, *Global Land Outlook 2*, p.xvi

tional techniques. The idyll never existed, and we have no desire at all to return to the backbreaking labour of traditional peasant societies, nor indeed to their parochial outlook and oppressive patriarchal values. The conversion of agriculture also implies a world wide conversion of the whole food processing industry, many of whose products are to all intents and purposes unfit for human consumption and largely responsible for the global pandemic of obesity, a pandemic which mostly affects the working classes and the poor.

Agriculture and food processing can only be rendered fit for purpose by combining the advanced sciences of ecology, genetics, molecular chemistry, soil structure and husbandry, with whatever still survives of the traditional farming knowledge acquired by millennia of observation and experiment.

Farming and eating – those most basic of human activities – will be at the heart of one key element in communism: the elimination of the contradiction between town and country.

Clearly, like the hero of the film *The Martian*, 'in the face of overwhelming odds, we have only one option. We're going to have to science the shit out of this'.[32]

Technique allied to knowledge has always been the means of human interaction with the rest of nature. Capitalism however has given birth to something new: science as a world wide, associated endeavour, a productive force in its own right.

'Science as a productive force' is not something abstract. It only 'produces' through the associated human labour[33] of research, shared knowledge, experiment – and education. One of the most tragic fetters that capitalism lays on the productive forces is the monstrous waste of human intelligence, curiosity, and creativity: the billions either excluded from the labour process altogether, or limited to mind-numbing repetitive tasks, or at best, with their imaginations stunted by over-specialisation.

To unchain science as a productive force will demand a vast effort of education which will take generations to accomplish. First and foremost it means calling on the talent of the young, awakening them to a knowledge of the world and – perhaps above all – giving them a perspective of finding a place in an adult society where they will be able to use their talents to the fullest by contributing them to society as a whole.

---

32   This appears in a short clip on YouTube: <https://youtu.be/BABM3EUo990> [accessed 10 January 2023].

33   It is worth recalling that the first version of the 'world wide web' which we all use, and which has become a critical tool in developing human interaction world wide, was developed by Tim Berners-Lee at CERN, as a means of interconnecting scientific knowledge through linked hyper-text.

The whole system of education must change. Today's schools are built on the factory principle: children as raw material, teachers as assembly line workers, and new workers as the finished product. The model of creative associated labour, no longer alienated but life's chief pleasure, will seek to integrate learning and labour so that biology will be learnt in the fields and gardens as much as in the classroom and the laboratory, physics in the factory as much as in the lecture theatre, and so on.

Nor will the educational effort be solely scientific and technical. All human societies are bound together by a common ethos. In class societies, the common ethos can only be deeply contradictory since it must both bind society as a whole, while at the same time containing and obfuscating the contradictions and violent conflicts between exploiting and exploited classes. Communism will no longer have to accommodate conflict between social classes; its common ethos will have to bind together the most diverse, widespread population of any human society with an infinity of different projects, proposals, hopes, desires and dreams. The construction of this common ethos is the necessary antidote to capitalism's atomisation, anomie, and absence of meaning.

In all human societies, art is the embodiment, the expression and the means of thinking the social ethos, from the cave paintings of Lascaux to the murals of Diego de Rivera, from the shaman's trance dances to the break dance of the modern city. Art will be as vital a part of the new world as science, and as vital a part of that education which aims to produce individuals of the greatest possible internal richness and diversity. Little by little, art must pervade every aspect of human existence, overturning the drab uniformity of life under capitalism, to the point where eventually, it will cease to be a specialised activity separated from daily life to become, like labour, one of life's chief joys.

This transformation will not be achieved by any government or power, be it ne'er so revolutionary. For as Rosa Luxemburg once wrote:[34]

> The negative, the tearing down, can be decreed; the building up, the positive, cannot [...] Only experience is capable of correcting and opening new ways. Only unobstructed, effervescing life falls into a thousand new forms and improvisations, brings to light creative new force, itself corrects all mistaken attempts [...] The whole mass of the people must take part in it.

---

34   Rosa Luxemburg, 'The Russian Revolution', in *Rosa Luxemburg Speaks* (Pathfinder Press, 1970), p.390

Main Sources

BBC 'Big Oil vs The World' (2022)

Bukharin, Nikolaï, *Historical Materialism* (1921)

Berners-Lee, Mike, *There is No Planet B* (Cambridge: Cambridge University Press, 2019)

Bloch, Marc, *La Société féodale* (Paris: Editions Albin Michel, 1939)

Chakrabarty, Dipesh, *The climate of history in a planetary age*, (University of Chicago Press, 2021)

Climate Files, <https://www.climatefiles.com/>

CMcl 'Has Capitalism entered its decadence since 1914?' (2021)

Communist Workers Organisation, *Refining the Concept of Decadence* (2005)

Davis M, *Planet of Slums* (Verso, 2006)

ER, 'For a Non-productivist Understanding of Capitalist Decadence' in *Internationalist Perspective* no. 44 (2005)

Engels, Friedrich
- *Socialism – Utopian and Scientific* (1880)
- *Dialectics of Nature* (Moscow: Progress Publishers, 1976)
- *Anti-Dühring* (1894) (Moscow: Progress Publishers, 1977)

Extinction Rebellion, *This is not a Drill* (London: Penguin Books, 2019)

Fromm, Eric, *Marx's concept of man* (1961)

Foster John Bellamy,
- 'Engels's Dialectics of Nature in the Anthropocene' in *Monthly Review* Vol 72 No 6 (2020)
- *Marx's Ecology* (New York: Monthly Review Press, 2000)

Gorter, Herman, *Historical Materialism for Workers* (1908)

Grossman, Henryk, *The Law of Accumulation and Breakdown of the Capitalist System* (London: Pluto Press 1992)

Guenther, Matthias, *Tricksters and Trancers* (Indiana University Press, 1999)

Hickel, Jason, *Less is More, How Degrowth will save the World* (Windmill Press, 2021)

International Communist Current
  - *The Decadence of Capitalism* (2005 Edition)
  - CDW, 'The alienation of labour is the premise for its emancipation', *International Review* n°70, 3rd Quarter 1992

International Labour Organisation, 'World Employment Social Outlook, Trends' (2020)

Knight, Chris, *Blood Relations* (Yale University Press, 1995)

Kautsky, Karl, 'Land hunger – feudal and capitalist', in *Thomas More and his Utopia* (1888)

Lenin, Vladimir Ilyich, *Imperialism, The Highest Stage of Capitalism*, (1916)

Luxemburg, Rosa
  - *The Accumulation of Capital* (1913)
  - 'The Russian Revolution', in *Rosa Luxemburg Speaks* (Pathfinder Press, 1970),
  - 'The Junius Pamphlet: The Crisis in the German Social Democracy' (1915), in *Rosa Luxemburg Speaks* (Pathfinder, 1970)

Maito E, in G. Carchedi & M. Roberts, *World in Crisis: A Global Analysis of Marx's Law of Profitability* (Haymarket, 2008)

Malaurie, Jean, *Les derniers rois de Thulé* (Plon, 1989)

Marx, Karl
  - *Preface to the Critique of Political Economy* (1859)
  - *Capital*, Volume 1 (1887)
  - Capital, Volume 3 (1883)
  - *Theories of Surplus Value Part II* (Lawrence and Wishart, 1969)

- *The Communist Manifesto* (1848)
- 'Estranged labour', in *Economic and Philosophical MS of 1844* (New York: International Publishers, 1972)
- *Grundrisse* (Penguin, 1973)
- *The German Ideology* (Moscow: Progress Publishers, 1976)

Mattick, Paul, *Marx and Keynes: The Limits of the Mixed Economy* (Merlin Press, 1974)

Mauss, Marcel, *Essai sur le Don* (Quadridge/PUF, 2007)

Mill, John Stuart, *On Liberty* (1859), (Random House, 2002)

More, Thomas, *Utopia* (1516), (Penguin Classics, 1965)

North American Congress on Latin America, 'The Food Weapon', NACLA's Latin America and Empire Report, 9:7, 12-17, 1975

Our World in Data, <https://ourworldindata.org>

Pannekoek, *The Theory of the Collapse of Capitalism* (1934)

Population Matters, 'Biodiversity' (2022)

Platform of the Communist International (1919), in J. Degras (ed.), *The Communist International 1919-1943: Documents*, vol. 1, Frank Cass, 1971

Saito, Kohei, *Capital, Nature and the Unfinished Critique of Political Economy* (2017)

Scott, J.C., *Against the Grain*, (Yale University Press, 2017)

Shiva, Vandana, *Who really feeds the world?*, (North Atlantic Books, 2016)

Sternberg, Fritz
- *Kapitalismus und Sozialismus vor dem Weltgericht*, (Hamburg, 1951)
- *Capitalism and socialism on trial* (Gollancz, 1951), (English translation)
- *Le conflit du siècle*, (Éditions du Seuil, 1956), (French translation)

Stites, Richard, *Revolutionary Dreams: utopian Vision and Experimental Life in the Russian Revolution* (Oxford University Press, 1989)

Stockholm Resilience Centre, 'Planetary Boundaries, 2022'

Testart, Alain

- *Avant l'Histoire* (Gallimard, 2012)
- *Le communisme primitif* (Éditions de la Maison des Sciences de l'Homme, 1985)
- *Les chasseurs-cueilleurs ou les origines des inégalités* (Société d'Ethnographie, 1982)

United Nations, 'Sustainable Development and Climate Action'

UNHCR, 'Global Trends: Forced Displacement' (2020)

World Economic Forum

- 'Earth could cross the global warming threshold as soon as 2027' (2021)
- 'Climate Change'

World Wildlife Fund

- 'Six Ways Loss of Arctic Ice Impacts Everyone' (2022)
- 'Climate'

Wallace-Wells, David, *The Uninhabitable Earth* (London: Penguin, 2019)

Printed in Great Britain
by Amazon

27103263R00145